# THE MOST MIGHTY BRANCH

# THE MOST MIGHTY BRANCH

## STORIES FROM THE LIFE OF 'ABDU'L-BAHÁ

by

Hitjo Garst

*Translated by Olive McKinley*

GEORGE RONALD
OXFORD

George Ronald, Publisher
www.grbooks.com

Original Dutch edition © Stichting Bahá'í Literatuur, The Hague 2005
First edition
All rights reserved

The Publisher acknowledges with gratitude the assistance of the
Continental Board of Counsellors for the Bahá'í Faith in Europe

A catalogue record for this book is available from the British Library

ISBN 978-0-85398-513-6

Printed and bound in Great Britain
by Biddles Ltd, King's Lynn, Norfolk

# Contents

vii

The object of this sacred verse is none other except
the Most Mighty Branch.
*Bahá'u'lláh*


The 'Most Mighty Branch' is one of the titles conferred by
Bahá'u'lláh on 'Abdu'l-Bahá.
*Kitáb-i-Aqdas, note* 145

# 1

# The Most Mighty Branch

The learned men of Baghdad were astonished! How could this be? They had been talking about questions they had studied all their lives and yet still could not answer. And now? Now this young boy sat there answering them all. He had been to school for one year, no more. He had done no further studies and He had certainly not read as many books as they had. And yet He could explain the most difficult subjects. They felt a great deal of respect for Him and loved Him because He was always so modest and friendly.

Who was this boy who, even while so young, possessed such knowledge and wisdom? He was one of the exiles from Persia. His Father, their leader, sometimes called this son 'the Mystery of God'. When the learned men asked the boy from whom He had learned all these things, His answer was always, 'from my Father'. The boy was 'Abdu'l-Bahá. 'Abdu'l-Bahá was the eldest son of Bahá'u'lláh. Bahá'u'lláh is God's Messenger for our time.

Every time a Messenger of God appears on earth He is preceded by someone who prepares people for His coming. John the Baptist prepared the Jewish people for the coming of Jesus. Before Muhammad revealed Himself there were four men who announced His coming. The Báb said that He would soon be followed by another divine Messenger, Bahá'u'lláh. God has always ensured that people are prepared for the coming of a divine Messenger.

And when the Messenger died? Were His followers prepared, then, too, for the task of carrying on the new faith? Although every Messenger appointed someone to be the leader after Him, these instructions were not written down. And so, after only a short time, the followers would no longer agree as to how the teachings of the Messenger should be explained and practised. There have even been wars among the followers of the same Messenger because of such differences of opinion.

The time for such differences is over. With the coming of Bahá'u'lláh the time of the unity of mankind has begun. Bahá'u'lláh has made this unity possible. He did something that no other Messenger of God had done before: Bahá'u'lláh wrote down clearly who should lead His faith after Him. That is 'Abdu'l-Bahá. In the Most Holy Book, the Kitáb-i-Aqdas, Bahá'u'lláh wrote, 'turn your faces toward Him Whom God hath purposed, Who hath branched from this Ancient Root'. In His Testament Bahá'u'lláh wrote, 'The object of this sacred verse is none other except the Most Mighty Branch.' The Most Mighty Branch is one of the titles Bahá'u'lláh gave 'Abdu'l-Bahá. Because of 'Abdu'l-Bahá the unity of the Bahá'í Faith has been safeguarded since the ascension of Bahá'u'lláh.

Bahá'u'lláh compared His sons to the branches of a tree. 'Abdu'l-Bahá is the mightiest branch on that tree, a branch that withstood many a storm. He went through many difficulties in His life. When He was a child he had to flee from home with His mother and younger sister and brother. As a young boy He saw how badly his Father was treated in prison. He went with His family, in the bitter cold, to Baghdad. Ten years later He again journeyed with His family for more than a hundred days through the hot desert and over high mountains. Finally He found Himself, with His Father and family, in the prison of 'Akká in Palestine. When He became Head of the Faith

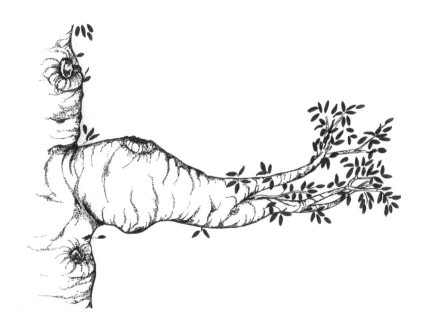

after the passing of Bahá'u'lláh, most of His family strenuously opposed Him. They were jealous and did not want to accept that Bahá'u'lláh had appointed Him as Head of the Faith. Several times they put His life in danger, and once it was only at the last minute that the danger was averted. He was a prisoner almost all His life; for fifty-six years He was a prisoner of the government. When He was finally freed, He was old and in poor health owing to all those years of imprisonment. Yet still He undertook the long journeys to Europe and America to tell people about His Father's teachings.

The name 'Abdu'l-Bahá means 'Servant of Bahá', the servant of Bahá'u'lláh. That was 'Abdu'l-Bahá's great purpose in life, both during Bahá'u'lláh's lifetime and after His passing. Day and night 'Abdu'l-Bahá was busy. When almost everyone else had gone to bed, He was often still working. And when nearly everyone was still asleep in the morning, He had already been back at work for hours.

To serve Bahá'u'lláh – that was all that mattered to 'Abdu'l-Bahá, even when He was still a young child who had to be taken to school. Taking 'Abdu'l-Bahá to school was the job of a loyal servant, Isfandíyár. Once, Isfandíyár had gone to the market and had not yet returned when it was time for 'Abdu'l-Bahá to leave for school. So Nabíl was asked to take Him. Nabíl put out his arms to pick up the child.

There was no question of that!

'We shall walk together,' said 'Abdu'l-Bahá, as He took hold of Nabíl's hand and led him out of the house. As they reached His classroom, He turned to him and said: 'Come again this afternoon and take me back to my home, for Isfandíyár is unable to fetch me. My Father will need him today.'

Although he was still very young, 'Abdu'l-Bahá was already Bahá'u'lláh's first servant.

# 2

# The Boy Who Gave Away His Father's Sheep

When 'Abdu'l-Bahá was born He was given the name of 'Abbás. He was called after His grandfather. 'Abbás's parents and grandparents were rich and prominent members of the nobility. They owned many acres of land and had large herds of animals. They lived in a beautiful big house with a garden full of lovely flowers and delicious fruits. 'Abbás, His sister and His younger brother could play there to their hearts' content.

Although 'Abbás's father and mother were indeed very rich, they did not wish to live like other rich people. The rich wanted to enjoy their money and their lives as much as they could. They often gave big parties that cost a lot of money. 'Abbás's father and mother did not do this. Instead of spending their money on their own pleasure they spent it on the poor and on people who needed help. These people could always come to them; no one was ever sent away. 'Abbás's parents were so kind to the people that His Father was called the 'Father of the Poor' and His mother the 'Mother of Consolation'.

'Abbás Himself was very generous too. This was seen when He was still a small boy. One day He was allowed to go into the mountains where the shepherds of Bahá'u'lláh's flocks were giving a great feast. It was a splendid trip, through lovely green valleys and meadows, through narrow mountain passes and along winding paths. They climbed a mountain and when they reached the top they had a wonderful view. They could see a green prairie below, full of horses, cattle and thousands of sheep and goats.

The shepherds gave them a warm welcome. They were having a big party there. They had their best clothes on and danced and sang, while the sheep they had slaughtered were roasted over huge camp fires. At lunch time they all sat down on the grass to eat the delicious roast meat. After the meal the shepherds said goodbye to 'Abbás. It was the custom for the landlord to give the shepherds presents, and so they were expecting something from Him. After all, 'Abbás was the landlord's son. But what was He to give them? He was only a small boy who had nothing and He had not brought anything with him either. What could He do?

Then He had an idea: I will give each shepherd some sheep from the flock. He said this to the chief shepherd. The shepherd thought this was a good suggestion and so he put it

into practice straight away. When they got home that evening the story was told to Bahá'u'lláh. What did He think of that? His little son had simply given away hundreds of His sheep! Bahá'u'lláh laughed heartily to hear it and said He would have to get someone to protect 'Abbás from His own generosity. 'Else, some day, He may give Himself away.'

You would think that, with such rich parents, 'Abbás had a very wonderful life. And so He had when He was a small boy. But when He was a bit older He heard about the terrible things that were happening in Persia. The Báb's followers, the Bábís, were being cruelly persecuted. Thousands were murdered by order of the Muslim clerics and the government. The Bábís hardly dared to go out on the street. If two Bábís met in the bazaar or on the street, they did not even dare to greet each other, so afraid were they that they would be recognized as Bábís and thrown into prison. If they wanted to meet, they had to do it in the night time and very secretly. No one must know.

'Abbás's Father also had to suffer persecution. Shortly after the Báb had declared Himself to His first follower, Bahá'u'lláh received a letter from the Báb. Immediately, Bahá'u'lláh began travelling through the villages and towns to call upon the people to become followers of the Báb. And just like the other Bábís, Bahá'u'lláh was taken prisoner and tortured. The Shah even wanted to have Him killed. He gave orders for Bahá'u'lláh to be arrested, but before that order could be carried out, the Shah died. The order for the arrest was then no longer in force.

The home of 'Abbás's parents now became a meeting place for the persecuted Bábís. 'Abbás was often there at the time.

And some guests and events would always be deeply etched in His memory. Even more than sixty years later, when He was travelling through America, He used to talk about them.

One visitor to their home that 'Abbás would remember all His life was Ṭáhirih, the greatest heroine of the Faith of the Báb. 'Abbás was then a little boy of five. Ṭáhirih loved to take Him on her lap. They were sitting like this one day in His mother's room. In the other part of the room, they could hear Vaḥíd talking to 'Abbás's Father. Vaḥíd was one of the most famous learned men of the land. Ṭáhirih was a courageous woman who was not afraid to speak her mind. Even to Vaḥíd. When she had listened for a while, she said: 'O Siyyid, this is not the time for arguments, for discussions, for idle repetitions of prophecies or traditions! It is the time for deeds! The day for words has passed! If you have courage, now is the appointed hour for manifesting it; if you are a man of deeds, show a proof of your manhood by proclaiming day and night: "The Promised Herald has come! He has come, the Qá'im, the Imám, the Awaited One has come! He has come!"'

Ṭáhirih called upon Vaḥíd to go throughout the country telling people that the Báb had appeared. This was very dangerous; the persecutions of the Bábís were getting worse all the time. Everywhere in Persia they were being persecuted, from north to south and from east to west. Yet Vaḥíd did what Ṭáhirih had urged him to do. Not long afterwards, hundreds of other Bábís were killed when defending themselves against a treacherous enemy. The Báb Himself was shot dead by a firing squad of seven hundred and fifty soldiers. 'Abbás's Father was forced to leave the country. He went to Karbila, a holy city in Iraq. For almost a year He was separated from His family.

When Bahá'u'lláh returned it was still dangerous for the followers of the Báb in Persia. And also for Bahá'u'lláh. Yet He and His family were still able to live in their large and beautiful house. But that would not be for long. From one day to the next everything would change.

# 3

# The Day Everything Changed

One day, one of the servants suddenly stormed into the house: 'The master, the master,' he cried, 'He is arrested – I have seen him! He has walked many miles! Oh, they have beaten him! They say he has suffered the torture of the bastinado! His feet are bleeding! He has no shoes on! His turban has gone! His clothes are torn! There are chains upon his neck!'

The face of 'Abbás's mother grew whiter and whiter when she heard this. 'Abbás and His sister Fáṭimih were terrified and began sobbing loudly.

What had happened? Because of the dreadful cruelties inflicted on the Báb and His followers, two young Bábís had become crazed. They no longer knew what they were doing: they shot at the Shah with a pistol. The Shah was only slightly wounded and not badly hurt. But this attack made things in Persia more difficult than ever for the followers of the Báb.

Only two Bábís were involved in the attack. The others knew nothing about it. If they had known of the plan, they would certainly not have agreed to it. But it seemed now that all the Bábís would have to suffer for it. Once more, the cruel persecutions broke out.

It was no wonder that 'Abbás's mother went deadly pale when she heard that Bahá'u'lláh had been taken prisoner. What awful things might happen to Him now?

Soldiers had brought Him to a ghastly prison, the Síyáh-Chál. This was an old underground reservoir. Only the worst criminals were thrown into it. It was cold inside, pitch dark and the smell was horrible. Bahá'u'lláh's feet were fastened into stocks and a very heavy chain was put around His neck.

And what would happen to 'Abbás's mother herself and her children now? They were soon to find out! All their relations, friends and servants – everyone fled from the house in terror.

Only two old servants dared to stay. Very quickly all kinds of people broke into the house to loot it. In a short time there was nothing left of their belongings. Their land and thousands of sheep were taken from them. 'Abbás's mother was only able to save a few of her treasures. The family were no longer safe in their own home. Stones were being thrown into it. Fortunately, Uncle Mírzá Músá was still there. He helped them to flee to the city, to Teheran, to a small house in a back street.

From one day to the next, the lives of 'Abbás, His mother, sister Fáṭimih and their little brother Mihdí were completely changed. Before, they had belonged to one of the richest families, now suddenly they were one of the poorest. Before, they had lived in a huge house with a beautiful garden, now they lived in a tiny house in a back street. Before, the poor used to come to them for help, now they themselves had to ask their relatives for help. Their mother had not enough for her children to eat. At one time, she could only give them a handful of flour; that was all she had.

And it was dangerous too! Once, 'Abbás was walking alone through the market. When He looked around, He saw that a

group of boys was following Him. They ran towards Him and
began throwing stones at Him and yelling: 'Bábí! Bábí!' 'Abbás
stopped. What was He to do, alone against such a large group?
He turned round and ran with such determination towards
them, that they were really scared and ran away. He could still
hear them yelling in the distance: 'The little Bábí is fast pursuing
us! He will surely overtake and slay us all!' As He continued
walking, He heard a man on the street, calling: 'Well done, you
brave and fearless child! No one of your age would ever have
been able, unaided, to withstand their attack.' From that day
onward, 'Abbás was never again molested by any of the boys on
the streets. Nor did they ever shout abuse at Him again.

But it was still dangerous! They had to stay in hiding and
were safe nowhere. Yet 'Abbás and his mother went into the
city every day to ask about Bahá'u'lláh. For every day one of
the Bábís was taken out of the prison and killed. And 'Abbás's

mother knew that any day it could be her husband.

And 'Abbás? What a lot of worries He had, as an 8-year-old boy. His Father had already had to suffer so much because He had openly proclaimed the new teachings of the Báb. And now He was in this dreadful prison. How was He? 'Abbás wanted to go and see Him. One of the prison guards was willing to help Him to do this. He took Him to the prison and carried Him on his shoulders down the steep steps. It was pitch dark down there. No matter how hard He looked, 'Abbás could make out no one. When they were halfway down the stairs they suddenly heard the voice of Bahá'u'lláh: 'Do not bring Him in here.'

Without having seen his Father, 'Abbás was taken up again. There, they told Him to wait outside because at noon the prisoners would be allowed out for a while. So then 'Abbás saw His Father. Bahá'u'lláh had a very heavy chain round His neck. He was chained to another prisoner. He could hardly walk, His clothes were in rags and He looked ill. It was a terrible sight. 'Abbás received such a shock that He fainted and was carried home, unconscious.

For four long months Bahá'u'lláh, who was innocent, was held in this dreadful prison. Then He was freed. How happy they were to have Him home again! But He was also in a bad way. The heavy chains had left deep, painful wounds. He was weak and ill. How could He be anything else after four months in such a filthy, unhealthy hole? He had to be looked after and He needed rest. But the government would not even let Him have that. He was ordered to leave Persia within one month.

And yet, even though Bahá'u'lláh was still so sick, He glowed with happiness. He had changed in the prison. Something very special must have happened there.

# 4

# A Dreadful Journey

'Abbás, at 8 years old, was going on a journey. His sister Fáṭimih, aged 6, was going too. But they had to leave behind their little brother Mírzá Mihdí, who was only 4. The journey would be too dangerous for him. Why did they have to make such a dangerous journey?

Their Father, Bahá'u'lláh, had only just been released from the Síyáh-Chál prison when the order came from the government. He had to leave Persia within the month. It was an unjust and cruel order. Ill, weak and with painful wounds, He had come home from the Síyáh-Chál. One month was not long enough at all to recover, never mind be able for a journey. Even though 'Abbás's mother and his aunt Maryam had looked after Him so very well.

The enemies of the Faith were glad. They had done all they could to get rid of the Faith of the Báb. The Báb had been executed and they had murdered thousands of His followers. And now they had also succeeded in getting Bahá'u'lláh put out of the country. Now the Bábí Faith would finally be gone for good.

Or so they thought!

God has a Plan for the world. He gives mankind a new divine Messenger. And then there are people who want to destroy that new Messenger's Faith. Can anyone do that? No, of course not! Whatever people do, the Plan of God goes on. And God's Plan was that nine years after the Báb, a new Revelation would begin.

And that is what happened. Just at a time when it all seemed so hopeless, when Bahá'u'lláh was a prisoner and might be killed any day, He received a vision in the Síyáh-Chál. In that vision He saw a heavenly Maiden, who pointed with her finger at His head. She spoke to all who were in heaven and all who were on earth in a marvellously sweet voice. She said that Bahá'u'lláh was the Best Beloved of the world, the Beauty of God, and the Mystery of God.

Fortunately, the enemies of the Faith did not know that Bahá'u'lláh was the new divine Messenger. Otherwise they would surely have killed Him! Now they had released Him and ordered Him to leave Persia, the land of His birth. It was up to Him how to manage this. While 'Abbás's mother was nursing Bahá'u'lláh, she also tried to prepare her family as well as she could for the journey. There was no money left. Everything had been stolen from them. She could only sell the few small things she had been able to save when the house was ransacked. But these did not bring in much money, not nearly enough to buy what they needed for the journey.

Yet they had to leave. They had not enough clothing. Bahá'u'lláh was still very weak. 'Abbás's mother was expecting a baby. And then they found that 'Abbás was sick too. He had tuberculosis, which is a serious disease of the lungs. The doctors had said that He would not get better. Yet they were not allowed to stay any longer in Persia. So they began the long and difficult journey in the middle of winter. They had to go over high mountains and often had to make a way for themselves through a deep layer of snow. They felt bitterly cold in their clothes which were far too thin, so cold that sometimes

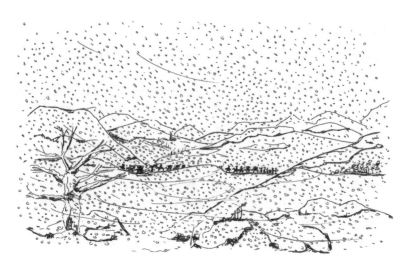

they could hardly move. 'Abbás's feet twice got frostbitten. His whole life, He had trouble as a result and later always had to wear extra large shoes.

After a terrible journey of three months they arrived exhausted in Baghdad. Now at last Bahá'u'lláh had a chance to grow stronger and for His wounds to heal. And how was 'Abbás now? In Baghdad He went to the doctor again. This doctor said that He was in the best of health. He had recovered completely from his deadly illness. It was as if a miracle had happened.

There was something else which was very different. 'Abbás saw that His Father had changed when He came out of the Síyáh-Chál. He was glowing with happiness. 'Abbás knew quite well that His Father was different to other fathers. Even much, much more than that. He was a divine Messenger. 'Abbás knew this Himself without having been told by anyone. It was still a great secret and at first Bahá'u'lláh did not let anyone know about it. Not until ten years later, in the Garden of Riḍván, did He tell this to a small group of followers.

But there was one to whom, shortly after arriving in Baghdad, Bahá'u'lláh told the secret. That was 'Abbás, then a boy of nine years old. 'Abbás immediately recognized Bahá'u'lláh. He threw Himself at His feet and begged Him earnestly for the privilege of sacrificing his life for Him.

Just imagine: a new divine Messenger comes from God. And the first person to whom He makes Himself known is a boy of nine. That boy must indeed be very special! And 'Abbás was. He was not only Bahá'u'lláh's first disciple but also became Bahá'u'lláh's first servant. From His boyhood He served Bahá'u'lláh all His life, day after day.

Later He said that He wished to be known as 'Abdu'l-Bahá. This name means Servant of Bahá, servant of Bahá'u'lláh. Therefore we shall not call him 'Abbás in this book any more, but 'Abdu'l-Bahá.

# 5

# The Wicked Half-brother

Bahá'u'lláh had been released from the Síyáh-Chál and had made the terrible journey with His family to Baghdad. How glad they were to be together again, especially 'Abdu'l-Bahá. He knew that Bahá'u'lláh was the Promised One that the Báb had repeatedly said would soon appear. 'Abdu'l-Bahá was, after all, the first one that Bahá'u'lláh had told. He wanted to serve Bahá'u'lláh in whatever way He could. And He wanted to be with Him as much as He possibly could.

A great many people wanted to go to see Bahá'u'lláh. He had only been living in Baghdad a short time but already He possessed a great power of attraction for its inhabitants. If He went to the coffee house, it was not long before that coffee house was packed with people. And many Bábís, followers of the Báb, came from Persia to visit Him.

It was a difficult time for the followers of the Báb. The Báb had been killed. Vahíd, Táhirih and the many others who could have led them had also been murdered. There was no one left to whom they could put their questions. And they had still so many questions to ask.

Many Bábís thought that Mírzá Yaḥyá, Bahá'u'lláh's half-brother, had been chosen by the Báb as His successor. So they asked Mírzá Yaḥyá to explain what they had not properly understood themselves. But he could not help them to solve their problems and could not give any proper answers to their questions. Mostly they got no answers at all because hardly anyone knew where he was. Mírzá Yaḥyá stayed in hiding as much as he could. He was very frightened that something might happen to him. When he heard of the martyrdom of the Báb, he disguised himself as a dervish, a poor wandering beggar. At another time he was a merchant selling shrouds or cotton cloth. Yet another time he went about disguised as a Jew selling shoes and sandals. He did all this so that no one would discover who he was. He was so scared. Could someone who was so scared be a good leader?

No, Mírzá Yaḥyá could not lead the Bábís. Yet he wanted them to see him as their leader. When he saw that so many people were going to Bahá'u'lláh, and respecting Him, Mírzá Yaḥyá became even more jealous than he already was. He himself wanted to be respected like that. He began spreading mean lies about Bahá'u'lláh. He said that Bahá'u'lláh was trying to destroy the Faith of the Báb. Mírzá Yaḥyá also sowed dissension among the Bábís. And all this out of pure envy.

Bahá'u'lláh wanted to build up the Faith of the Báb once more. But He saw how it was being pulled down before His eyes. And this was being done by His own half-brother. Bahá'u'lláh's sorrow knew no bounds. He did not wish to be the source of disharmony and disunity and so decided to withdraw Himself. One morning He suddenly disappeared. No one knew where He was, not even His own family!

'Abdu'l-Bahá was again without his Father. How sad it made him, as it did his mother and little sister Fáṭimih. He and his sister helped their mother as much as they could. As a boy of about ten now, He also looked after things as his Father used to do. He sometimes took on tasks which even grown-up people would have found too difficult.

Their life was very hard. Something else happened which made it even harder than it was already. Mírzá Yaḥyá and his family had come to live in their house with them. They did their very best to make him welcome. Mírzá Yaḥyá always got the best and nicest food. Yet He always grumbled about his food. He was never grateful or contented, and he never offered to help. As well, he was always afraid that people would find out where he was. Fáṭimih was not even allowed to play with the girls next door. If she even opened the door a little to look out at the other children, Mírzá Yaḥyá came out angrily to close it again. And he did not want anyone to come to visit them. Shortly after their arrival in Baghdad, another little brother was born. When this baby was sick, Mírzá Yaḥyá would not let anyone call a doctor. When the little boy died, they were not even allowed to bury him. A man came to fetch the little body. They never knew where it was buried.

How 'Abdu'l-Bahá longed for His Father to come back. He prayed unceasingly for His return, sometimes all night long. Once, when He had said prayers the whole night, He heard from some travellers about a wonderfully wise man who lived somewhere far away in the mountains of Kurdistan. Who else could that be but Bahá'u'lláh? 'Abdu'l-Bahá and His uncle Mírzá Músá immediately sent someone off to look for Him and to beg Him to come back. They waited anxiously. At last, there He was! After two long years, Bahá'u'lláh was back in Baghdad. What joy it was for them to see Him again. 'Abdu'l-Bahá was perhaps the happiest of all. He almost hid Himself in His Father's clothing, He crept so closely up to Him. He held His hand so tightly that it seemed as if He would never let Him go again.

# 6

## The Mystery of God

For two whole years, Bahá'u'lláh had been away from Baghdad. For two whole years Mírzá Yaḥyá had had the opportunity to show that he was capable of leading the Bábís. After all, he really wanted so much to be the leader. But was he capable of it? No, definitely not! The Faith of the Báb had declined even more. In the time of the Báb, His followers had been brave and honest people. They would give anything for their Faith, even their lives. Now there was nothing of that spirit left. The Bábís had become frightened people and they were simply laughed at in the street. No one had any respect for them now.

It was becoming clearer to the Bábís that Mírzá Yaḥyá could not possibly be their leader. But then, who was? Some Bábís who thought that it was them stood up and said they were the divine leader about whom the Báb had spoken. There were about twenty-five of them! This did not, of course, improve matters at all. No, the confusion and disunity only got worse. The Faith of the Báb seemed to be lost beyond saving.

How hard it must have been for 'Abdu'l-Bahá to see the Faith of the Báb going backward so quickly. He knew well Who the Promised One was that the Báb had foretold: Bahá'u'lláh. No one else. 'Abdu'l-Bahá was, after all, the first one to whom Bahá'u'lláh had told this, soon after they had arrived in Baghdad from Persia. 'Abdu'l-Bahá knew that only His Father could bring back unity among the Bábís and that only Bahá'u'lláh would be able to save the Faith of the Báb.

Thankfully, Bahá'u'lláh was now back in Baghdad. When He saw how badly things were going with the followers of the Báb, He became very sorrowful. He withdrew Himself for a while and would see no one. But soon Bahá'u'lláh began once more to lead the Bábís. He wrote letters to them and revealed Tablets for them. That meant a lot of work for 'Abdu'l-Bahá as well. Because those letters and Tablets, and even books, had to be copied out before they were sent. Such as the Book of Certitude, a book of a hundred and fifty pages, which 'Abdu'l-Bahá copied out very carefully by hand.

Bahá'u'lláh also went to the meetings of the Bábís. These were often held on the banks of the river Tigris. And 'Abdu'l-Bahá just loved to go with Him. He listened attentively to what Bahá'u'lláh taught the Bábís. Who could understand Bahá'u'lláh's words better than he? He also went along to the meetings of the divines. They were astonished that such a young boy could explain the most difficult things that they themselves had never properly understood. When they asked

23

Him from whom He had learned all this, His answer was always: 'From my Father'.

He thought a lot about the words of Bahá'u'lláh. He could see what would happen if people followed Bahá'u'lláh's teachings. The world would then become a very different world. Then prejudices would disappear and the Most Great Peace would reign. Then the Kingdom of God would exist on earth – for which people had been praying for nearly two thousand years. Then there would be no more war, then everyone would have a house to live in and everyone would have enough to eat.

'Abdu'l-Bahá was also like a shield that protected his Father. When visitors came, He decided who should and who should not be allowed to see Bahá'u'lláh. He was a good judge of people. He knew exactly who were the sincere seekers after truth and who were those only coming out of curiosity. Those who only came out of curiosity were not allowed to see Bahá'u'lláh.

Even when He was very young, He helped to teach the Faith. Sixty years later, on His travels through Germany, He said this about it:

'It is good to be a spreader of the Teachings of God in childhood. I was a teacher in this Cause at the age of this child.' He pointed to a child of eight or nine and told the following story of an event in his childhood:

There was a man, highly educated, but not a Bahá'í. I, but a child, was to make of him a believer. The brother of this man brought him to me. I stayed with him, to teach him. He said, 'I am not convinced, I am not satisfied.' I answered, 'If water were offered to a thirsty one, he would drink and be satisfied. He would take the glass. But you are not thirsty. Were you thirsty, then you too would be satisfied. A man with seeing eyes sees. I can speak of the sun to every seeing one, and say it is a sign

24

of the day; but a blind person would not be convinced because he cannot see the sun. If I say to a man with good hearing, listen to the beautiful music, he would then listen and be made happy thereby. But if you play the most beautiful music in the presence of a deaf man, he would hear nothing. Now go and receive seeing eyes and hearing ears, then I will speak further with you on this subject.' He went; but later he returned. Then he understood and became a good Bahá'í. This happened when I was very young.

When 'Abdu'l-Bahá was about twelve, Bahá'u'lláh told everyone to call Him 'the Master'. Bahá'u'lláh also called Him 'the Mystery of God'. A mystery is something that we cannot explain. People cannot understand how someone can be like 'Abdu'l-Bahá. He is Bahá'u'lláh's gift to mankind. His true station is something we will never be able to understand.

'Abdu'l-Bahá experienced great changes in Baghdad. They had arrived as penniless refugees. How much He missed His Father when He had then gone alone into the desert for two whole years. Things had looked so hopeless for the Faith then. After His return the Faith was again going forward. The Bábís were once more the loyal, honest people that they had been before. When the Bábís in Persia heard that Bahá'u'lláh was back in Baghdad, many came to see Him. But among all the people who came to see Him, there was hardly anyone who knew who Bahá'u'lláh really was. For most of the Bábís, Bahá'u'lláh was a prominent follower of the Báb. He had told no one but 'Abdu'l-Bahá that He was the new Promised One. However, there were some believers who had discovered this for themselves. To them Bahá'u'lláh had said that they should not yet make it known. When would Bahá'u'lláh also reveal it to other people?

# 7

# A Journey of More Than a Hundred Days

In Baghdad the people were drawn as by a magnet to
Bahá'u'lláh. His house was the point of attraction for all kinds
of visitors. People came who had been unjustly treated. They
asked Him to help in the hope of repair for the injustice
done. Bábís from Persia came. Their only purpose was to
be with Bahá'u'lláh. Refugees from Persia came who had
been constantly threatened in their own country. They were
seeking safety. If Bahá'u'lláh went to any of the coffee houses in
Baghdad, many important people of the city hurried off there
too. They wanted so much to be with Him. Even the British
Consul began a friendly correspondence with Bahá'u'lláh. The
Consul even offered to help Bahá'u'lláh to travel to another
country where He would be safe.

For the Muslim clergy, the mullahs, it was a thorn in the
side that Bahá'u'lláh was so respected and so popular. They
were jealous. First, by telling all kinds of lies about Bahá'u'lláh,
they tried to make Him leave Baghdad. This failed. Then they
tried to stir up the inhabitants against Him, in the hope that
the Bábís would take revenge on them. Then they would have
a reason to get rid of Bahá'u'lláh from Baghdad. The Bábís did
not let themselves be tempted to take revenge. The mullahs
even hired someone to kill Bahá'u'lláh. That failed too.

The mullahs kept on trying. They also tried to make Bahá'u'lláh
look bad in the eyes of the Persian government. No lies were too
barefaced for them to tell. They even claimed that Bahá'u'lláh

was in a position to mobilize an army of a hundred thousand soldiers in one day! In this way they tried to frighten the Persian government. And at last their efforts succeeded: Bahá'u'lláh received a request to go to Istanbul, the capital of the Turkish Empire known at that time to Westerners as Constantinople. That was a very long way from Persia, over a hundred days' journey. It looked as if the enemies of the Faith had triumphed at last. But was this the case? Or had they, without knowing it themselves, done exactly what was part of the Plan of God?

Ten years earlier, when Bahá'u'lláh had been a prisoner in Teheran in the Síyáh-Chál, that dark, filthy hole, it also looked as if the enemies of the Faith had triumphed. But just then Bahá'u'lláh had the vision of the heavenly Maiden. For ten years it had to remain a secret that Bahá'u'lláh was the new divine Messenger. And now, now the enemies of the Faith again thought that they had won a great victory because Bahá'u'lláh had to leave Baghdad, just now the moment had come to reveal that long-kept secret. In the Garden of Riḍván, Bahá'u'lláh told a small group of followers that He was the Promised Messenger. The divine Messenger who, as the Báb had foretold, would soon appear.

Bahá'u'lláh stayed in the Garden of Riḍván for twelve days. These were days of intense joy. It was the start of the holiest and most important feast in the Bahá'í Faith, the Festival of Riḍván. They were, at the same time, days of sadness, because Bahá'u'lláh had to leave Baghdad! The people of Baghdad were filled with deep sorrow. Overwhelmingly great was the sorrow of the Bábís who had to stay behind in Baghdad. They felt desperate. Some of them would even have killed themselves if Bahá'u'lláh had not prevented it.

The enemies had wanted to humiliate Bahá'u'lláh. But this humiliation turned into a great victory. For, when Bahá'u'lláh left Baghdad, it did not look as if He was a prisoner at all. It looked much more as if a king were leaving the city. The whole of Baghdad was on the street to see Bahá'u'lláh off. That is how much He was respected by the inhabitants.

It would be a long, difficult journey for Bahá'u'lláh's family and the twenty-six followers who went with them. Ten Turkish soldiers also went along to protect them from highway robbers. The journey was over high, narrow mountain passes and through hot desert areas. So hot, that they could not even travel by day. So they often travelled by night, sometimes in the pitch dark. Once it happened that they had to stop to mend something. One of the men in the group, Áqá Riḍá, was so tired that he went to sit somewhere to rest. He promptly fell asleep and when he woke up five hours later, he found to his horror that they had all gone. They had forgotten him in the dark. Only hours later they discovered he was not with them. They were just about to go looking for him when he turned up, having found them again himself.

It was a tiring journey. They had to walk for hours at a stretch, sometimes even 20 or 25 miles in one day or one night. When they had reached their destination at the end of another of those long treks, most of them fell straight away into a deep sleep. When their food was ready, they had to be shaken awake, but as soon as they had eaten they immediately went back to sleep.

It was also a dangerous journey. Once, they had to cross a fast-flowing river. Two mules were carried away by the current. This was so strong that it was not possible to save them. Another time they were going over a high, narrow mountain pass. Just for a moment, they lost control of the mule carrying Bahá'u'lláh's litter. The animal slipped down the slope and everyone could see what would happen: with Bahá'u'lláh on its back it would fall into the abyss. But as if by some miracle the mule regained its balance and scrambled back up. What a fright they had! And how glad they were that Bahá'u'lláh had escaped such great danger.

'Abdu'l-Bahá was busy every day helping everyone as much as He could. At the end of a day's journey, He went to the surrounding villages to try to buy food for the people and the animals. This was a difficult task, as there was a famine in some of those regions. Sometimes it took until midnight for Him to find enough to buy. In the morning He was always the first one up, to help with taking down the tents and packing up their belongings so that they could go on. During the day or at night He often walked beside the mule carrying Bahá'u'lláh's litter, just to make sure that the journey was as comfortable as possible for Bahá'u'lláh. To be able to take some rest Himself,

'Abdu'l-Bahá sometimes rode on His horse a good way farther on. He saw that the horse could lie down and then went to sleep himself with His head on the horse's neck. When the horse heard the rest of the group coming, it would shake 'Abdu'l-Bahá awake.

The animals, too, suffered under such a difficult journey, especially as it was not possible to buy enough feed for them. The horses and mules got so much thinner that it was harder and harder for them to go on. But when they reached the little town of Khárpút the governor of that town sent them ten cartloads of fodder. 'Abdu'l-Bahá said afterwards that it was a gift from God. They nearly always refused gifts and bought the food themselves but this time the gift was gratefully accepted. They were able to stay there for a whole week to recover from their exhaustion. They really needed that. 'Abdu'l-Bahá was so tired that He slept for two days and two nights almost without waking up at all.

After this they departed once more. Through the high, cold mountains and dense forests of Turkey until, after more than a hundred days, they reached the port of Samsun. There they continued their journey on a steamship to Istanbul.

In Baghdad, Bahá'u'lláh had foretold that great tests awaited Him and His followers. This prediction would very soon come true in Istanbul.

# 8

## The Dead Branch is Cut From the Tree

'Abdu'l-Bahá was nineteen when He arrived in Istanbul with his Father and his family. He was still young, but He had already seen Bahá'u'lláh suffer so much. As a boy of nine He had seen in what a miserable state Bahá'u'lláh had been when He was held a prisoner in the Síyáh-Chál. Then Bahá'u'lláh and His family had to leave Teheran for Baghdad, in the bitter cold, over high mountains. In Baghdad, Bahá'u'lláh had gone alone into the desert because the jealous Mírzá Yaḥyá wanted to be the leader. Later, when Bahá'u'lláh was back in Baghdad and many came to visit him, the Persian ambassador got Him banished to Istanbul. After that followed the long, difficult journey of more than a hundred days.

In Istanbul things turned out as Bahá'u'lláh had predicted: very soon there was more trouble. Once again this was caused by the Persian ambassador. He had earlier done his best to make Bahá'u'lláh leave Baghdad. Now he wanted to get rid of Bahá'u'lláh from Istanbul too. He tried his best to damage Bahá'u'lláh's reputation in the eyes of the government. And once again he got what he wanted. The government decided to banish Bahá'u'lláh to Edirne. This was a far-off town on the extreme edge of the huge Ottoman Empire, as far away as possible from Persia, known at that time to Westerners as Adrianople.

So, not even four months later, Bahá'u'lláh with His family and some followers had to make another journey. From

Istanbul to Edirne. Just like their first banishment from Teheran to Baghdad. It was icy cold winter weather and now, too, they had not enough warm clothing to protect them from the cold. It was such a hard winter that even the oldest people could not remember having had such a cold one. If they needed water, they first had to light a fire to melt some ice. Sometimes they saw people lying at the roadside who had frozen to death. This most dreadful journey lasted for twelve days.

In Edirne, Bahá'u'lláh found more opposition. Now it was mainly Mírzá Yaḥyá who caused Bahá'u'lláh a great deal of sorrow. He was again trying to become the leader of the Faith. In Baghdad it had become very clear that he was not capable of leadership. But Mírzá Yaḥyá's greed for power knew no bounds. He tried to murder Bahá'u'lláh by smearing poison in His teacup. He poisoned the well, so that the whole family fell sick. He told Bahá'u'lláh's barber that he must kill Him when he was giving Him His bath. He encouraged all kinds of malicious gossip to be spread about Bahá'u'lláh. Mírzá Yaḥyá even went so far as to say that he himself was a messenger from God and that all the people in the world must obey him.

For years, Bahá'u'lláh had always given protection to Mírzá

Yaḥyá. Every time he did something nasty, Baháʼuʼlláh told His family and followers to keep it quiet. They must not talk to anyone about it. But when Mírzá Yaḥyá said that he himself was a messenger from God, that was the end of it. Up to that time, Mírzá Yaḥyá was respected by the Baháʼís because he was a member of the Holy Family. And up to that time he was regarded by almost everyone as a faithful Baháʼí and allowed to be anywhere the Baháʼís gathered. Now that was finished. Mírzá Yaḥyá and his small group of helpers were separated from the faithful believers. They no longer belonged. They were like dead branches which were cut from the living tree.

Baháʼuʼlláh had such a lot to bear! But even though His suffering was so great, He still went on giving His divine Message to the people. Nothing can stop a Messenger of God from carrying out His mission. It was actually in those terribly difficult years in Edirne that Baháʼuʼlláh revealed very important letters. We call such letters from Baháʼuʼlláh Tablets. Like the Súriy-i-Mulúk, the letter to the kings and rulers of that time. In this and other Tablets He announced His Mission and urged the kings to accept His message. Baháʼuʼlláh assured the kings that His Faith would conquer the world even if not a single king became a follower of His Faith. Day and night Baháʼuʼlláh revealed new Tablets. His secretary, who could write really fast, wrote them down. Others were busy all the time, copying them. ʻAbduʼl-Bahá, too, was busy day and night doing this. There was not a minute to lose. But even though they worked so hard, they could not keep up. A great many of the Tablets could not be copied out.

In Edirne Baháʼuʼlláh revealed another important Tablet. This was the Tablet about ʻAbduʼl-Bahá: 'Tablet of the Branch' (in Arabic: 'Súriy-i-Ghuṣn'). In this, Baháʼuʼlláh writes of the high station of 'Abdu'l-Bahá. For example, He calls him the 'Branch of Holiness' and the 'Limb of the Law of God'. Bahá'u'lláh declared in this Tablet also how important it would later be to obey 'Abdu'l-Bahá. He wrote, 'Whoso turneth towards Him hath turned towards God, and whoso turneth away from Him hath turned away from My Beauty, hath repudiated My Proof, and transgressed against Me.' That means that everyone who later disobeyed 'Abdu'l-Bahá was not being obedient to Bahá'u'lláh either.

For 'Abdu'l-Bahá too, the years in Edirne were very difficult. For who could understand better than 'Abdu'l-Bahá how much Bahá'u'lláh had to suffer? And 'Abdu'l-Bahá probably knew that the time would come that Bahá'u'lláh would have to suffer even more. That time would not be far away.

The Persian ambassador and the ministers in Istanbul saw that the Faith was still gaining more followers. Even Bahá'u'lláh's banishment to such an out-of-the-way place as Edirne could not stop the growth of the Faith. They were becoming worried. And their worries were increased by the lies which Mírzá Yaḥyá and his fellow-conspirators were still spreading about Bahá'u'lláh. They even started a rumour that Bahá'u'lláh was plotting with Bulgarian military leaders and those in other European countries to take the capital city of Istanbul.

The ministers did not try to find out the truth of these rumours first. They were not so concerned about the truth. Especially if they could use such lies to carry out their own evil plans. They decided to banish Bahá'u'lláh once again. This time to 'Akká, a dreadful prison city to which only the worst criminals were sent.

34

# 9

## In the Prison City of 'Akká

The people of 'Akká were filled with curiosity as they watched Bahá'u'lláh arriving in 'Akká with His family and companions. They wanted to see the 'God of the Persians'. That's what they called Bahá'u'lláh. All kinds of wild rumours were going around 'Akká about Him and His followers. They were said to be bad people, criminals of the worst kind. Even in the mosques, people were told not to have anything to do with these prisoners. They jeered at the prisoners when they walked through the streets and did not hide their contemptuous and hostile feelings. No, it was not in the least a friendly reception.

What awaited the exiles in the prison itself was not very pleasant either. The first night, especially, was dreadful. It had been a stiflingly hot day and they had spent the whole of it sitting on the boat in the burning sun. They were dying of thirst, but they got nothing to drink. 'Abdu'l-Bahá begged the guards several times for water, especially for the children. But it was no use. Not until next morning did they get any water or bread.

For the first months things were little better. The food was bad, there was not enough of it and the drinking water was not very good either. It was not very long before all the prisoners became ill. Only 'Abdu'l-Bahá and one of the other Bahá'ís were left to look after the sick. Day and night they were kept busy. At last 'Abdu'l-Bahá Himself became very ill. But luckily He got better.

The Sultan in Istanbul had given strict orders: the exiles

35

must have no contact with anyone in 'Akká. Bahá'u'lláh was only allowed to speak to members of His family. When they went into the city to buy anything the guards had to go with them. In those first months, things were so bad that the guards even had to go with them when they wanted to have a bath. The guards were cruel and grasping. They treated the prisoners very unkindly. They had heard such bad things about them! But however badly or unkindly the Bahá'ís were treated, they never did anything mean or unkind in return. They were guided in this by 'Abdu'l-Bahá. He always remained kind and patient no matter what the guards did. Even under the most difficult circumstances, 'Abdu'l-Bahá showed a good example to the Bahá'ís. This changed the prison guards, too. Very slowly, they became a little kinder. How could they stay so unkind to such people who never did anything mean in return? Still, life in the prison remained very difficult. Then a serious accident happened as well.

Mírzá Mihdí, 'Abdu'l-Bahá's younger brother, was walking on the roof saying his prayers. For a moment he was not paying attention, and fell through the skylight. He was so badly hurt that the doctor who was called could do nothing for him. 'Abdu'l-Bahá threw Himself at Bahá'u'lláh's feet and begged for his brother's recovery. Bahá'u'lláh spoke to Mírzá Mihdí and said that if he himself wanted it, God could make him better. But Mírzá Mihdí asked Bahá'u'lláh if he could give his life. For the pilgrims. Because when they arrived in 'Akká after a long, dangerous and tiring journey, they were not allowed into the city and could not visit Bahá'u'lláh. Mírzá Mihdí thought this was dreadful for the pilgrims. So he wanted to give his life for this, so that the city gates would be opened and the pilgrims could visit their Lord. The day after the accident Mírzá Mihdí died. He was only 22 years old.

Four months later the exiles were allowed to leave the prison building. That did not mean that they were free. They had to remain in 'Akká. They were given houses but these were much too small. For a while, thirteen people – men and women – had to sleep in one room.

Some of the Bahá'ís went, like 'Abdu'l-Bahá, to live at the caravanserai. The rooms were damp and dirty. 'Abdu'l-Bahá had sold a gift He had once received in Baghdad and with this money He had the rooms done up. He left his own room to the last but when they came to that, the money was all gone. So 'Abdu'l-Bahá had a room with a leaking roof, damp walls and a dirty floor. He had only a mat on which He could sit and sleep. And there was another nasty thing: the room was full of fleas. When 'Abdu'l-Bahá went to sleep under his sheepskin, the fleas were able to get inside to bite him. But He found a way to deal with them. Every time they had almost got inside the sheepskin, 'Abdu'l-Bahá woke up, turned the sheepskin inside out and went back to sleep. He had to turn the sheepskin about ten times every night.

Even though they were no longer in the prison, Bahá'u'lláh and His followers were still prisoners in 'Akká. The Sultan's strict order that they were not to leave 'Akká was still in force. And the people living in 'Akká still thought that they were criminals and infidels with whom it would be best not to mix. This was made worse by Siyyid Muḥammad, the man who had always encouraged Mírzá Yaḥyá to make trouble. Mírzá Yaḥyá himself gave them no further trouble, for he had been exiled to the island of Cyprus. They would never see him again.

But the Sultan had decided that Siyyid Muḥammad had to go with them to 'Akká. There, he did everything he could think of to poison the lives of Bahá'u'lláh and His followers. Siyyid Muḥammad was always spreading slander. He even altered the words of Bahá'u'lláh's Writings and made sure that the falsified texts were read by the people. He changed them in such a way that they would be bound to arouse the anger of the residents of 'Akká. By such mean tricks he tried to stir up the people and the authorities of 'Akká more and more against Bahá'u'lláh. Bahá'u'lláh and His followers suffered dreadfully because of the scheming Siyyid Muḥammad.

Some of the Bahá'ís became very angry about this. They could not bear seeing Bahá'u'lláh suffering because of all this slander. But Bahá'u'lláh and 'Abdu'l-Bahá remained extremely patient and told the Bahá'ís that they should do the same. They were absolutely not to take revenge. But a small group of disobedient followers did that anyway; they shot Siyyid Muḥammad and two of his friends dead.

The consequences were frightful. Bahá'u'lláh and 'Abdu'l-Bahá had to appear in court and many Bahá'ís in 'Akká were thrown into prison. The hatred and contempt which the people of 'Akká had for the prisoners became greater than ever. They were blamed for everything. They were considered to be godless people, heretics and people who claimed there was no God. Insults were openly hurled at them in the street. Bahá'u'lláh's neighbour had become so frightened that he had the wall between their houses reinforced. Even the Bahá'í children hardly dared to appear on the street. They were pursued, called names and had stones thrown at them. This is how much the people of 'Akká hated the Bahá'ís.

Fortunately it would not remain like this. It was God's will that it should change. After a while the residents of the city realized that Bahá'u'lláh was innocent of the murder. Their hostile attitude slowly began to change. It was mainly 'Abdu'l-Bahá who made this happen. He mixed with everyone, high and low, rich and poor. He had a gentle and kindly character. He was always extremely patient. Through 'Abdu'l-Bahá, the people began to realize that the Bahá'ís were not criminals as they had always been told. On the contrary, Bahá'ís were honest, kind people. Their hatred and contempt gradually changed into respect.

And what about the pilgrims who could not enter 'Akká? The pilgrims for whom Mírzá Mihdí had sacrificed his life? Their despair was also about to change. A new governor was sent to 'Akká, Aḥmad Big Tawfig, a just man. He knew about the Sultan's order that Bahá'u'lláh and 'Abdu'l-Bahá were not allowed any visitors. But nevertheless he allowed the pilgrims to visit Bahá'u'lláh.

So Mírzá Mihdí's wish was granted. He had not given his life in vain!

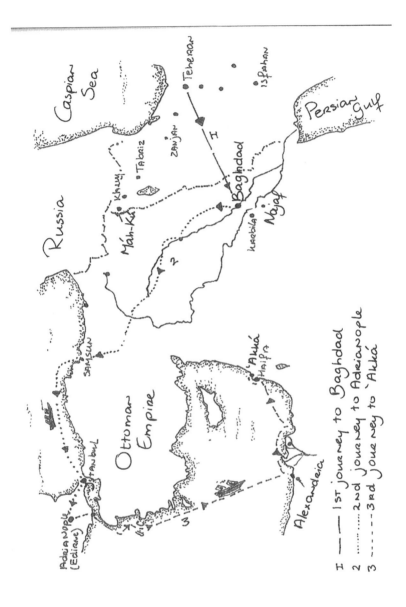

Caspian Sea

Persian Gulf

Russia

Teheran

Isfahan

Zanjan

Tabriz

Khuy.

Máh-Kú

Baghdad

Najaf

Karbilá

I

2

Samsun

Istanbul

Ottoman Empire

'Akká
Haifa

'Akká

Adrianople
(Edirne)

3

Alexandria

I ——— 1st journey to Baghdad
2 ············ 2nd journey to Adrianople
3 - - - - - 3rd Journey to 'Akká

41

# 10

# Munírih Khánum (I)

The Bahá'ís were filled with curiosity. 'Abdu'l-Bahá was a young man of 25, and still not married. Who would be his wife? At that time it was the custom in Persia that a boy and girl did not themselves choose whom they would marry. Their parents did this for them, often when they were very young. This had also happened with 'Abdu'l-Bahá. When He was still a child, His parents arranged that He would later marry His young cousin, Shar-Bánú.

Fifteen years later, Bahá'u'lláh sent a message to Teheran: Shar-Bánú could travel to Adrianople to marry 'Abdu'l-Bahá. One of Bahá'u'lláh's sisters heard about this. She was hostile to Him and did not miss this opportunity to work against Bahá'u'lláh. She took Shar-Bánú into her own house and forced her against her will to marry someone else.

Some time later, Bahá'u'lláh had a dream. He saw the face of Shar-Bánú before Him but it began to grow fainter and fainter. In its place the face of another girl appeared, with shining eyes and a radiant heart. Bahá'u'lláh chose her to become the wife of 'Abdu'l-Bahá.

The birth of this girl was a miracle which happened in the time when the Báb was still living. In Isfahan, a large city in Persia, a feast was being given in honour of the Báb by some of His followers. During this feast, the host went to the Báb and said, 'My brother, Mírzá Muḥammad-'Alí, has no child. I beg You to intercede on his behalf and to grant his heart's desire.'

The Báb at once took part of the food that was reserved for Him, placed it Himself upon a dish, handed it to His host and asked him to take it to Mírzá Muḥammad-'Alí and his wife. 'Let them both partake of this,' He said; 'their wish will be fulfilled.' Less than a year later they had a daughter: Fáṭimih. When Fáṭimih had grown to be a young woman, her marriage was also arranged by the family. She was going to marry a cousin. The family was rich and the wedding day was a wonderful occasion. But the lovely day ended very sadly. When the bride and groom were going home together, something very strange happened. Just as they were about to enter the house, the bridegroom collapsed. They had to help him to his feet. He seemed to be overcome by some power no one could explain. He became seriously ill and died a short time later. Fáṭimih was left alone and withdrew herself from the world around her. She spent her days in prayer and meditation.

Some months later, Shaykh Salmán arrived in Isfahan. He was Bahá'u'lláh's courier, who made journeys of thousands of miles on foot to deliver the letters from Bahá'u'lláh to the Bahá'ís in Persia. Shaykh Salmán had come now, too, from Bahá'u'lláh. So he knew what was happening to Him and to the Bahá'ís who had been banished with Him to 'Akká. The Bahá'ís in Isfahan were dying of curiosity, since at that time they heard very little news of Bahá'u'lláh. They hung upon every word spoken by Shaykh Salmán. They wanted to know everything, even the smallest details.

An aunt of Fáṭimih's had another question: had Shaykh Salmán ever heard that anyone had spoken in Bahá'u'lláh's presence of a wife for the Master, 'Abdu'l-Bahá?

'No,' he replied. But he did tell Fáṭimih's aunt about Bahá'u'lláh's dream. The dream in which the image of Shar-Bánú kept getting fainter and the image of another girl began to appear – the girl that Bahá'u'lláh had chosen to become the wife of 'Abdu'l-Bahá.

As soon as <u>Sh</u>ay<u>kh</u> Salmán had spoken of the dream, Fáṭimih's aunt knew that Fáṭimih was that girl. When they told her this, Fáṭimih began to cry and said, 'Far be it, for I am not worthy of such a bounty. I beg you never to breathe a word of this again; do not speak of it.'

Some months later it appeared that Fáṭimih's aunt was right after all. <u>Sh</u>ay<u>kh</u> Salmán had been ordered by Bahá'u'lláh to bring Fáṭimih to 'Akká. It would be a dangerous and difficult journey. The preparations had to be made in secret. No one was to find out that they were Bahá'ís who were on their way to 'Akká, to Bahá'u'lláh. So Bahá'u'lláh ordered that they should first go on pilgrimage to Mecca, the holiest place of Islám. From there they would have to go on quietly to 'Akká. There were four of them: <u>Sh</u>ay<u>kh</u> Salmán, Fáṭimih, her brother and a servant.

It was a journey full of uncertainties. Would they ever reach 'Akká? On the way they heard the bad news that not a single Bahá'í could get into or out of 'Akká. Three men had been killed in 'Akká and the governor of the city thought that Bahá'u'lláh had given the order for this. Nearly all the Bahá'ís in 'Akká had been thrown into prison. The Bahá'ís whom they met on the way urged them to go back. They would not get into 'Akká.

<u>Sh</u>ay<u>kh</u> Salmán never doubted for a moment that they would certainly reach their goal. He reassured them and said that this situation did not apply to them. He gave them confidence that they would arrive easily and peacefully in the Holy Land. Even if all the Bahá'ís were chained up in prison. Bahá'u'lláh Himself had invited Fáṭimih, hadn't He?

So they travelled on to Alexandria, in Egypt. There they

received permission from Bahá'u'lláh to travel by ship to 'Akká. They had to take an Austrian ship and when the ship reached the port of 'Akká, they had to wait until they were met by someone. The ship dropped anchor outside the harbour of 'Akká. The other passengers disembarked. Fáṭimih and her travelling companions waited for someone to come for them. But no one came. By this time darkness had fallen, the ladder for the passengers to go down into the little boats had already been hauled up and the ship was almost ready to leave. Now that they were so close to their goal, could something still go wrong?

Then, at the last minute, a small boat arrived. The men in it called: 'Sha<u>kh</u> Salmán, Sha<u>ykh</u> Salmán!' Just in time. In pitch dark they got off the big ship and were taken ashore in the small boat. Sha<u>ykh</u> Salmán had been right. They had arrived safely in 'Akká.

# 11

## Munírih Khánum (II)

When Fáṭimih was still a child, she often thought about the lives of Christ, Muhammad and the other Messengers of God. How she would have loved to be with them! Sometimes she cried because she had not lived in their time. And now she had been invited by Bahá'u'lláh to come to 'Akká. All during the long journey she was always thinking about the fact that she would be with Him. She was so filled with gladness and joy that she did not mind the hardships of the journey.

The very next day after her arrival in 'Akká, what Fáṭimih had so ardently longed for happened, and she was invited to come to meet Bahá'u'lláh. The first thing Bahá'u'lláh spoke to her about was the journey and the rumours on the way that Fáṭimih would never be able to get to 'Akká. He said, 'We have brought you into the Prison at such a time when the door of meeting is closed to all the believers. This is for no other reason than to prove to everyone the Power and Might of God.'

Fáṭimih was allowed to visit Bahá'u'lláh very often. How happy she was in the presence of Bahá'u'lláh. Each time it was as if her soul was floating in a heavenly atmosphere of peace and love. Her happiness and joy were so great that she would never be able to express them in words.

At first, Fáṭimih lived in the house of Mírzá Músá, Bahá'u'lláh's brother. This was a house which had a view of the sea. That was nice for her. For 'Abdu'l-Bahá sometimes went swimming in the sea and she could see Him from her window.

How strong He was and what a good swimmer!

Fáṭimih often received little presents from Bahá'u'lláh. Every time when Mírzá Músá had been to see Bahá'u'lláh, he brought something back for her. Then he came home one day with a beaming face and said, 'I have brought a most wonderful gift for you. It is this – a new name has been given you and that name is Munírih.' Munírih means 'Illumined'. This was the name Bahá'u'lláh had given her.

From then on Fáṭimih was called Munírih <u>Kh</u>ánum. <u>Kh</u>ánum is a title of respect given to women.

Munírih <u>Kh</u>ánum had come to 'Akká as the future bride of 'Abdu'l-Bahá. But after five months she was still living at the house of Mírzá Músá. Why was this? Why were they not getting married?

The neighbour of the Holy Family, 'Abbúd, also thought it was strange. He knew why Munírih had come to 'Akká. So he tried to find out why they were not getting married. But there was no one who would tell him. He kept on trying and finally he discovered the reason: there was no suitable place for them to live. When he heard this, he immediately had the solution. He had a spare room in his house. The room was right next to the house where the Holy Family lived. A door between the two houses could be made and then 'Abdu'l-Bahá and Munírih could have that room. As soon as Bahá'u'lláh had approved of this suggestion, 'Abbúd got busy and made sure that the bridal pair would have a nicely furnished room.

When the room was ready, Munírih <u>Kh</u>ánum went – as she often did – to visit the Holy Family again. But this time Bahá'u'lláh had given her instructions not to return to the home of Mírzá Músá. And He told 'Abdu'l-Bahá that He should come back home early that afternoon. The wedding would take place that same evening. 'Abdu'l-Bahá's mother and sister already had a wedding dress ready for the bride. The great moment had arrived! Now 'Abdu'l-Bahá and Munírih Khánum were getting married. It was a very unusual marriage ceremony, but the most beautiful that a bride and groom could wish for. Bahá'u'lláh was present. He spoke the following words to Munírih:

Oh Munírih! Oh my leaf! I have destined you for the wife of My Greatest Branch. This is the bounty of God to you. In earth or heaven there is no greater gift . . . Oh Munírih! Be worthy of Him, and of Our generosity to you.

Then Munírih chanted in her sweet voice the Tablet that Bahá'u'lláh had revealed for her and 'Abdu'l-Bahá. Bahá'u'lláh Himself also chanted some prayers.

They were wrapped in a great spiritual joy. It looked like a very simple marriage ceremony. There were very few guests. There were no decorations and no wedding cake. There was just tea. Yet it was the most beautiful wedding that Munírih Khánum could have imagined. She felt so happy that she would have liked to hold on to that hour for always. How greatly she loved 'Abdu'l-Bahá and His noble character. He was always cheerful and loved jokes. He was always ready to help others and had great patience with everyone. She thanked God that He had brought her to Him.

Munírih, even though she was very happy, was not going to have an easy life. No day passed without trouble of some kind. When they married, 'Abdu'l-Bahá was a prisoner of the Ottoman government and it would be thirty-five more years before He would be free. All those years Munírih Khánum

shared His exile. Sometimes the Sultan's orders were strictly obeyed by the guards. 'Abdu'l-Bahá had then to stay within the walls of 'Akká.

They were often poor. Then they could only buy the absolute necessities. And sometimes they could not even do that. 'Abdu'l-Bahá and Munírih Khánum had many sorrows. Of the nine children that they had, five died young. Only four daughters lived. And what difficult times they had because 'Abdu'l-Bahá's own relatives worked against Him so much.

Munírih Khánum always thought of other people first even if she herself was in trouble. And as soon as she saw that others had problems or were sad she went to them to help and comfort them. She was always ready to help everyone, with a heart glowing with love. That's why so many people called her the Holy Mother.

Even though her life in prison was a life full of difficulties, yet Munírih Khánum was eternally grateful that she was allowed to be the wife of 'Abdu'l-Bahá. Every day she thanked God that He had blessed her so richly. Munírih Khánum would never have wanted to exchange her life in prison with 'Abdu'l-Bahá for a life of freedom with luxuries and wealth. Together, they went through a great deal in the fifty years that they were married. Munírih Khánum once said that if she were to write all of it down, she would need at least fifty more years to do it. And if all the water in the sea were turned into ink and all the leaves of the forest into paper, it would still not be enough to write everything down.

# 12

## Enemies Become Friends

Do you remember the hate and contempt the inhabitants of 'Akká had for Bahá'ís? Especially after the murder of Siyyid Muḥammad and his accomplices. On the street, so that everyone could hear, the most horrible things were said against them.

The people of 'Akká had another way of showing their contempt, too. Like the Christian merchant. He, like the others, had heard little that was good about the Persian prisoners and so he had little respect for them either. Once, he saw a load of charcoal and heard that this belonged to the Bahá'ís. This was fuel of good quality. He himself could very well do with this and so he just kept it. It only belonged to those Bahá'ís after all. They were not really decent people so it was all right to take their stuff. At least that is what he thought.

When 'Abdu'l-Bahá heard about it, He went to the merchant to ask for the charcoal back. There were a lot of people there, but there was no one who paid Him any attention. What did 'Abdu'l-Bahá do? He went to sit down somewhere in the shop and He waited. A long time and very patiently. Three hours passed and 'Abdu'l-Bahá was still sitting there.

Then the merchant at last began to speak to Him and asked, 'Are you one of the prisoners in this town?'

'Yes,' said 'Abdu'l-Bahá.

The merchant asked, 'What was the crime for which you were imprisoned?'

'The same crime for which Christ was indicted.'

The merchant was indignant. He was, after all, a Christian and here was someone saying He was doing the same as what Christ had done.

'What can you know of Christ?', he asked 'Abdu'l-Bahá.

Then 'Abdu'l-Bahá began to tell him.

It was not long before the merchant was deeply affected by 'Abdu'l-Bahá. He discovered how arrogant he himself was and how patient was 'Abdu'l-Bahá. When a little later 'Abdu'l-Bahá stood up to leave, the merchant respectfully showed him to the door. At first he had regarded the Bahá'ís as suspicious prisoners. From that day on he was a friend to the Bahá'ís. And of course they got the money for the charcoal back.

More and more people in 'Akká were changed like that merchant. When they got to know the Bahá'ís better, they dropped their hostile attitude. They discovered that there was no truth in the unfavourable reports they had heard in the beginning about the Bahá'ís. The opposite was true; they appeared to be nice friendly people. And, in particular, you could always trust them, they would never cheat anyone.

'Abdu'l-Bahá was especially highly regarded by them. The people of 'Akká discovered that they could go to Him to ask for advice and help. Everyone could go to Him and no one ever went away disappointed. Even the governer of 'Akká went to visit 'Abdu'l-Bahá to discuss his most difficult problems with Him.

There was another great change. This too came about gradually. At first, when they had only just come to 'Akká, guards had to go with them if the Bahá'ís went into the city to do their shopping. After a few years, they were being treated less and less like prisoners and allowed to do more and more what they themselves wanted to. Finally they had so much freedom that they could even have their own little shops. No one placed the slightest obstacle in their way. And all the time the strict command of the Sultan was still officially in force; officially the Bahá'ís were not supposed to speak to anyone in 'Akká.

For Bahá'u'lláh, too, a great change was to come. Bahá'u'lláh loved life in the country. When He was young in the land of His birth, Persia, He used to take His horse and ride sometimes for days through the mountains. Now He had been shut in for years in 'Akká. Then one day He said that He had not seen anything green for nine years. 'Abdu'l-Bahá immediately understood what this meant. Bahá'u'lláh was longing to live in the country.

'Abdu'l-Bahá was sure that everything He would do to arrange that somehow, would also succeed. He rented a country house by a stream in Mazra'ih, four miles outside the city. He had the house done up and arranged for a carriage to take Bahá'u'lláh to it.

But how was 'Abdu'l-Bahá to manage about the order that none of the Bahá'ís could leave 'Akká? Not even 'Abdu'l-Bahá himself. What would happen if He did that anyway? He decided to try it and went to Mazra'ih himself to take a look. When He walked through the city gate, the soldiers were just standing there. No one stopped him. The next day He tried it again, this time with some officials and friends. There were soldiers standing guard on each side of the gate. No one said anything. A few days later He tried it again; He had organized a picnic in the country and even invited the city authorities to come. Once again no one stopped them.

Then 'Abdu'l-Bahá went to Bahá'u'lláh and said, 'The palace

at Mazra'ih is ready for you, and a carriage to drive you there.'
But Bahá'u'lláh refused. He said, 'I am a prisoner.'

'Abdu'l-Bahá tried a second time, and a third. Bahá'u'lláh
still refused. What could 'Abdu'l-Bahá do now? He did not
dare to insist any longer.

He went to the mufti of 'Akká. A mufti is someone who
explains the laws of Islam to others. Someone therefore who
understood very well what the Sultan's order meant: none of
the Bahá'ís was allowed to leave 'Akká. 'Abdu'l-Bahá asked the
mufti to go to Bahá'u'lláh, to kneel before Him, to take His
hands in his and not to let go before He had agreed to leave
the city.

The mufti went at once to Bahá'u'lláh. He knelt before Him,
grasped His hands, kissed them and asked, 'Why do you not
leave the city?'

'I am a prisoner,' replied Bahá'u'lláh.

'God forbid! Who has the power to make you a prisoner?
You have kept yourself in prison!'

The mufti kept begging Bahá'u'lláh to go to the country

house, telling Him how beautiful and green it was there. 'The trees are lovely, and the oranges like balls of fire!'

Again and again as Bahá'u'lláh said, 'I am a prisoner, it cannot be,' the mufti grabbed Bahá'u'lláh's hands and kissed them. Over and over again, for a whole hour. Until at last Bahá'u'lláh said, 'Very well.'

The very next day the carriage was driven up to take Bahá'u'lláh to Mazra'ih.

# 13

# The Shield that Protected Bahá'u'lláh

For nine long years, Bahá'u'lláh had been confined in 'Akká, the prison city. Happily that was now over. He had moved to Mazra'ih and was living in a house in the country. Two years later, 'Abdu'l-Bahá rented an even bigger house for his Father. That was the magnificent mansion of Bahjí. This was where Bahá'u'lláh lived until the end of His life on earth.

'Abdu'l-Bahá was still living with his family in 'Akká. Would He not have wanted to live in the country instead of in the city? He probably would. Then He could be with Bahá'u'lláh every day. Yet He did not move. 'Abdu'l-Bahá chose to live where He could best serve Bahá'u'lláh. And that was in 'Akká.

Formerly, when the Holy Family were still living in Baghdad, Bahá'u'lláh used to mix regularly with the people. In 'Akká that did not happen any longer; there it was 'Abdu'l-Bahá who went about on behalf of Bahá'u'lláh. 'Abdu'l-Bahá spoke to the government officials and made sure that all kinds of things were taken care of. If there were people who wished to visit Bahá'u'lláh, 'Abdu'l-Bahá decided who should see Him and who should not. Bahá'u'lláh only received the Bahá'ís. Very occasionally He received someone else if that person expressly requested it.

In the whole area, 'Abdu'l-Bahá began to be better known for His wisdom and knowledge. All kinds of people came to Him for advice, rich and poor, high and low. Even the governor of 'Akká often came to visit Him. He had so much respect for

'Abdu'l-Bahá that he took off his shoes before he entered His room. Even the authorities in the neighbouring towns were greatly impressed by Him. They came to visit Him and invited Him to come out of the city. Once, He was invited by one of the cleverest statesmen of that time to go to Beirut. There He spoke to some very prominent people.

Just imagine: 'Abdu'l-Bahá, the prisoner! The powerful Sultan of the great Ottoman Empire had forbidden Him to leave 'Akká. But the governors of that same Sultan were inviting Him to go to other cities! And the governor of his own city took off his shoes when he entered His room! That was how much respect they had for that prisoner!

And just imagine: 'Abdu'l-Bahá had hardly spent one year at school when He was a child. Yet because of His wisdom and knowledge, He received an invitation from Midḥát Páshá, the cleverest statesman of the time. And from other prominent people, who had all been well educated. Earlier, in Baghdad, when He was still a child, He had already amazed the learned with His knowledge and wisdom. Do you remember what He replied when they asked Him from whom He had learned it? 'From my Father.'

'Abdu'l-Bahá was there for everyone, especially for the poor people and those who needed help. He was always thinking of them. If necessary He would visit them Himself, even if they lived in the poorest little houses. If they were sick, He would look after them and if a doctor had to be called, He would pay him.

'Abdu'l-Bahá was also in 'Akká to help the pilgrims. After their long, tiring journey, they arrived exhausted in 'Akká. 'Abdu'l-Bahá made sure they had good lodgings. He prepared them for the greatest moment of their lives, the meeting with Bahá'u'lláh. Sometimes He inspected their clothes. If these

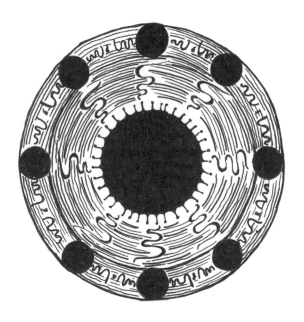

were worn or not suitable, He obtained other clothes so that they were properly dressed to go to Bahá'u'lláh.

By staying in 'Akká, 'Abdu'l-Bahá was able to save Bahá'u'lláh from having to bother about all the day-to-day worries. In this way He was the shield that protected Bahá'u'lláh. In this way, Bahá'u'lláh had the time and opportunity to reveal books and Tablets, and to write letters to the Bahá'ís.

'Abdu'l-Bahá had great reverence for Bahá'u'lláh. As often as possible, He went to visit Him. And as soon as He caught sight of the house where Bahá'u'lláh lived, 'Abdu'l-Bahá got out of His carriage or off His mule. He bowed low with His forehead to the ground, even if it was wet with rain. Then, out of reverence for Bahá'u'lláh He would walk the rest of the way. When He was with Bahá'u'lláh, He showed nothing but respect and humility.

Bahá'u'lláh taught His followers to have great respect for 'Abdu'l-Bahá. Bahá'u'lláh praised Him a lot. He called Him 'Áqá', 'the Master', and taught His family and followers to called Him the Master, too. When 'Abdu'l-Bahá visited Bahá'u'lláh, and Bahá'u'lláh saw Him coming in the distance, He told His family and followers to go and meet Him. That was a way to honour someone in the East.

Once He indicated to one of the pilgrims that meeting 'Abdu'l-Bahá was as if he were meeting Bahá'u'lláh Himself. This happened in the last year of Bahá'u'lláh's life on earth. The pilgrim, a youth of sixteen called Ṭarázu'lláh, had not been invited to meet Bahá'u'lláh for some days. At a moment when he was sure that Bahá'u'lláh was alone, he asked one of the children of the Holy Family if she would take a letter to Bahá'u'lláh. In this he asked for the bounty of being able to see Bahá'u'lláh again. When he was allowed to visit Him, Bahá'u'lláh asked him, 'Do you not meet the Master every day?'

'Yes,' replied Ṭarázu'lláh.

'Then why do you say that you have not been in My presence for days, while you have been with the Master every day and had the honour of being in his company?'

In this way Bahá'u'lláh made it clear that being with 'Abdu'l-Bahá was the same as being with Bahá'u'lláh. And thus Bahá'u'lláh was preparing His family and His followers for the time when He would no longer be on this earth.

# 14

## 'The Sun of Bahá Has Set'

The Sultan of the great Ottoman Empire was pleased. And so was the Shah of Persia. The Sultan had received a telegram from 'Abdu'l-Bahá which began with the words 'The Sun of Bahá has set'. That meant that Bahá'u'lláh had died. How could they be so pleased about that?

The Sultan and the Shah were the rulers of two great, powerful empires. They had both gone to a lot of trouble to destroy the Faith. In Persia the Báb and thousands of His followers had been killed. Bahá'u'lláh had been exiled by the Shah and the Sultan from one place to another, until He was finally sent to the Most Great Prison in 'Akká. They thought that they could destroy the Faith in this way. But they did not succeed. Just the opposite happened; the more intense the persecutions became, the faster the Faith grew. And its fame was spreading to more and more countries.

And now there was this telegram: 'The Sun of Bahá has set.'

The Sultan and the Shah became hopeful again; now that the leader had died things might still turn out as they had always wanted. Perhaps it would not be so long until the Bahá'í Faith would be no more!

For the Bahá'ís the news that Bahá'u'lláh had passed away was very sad. They were overcome by sorrow. How they would miss Him! How would they be able to go on living without Him? Who could ever fill the emptiness that Bahá'u'lláh had left behind? They were not only very sorrowful, they were also worried. What would happen now to the Faith? Who would be their leader now? Could the Faith really exist without Bahá'u'lláh?

Fortunately, Bahá'u'lláh Himself had made arrangements for the Faith to go on existing. He had made a Will. In a Will people write down what should happen to their possessions, like their money and their house, when they die. Bahá'u'lláh also wrote in His Will what was to happen after His death. Only He had no money to leave, for whatever He was given, He always gave to the poor. He Himself says in His Will: 'Earthly treasures We have not bequeathed . . .' Bahá'u'lláh wrote things in His Will that are much more important than money. His Will is a Covenant, an agreement with His followers. Bahá'u'lláh asks His followers to accept 'Abdu'l-Bahá as His successor and to obey Him. Bahá'u'lláh says that 'Abdu'l-Bahá is the Interpreter of His Book and the Centre of His Covenant. If they do not understand something or if there is a difference of opinion, the Bahá'ís must then ask 'Abdu'l-Bahá to help them to solve their problem. If His followers are obedient to the Covenant, the Faith will remain pure and unified. If they do not do this, disunity will be created. The Bahá'ís will then be split up and the Faith will lose its power.

The Covenant of Bahá'u'lláh is something very special. Never before had a Messenger of God written down who should lead the Faith after Him. After His death there was always disunity and disagreement among the followers. Often the disagreement and disunity was so great that they murdered each other and went to war against each other.

61

Through the Will and Testament and the Covenant of Bahá'u'lláh, there will be unity between the Bahá'ís. Is that possible? Something which has never happened before? Yes, it is! Because it is God's will that this unity now exists. And nothing or no one can oppose the will of God.

There were, however, evil influences which tried to break up that unity. Especially 'Abdu'l-Bahá's half-brother Mírzá Muḥammad-'Alí. Bahá'u'lláh had only just passed away and the family was still preparing His body for burial. Already Mírzá Muḥammad-'Alí was trying to steal the Will and Testament of Bahá'u'lláh. Luckily, 'Abdu'l-Bahá had kept it in a safe place!

The Sultan and the Shah had made a big mistake. What they were hoping would not happen. The Faith was not going to disappear at all. It was going to go on growing and shortly after the Ascension of Bahá'u'lláh the first Bahá'ís went to America to make the Faith known there. And later it would be spread from America to every part of the world.

And what happened to the two powerful rulers who worked so much against Bahá'u'lláh? A few years later the Shah was killed in his own country on the day that a great feast in his honour was to be held in Persia. The Sultan's empire became weaker and weaker. The once so powerful Ottoman Empire began to be called the 'sick man of Europe'. The Sultan was deposed from his throne and killed soon afterwards. That is what happened to Bahá'u'lláh's two most powerful enemies.

# 15

## The Stolen Satchels

During His last illness Bahá'u'lláh had given His Will and Testament to 'Abdu'l-Bahá. Who better could He trust? He knew that 'Abdu'l-Bahá had always been obedient to Him and would take great care to do exactly what He had written in His Will and Testament. It would soon be obvious how necessary that was.

Bahá'u'lláh's health began to deteriorate. 'Abdu'l-Bahá was busy day and night in looking after Him. 'Abdu'l-Bahá knew that Bahá'u'lláh would only be with Him for a short while longer. This thought made Him very sad. Then, one day, Bahá'u'lláh said to 'Abdu'l-Bahá that He should collect all the papers and seals which were in Bahá'u'lláh's room and put them away in two satchels. This had happened before. Whenever Bahá'u'lláh left His house for a few days, His papers had to be put away in those satchels. But now He could not go away; He was too ill for that. And yet His papers had to be put away.

'Abdu'l-Bahá understood very well what that meant. This made Him even sadder. Now it would not be very long at all before Bahá'u'lláh would die. He was so upset that Bahá'u'lláh had to ask Him again. With tears in His eyes and trembling hands, 'Abdu'l-Bahá began to put the papers away.

While 'Abdu'l-Bahá was doing this, Majdu'd-Dín came in. Majdu'd-Dín was a cousin of 'Abdu'l-Bahá's. He was a proud and treacherous man. It had often been noticed that he was not to be trusted. He was friendly with Mírzá Muḥammad-'Alí,

63

the half-brother of 'Abdu'l-Bahá. When Bahá'u'lláh was still alive, Mírzá Muḥammad-'Alí pretended to be a loyal follower of Bahá'u'lláh. But nevertheless he and Majdu'd-Dín together had given Bahá'u'lláh a lot of trouble.

'Abdu'l-Bahá asked Majdu'd-Dín to help Him put the papers and other valuable things belonging to Bahá'u'lláh into the satchels. When everything was packed up, Bahá'u'lláh told 'Abdu'l-Bahá that these satchels were now His. 'Abdu'l-Bahá became even more sorrowful at this. These words meant, after all, that the end of Bahá'u'lláh's life on earth was now very close. Shortly afterwards Bahá'u'lláh died. That was early in the morning of 29 May 1892.

Bahá'u'lláh had only just died when Mírzá Muḥammad-'Alí began to show his true character. The family were going to wash and prepare the body of Bahá'u'lláh for burial. The satchels containing the papers and seals, which 'Abdu'l-Bahá and Majdu'd-Dín had packed together, stood beside Bahá'u'lláh's bed. Mírzá Muḥammad-'Alí suggested to 'Abdu'l-Bahá that they should take the two satchels to another room. Because here they might get wet and then the papers in them might be damaged. At that moment, just after the death of Bahá'u'lláh, 'Abdu'l-Bahá was so shocked and full of sorrow that He was not really aware of what was going on around Him. He never thought for a moment that there would be a treacherous plan behind Mírzá Muḥammad-'Alí's suggestion. So He agreed and the bags were then taken to another room.

In the first few days after the funeral 'Abdu'l-Bahá was overcome with sorrow. The Light of the World was no longer on this earth and everything around him had become dark. At times He wept for hours on end. Three days later He had still not closed his eyes in sleep. The fourth night He still could

not sleep. He got up from his bed to walk up and down a bit. Perhaps that would help him. As He was walking in his room He looked out of the window and suddenly saw something His eyes could hardly believe. His brothers had opened the satchels and were going through the papers. Those same papers which Bahá'u'lláh had told 'Abdu'l-Bahá now belonged to Him!

'Abdu'l-Bahá did not want his brothers to know what He had seen. He went straight back to bed. The behaviour of his brothers made His sorrow even worse than it already was. He thought to himself that they were doing this because they did not yet know what Bahá'u'lláh had written in His Will and Testament. When they know that, He thought, they will soon stop their treacherous behaviour.

On the ninth day after the ascension of Bahá'u'lláh, the Will and Testament was read. This said it very clearly! 'The Will of the divine Testator is this: It is incumbent upon the Aghsán, the Afnán and My kindred' – by which are meant Bahá'u'lláh's family and blood relations – 'to turn, one and all, their faces towards the Most Mighty Branch.' And a little later Bahá'u'lláh writes: '. . . turn your faces toward Him Whom God hath purposed, Who hath branched from this Ancient Root. The object of this sacred Verse is none other except the Most Mighty Branch.' Everyone who heard it knew that by the Most Mighty Branch, 'Abdu'l-Bahá was meant. It could not be clearer. 'Abdu'l-Bahá must lead the Faith from now on, no one else. Everyone understood this. Even Mírzá Muhammad-'Alí. But did he want to understand it? That emerged a few days later!

One of the Bahá'ís had a Tablet which Bahá'u'lláh had revealed specially for him. A precious possession! He asked 'Abdu'l-Bahá if he could have a stamp with the seal of Bahá'u'lláh on it. Those seals were in the satchels which had been taken by Mírzá Muhammad-'Alí to another room when the family was busy washing the body of Bahá'u'lláh. So 'Abdu'l-Bahá asked his brother if He could have them back.

What was the reply? 'Abdu'l-Bahá's brothers said that they knew nothing about any satchels! When 'Abdu'l-Bahá heard that, His whole body began to tremble. He was deeply shocked and saddened. He knew then that they were still going to make things terribly difficult for Him.

And what about Bahá'u'lláh's faithful followers? Of course they were also sorrowful because Bahá'u'lláh was no longer with them. But after the reading of the Will and Testament they were relieved that Bahá'u'lláh had named the Most Great Branch, 'Abdu'l-Bahá, to lead the Faith. If they needed help, they could go to 'Abdu'l-Bahá. They put their whole trust in Him!

# 16

## The Beginning in America

Bahá'u'lláh had been a prisoner for forty long years. He had never had the opportunity to travel to other countries to teach His Faith there. But in spite of that, when He passed away there were quite a lot of countries where Bahá'ís lived. In Persia of course, where the Báb had lived and where Bahá'u'lláh was born. In Iraq, Turkey and the Holy Land, the countries where Bahá'u'lláh had lived as an exile. And in a few other countries: India, Russia, Syria and Egypt.

Soon after Bahá'u'lláh's ascension, His Faith would be spread much farther around the world. To Europe and especially to faraway America. When a Messenger of God comes with a new faith, then that new faith has to become known. Just as in Spring the flowers begin to bloom and leaves appear on the trees. No one can stop this happening.

Already in the year of Bahá'u'lláh's ascension, the first Bahá'ís went to America. One of these was Ibráhím Khayru'lláh. He was born in Syria and had been to a Christian school there. When he left school he went to Egypt. There he met a Persian Bahá'í who told him about Bahá'u'lláh. Two years later Ibráhím Khayru'lláh was visiting his Persian Bahá'í friend regularly. Then he decided to become a Bahá'í. He enthusiastically told one of his friends, Anton Haddad, about his new faith. Anton Haddad also began to visit the Persian Bahá'í and he, too, became a Bahá'í.

Ibráhím Khayru'lláh and Anton Haddad were the first Bahá'ís from the East who went to America. Ibráhím Khayru'lláh went to New York. He wanted to become a businessman. But this was not a success and two years later he settled in Chicago. He thought that he possessed special powers to heal the sick. He bought a diploma for himself so that he could call himself a doctor even though he had never studied medicine. In Chicago he tried to find people who were interested in the new Faith. He was very successful in this, because after only a few months there were the first Bahá'ís.

Ibráhím Khayru'lláh had a special way of going about his work. He gave courses of thirteen lessons. For thirteen weeks, one evening in the week. The first lessons were about the spirit of man and his immortal soul. Then he taught about the Prophets of God, especially a good deal about the Bible. He could easily do this since in his native land, Syria, he had been to a Christian school. In this way he prepared his students for his final lessons. These were the most important because then he told them that Bahá'u'lláh had come. He told his students that, with the coming of Bahá'u'lláh, the Bible prophecies had been fulfilled. As the Christians regard the Bible as the Word of God, they could not fail to regard Bahá'u'lláh as the Messenger of God Who had been promised in the Bible. Almost all the students accepted Bahá'u'lláh. The last lesson was the high point of the course. Then the students learned the Greatest Name: Alláh-u-Abhá. A solemn moment, which made a deep impression on the new believers.

In the time of Khayru'lláh there were very few Bahá'í books. This is why he did not know so much about the Faith and sometimes taught the Americans things that were not correct. He told them, for example, that Christianity was better than the other religions and that there were already 40 million Bahá'ís. He did not understand, either, who 'Abdu'l-Bahá was and said that 'Abdu'l-Bahá was the return of Christ.

He was rather secretive about his lessons. His students were not allowed to talk to others about them. They were only allowed to tell others if they were worthy of it and if they had Khayru'lláh's permission. Because of this secretive method the first Bahá'ís in some places in America were not even called Bahá'ís, but 'Seekers after Truth', or 'Knowers of Truth'.

Ibráhím Khayru'lláh was very strict with his students. He would not be contradicted. If one of his students said that he did not agree with him, he could pack his things and leave the class. He would not be allowed back.

Many Americans heard about the classes from friends or acquaintances who were taking the course. They became interested and then they, too, began to join the courses. In this way there were very soon many more Bahá'ís in America. Sometimes a person came in touch with the Faith in a very unusual way. One of these was Charlotte Dixon.

She had had a vision. Through this, she knew that there was a new Revelation. But so far she had not found anyone to tell her about it. Kneeling with her forehead on the floor, she begged God to send her someone who knew about this new Revelation. One day when she was praying again, there was a ring at the door. It was a woman who was asking for something and because it was such a dreadfully hot day, Charlotte Dixon asked her in to have a cool drink. While they sat talking, her visitor said that she had to visit a certain Mrs Reed, who did a great deal for the poor. Charlotte Dixon at once felt that she ought to do that too, and went there the same afternoon.

Mrs Reed was not at home, nor the following day either. When she tried the third day, again she wasn't there. So Charlotte Dixon spoke to one of Mrs Reed's neighbours. For a while the woman did not say anything and then she said,

'God sent you here, you are not seeking Mrs Reed. We have the greatest message since Christ.'

This neighbour of Mrs Reed's had followed the lectures given by Khayru'lláh. With tears in her eyes she spoke of the new Faith. She said that someone had come to Chicago from the Holy Land to teach people about the new Faith. This was Ibráhím Khayru'lláh. Charlotte Dixon did not waste any time. She looked him up and was also allowed to follow the lectures. A few months later she became a Bahá'í.

For years, Khayru'lláh taught the Faith in this way. He travelled to many cities to give his lectures. By the end of five years there were fifteen hundred Bahá'ís in America! Khayru'lláh had told his students many things about 'Abdu'l-Bahá. They would love to meet Him. But they knew that He was a prisoner and could not come to America. So a small group decided to go to visit 'Abdu'l-Bahá themselves in the Holy Land. Khayru'lláh was also invited to join them.

After this, things went wrong for Ibráhím Khayru'lláh. He wished to be the leader of the Bahá'ís of America. But Bahá'u'lláh had very clearly appointed 'Abdu'l-Bahá as the Centre of the Covenant. No one besides 'Abdu'l-Bahá could be the leader. Later we will hear what happened to Khayru'lláh in the end.

# 17

## Rúḥu'lláh (I)

For decades, the followers of the Báb and Bahá'u'lláh in Persia were persecuted. Though innocent, they were thrown into prison, their homes ransacked and thousands of them were killed. Even children were murdered because they were Bahá'ís. One of them was Rúḥu'lláh.

Rúḥu'lláh came from a family of brave and loyal Bahá'ís. His grandfather did not care that it was dangerous in a Muslim country like Persia to teach the Faith of Bahá'u'lláh. He knew the history and traditions of Islám better than anyone. So he was able to prove to the Muslims that the Báb and Bahá'u'lláh were Messengers of God and that through their coming the prophecies of Islám had been fulfilled. Everyone in the town knew that Rúḥu'lláh's grandfather was a Bahá'í. He had gained so much influence over the people that the mullahs felt he should be put to death. Fortunately there was a just judge who forbade that. But he had to leave the city. He then decided to make a pilgrimage; he wanted to go to 'Akká, to meet Bahá'u'lláh. Actually he was too old and weak for such a difficult journey over the high mountains and through the burning deserts. Yet Rúḥu'lláh's grandfather wanted to go to Bahá'u'lláh anyway. His longing to be with Him was so great that nothing could stop him. And even though he was often very tired during the journey, he still began to teach the Faith in every town and every village they passed through. He managed with great difficulty to get as far as Beirut. He could hardly move at all, he was so exhausted. But he was now so close to Bahá'u'lláh, he had to go on. His body, however, was too weak for this and he died within only a few yards of the house of Bahá'u'lláh.

Rúḥu'lláh's father, Varqá, was also a brave Bahá'í. He travelled a lot through Persia to teach the Faith. He knew it was dangerous and that it might land him in prison. And that is what happened; in his home town he spent a whole year in prison because he was a Bahá'í. Varqá was also a poet and wrote fine poems about Bahá'u'lláh and 'Abdu'l-Bahá.

Rúḥu'lláh's grandmother was quite different. She wanted nothing to do with the Faith and could not bear that her husband and son-in-law were devoted Bahá'ís. In her eyes they were disloyal to Islám. She actually went so far as wanting to have Rúḥu'lláh's father killed. She went to one of her servants, Khalíl, and promised him a horse worth 25 tumans if he would kill Varqá. But there was something that Rúḥu'lláh's grandmother did not know: Khalíl had also become a Bahá'í! And instead of killing Varqá, Khalíl went to him and told him about the evil plot his mother-in-law had hatched.

Then Varqá realized that it would be better for him to escape. But how? He lived in the same house as his mother-in-law and she, of course, watched him carefully. Varqá knew what to do. In the middle of the night he threw the things he wanted to take with him out the window on to the street. Then he just went out as if nothing was going on. He gathered up the things he had thrown out the window and fled from the city. When his mother-in-law noticed that he had escaped, it was too late. Varqá was already so far away that they could never catch up with him.

She was furious and she was not intending to leave things

like that. She went to the mujtahid – that's a Muslim judge. She asked him to write a letter containing the death sentence for Varqá on the grounds that he was a Baháʼí. 'My son-in-law', she said, 'ought to be put to death.' But the mujtahid refused her request. Then she ran off to fetch Rúḥuʼlláh. She said to the mujtahid, 'I will prove to you through this child the apostasy of my son-in-law.' They asked Rúḥuʼlláh to say his daily prayer. Rúḥuʼlláh made his ablutions and then in a melodious voice chanted a Baháʼí prayer. The mujtahid was greatly impressed by the way in which the young Rúḥuʼlláh had said his prayer. He said to Rúḥuʼlláh's grandmother that it would be dreadful and unforgiveable to kill a father who had such a special son.

Fortunately for Rúḥu'lláh, he was able soon after that to go and live with his father in the city of Zanján.

About a year before the ascension of Bahá'u'lláh, Varqá went on pilgrimage to 'Akká. Rúḥu'lláh and his brother went with their father. It was a long and difficult journey. Just imagine a little boy of seven or eight having to walk over 600 miles through that hot desert and over those steep mountains!

In 'Akká, Bahá'u'lláh often spoke with Varqá and his sons. Once He told them about 'Abdu'l-Bahá. He praised Him for His divine qualities. Bahá'u'lláh said that in this world of existence there is a very special power, the 'Divine Elixir'. Anyone who possesses this power can exercise an enormous influence in his work in this world. He can do anything he wants. Look at Jesus Christ; after His crucifixion the Jews had paid no further attention to Him. His name did not even appear in their books. But because Christ had this power, He could not remain unknown. Through Him, the world was changed. Bahá'u'lláh told Varqá that 'Abdu'l-Bahá also possessed this power and would have an immeasurably great influence upon the world. When Varqá heard this, he was so full of joy and he threw himself at Bahá'u'lláh's feet. He begged Bahá'u'lláh that he might sacrifice his life and the life of one of his sons for 'Abdu'l-Bahá. Bahá'u'lláh gave His permission.

How did Rúḥu'lláh like being with Bahá'u'lláh? Just as we bask in the warmth of the sun, Rúḥu'lláh basked in the spiritual Sun of Bahá'u'lláh. It made him deeply happy to be so close to Bahá'u'lláh and his faith became even stronger than it was already.

Once time when Rúḥu'lláh was with Bahá'u'lláh, Bahá'u'lláh asked him, 'What have you been doing today?'

74

Rúḥu'lláh replied that he had been having his lessons that day.

'What were the lessons about?' asked Baháʼuʼlláh.

'About the return of the prophets.'

'Can you explain what that means?'

'By return it means the realities and qualities will come back,' answered Rúḥu'lláh.

'Those are exactly the words your teacher used and you are repeating them like a parrot. Tell Me in your own words what you understand on this subject.'

'It's like a flower that you cut from a plant this year,' said Rúḥu'lláh. 'The flower next year will look just like it but it's not the same flower.'

When Varqá was back in Persia after his pilgrimage, he wrote Baháʼuʼlláh a letter. In it he begged again that he and one of his sons might offer their lives as martyrs for the Faith. Again Baháʼuʼlláh gave His permission.

# 18

# Rúḥu'lláh (II)

A few years after the ascension of Bahá'u'lláh, Rúḥu'lláh again went on pilgrimage with his father and brother. There he spoke again with 'Abdu'l-Bahá and His sister, Bahíyyih Khánum. She admired him and loved to talk to him. One day Bahíyyih Khánum saw that Rúḥu'lláh was playing with others in the garden. She called him to her and asked him what they were saying to the people they were teaching the Faith to. Rúḥu'lláh replied, 'We tell them that God has manifested Himself.'

Bahíyyih Khánum was amazed and told him that they should not just say that straight out to people.

'We don't say that to everyone; we only say it to people who have the capacity to hear such a statement.'

'How do you know who those people are?' asked Bahíyyih Khánum.

'We look them in the eyes and then we know whether we can give them the Message,' answered Rúḥu'lláh.

Rúḥu'lláh was an unusually gifted boy who began teaching the Faith when he was very young. When he was ten, he was already writing beautiful poems about Bahá'u'lláh and 'Abdu'l-Bahá. He knew a great deal about the Faith and could answer the most difficult questions. Sometimes he went with his father to the meetings of divines. These divines would not believe that the Báb and Bahá'u'lláh were Messengers of God. But Rúḥu'lláh was able to prove to them with texts from the Qur'án that this was so. He could explain it so clearly that they were unable to argue with it. Out of revenge, they would rather have had Varqá and Rúḥu'lláh put to death. Luckily, they did not get the chance.

Zanján, the city where Varqá had gone to live after he had fled from his mother-in-law's house, was a dangerous place for the Baháʼís. It had been like that for a very long time. In the time of the Báb, almost two thousand Bábís were killed there. They had had to retreat into a fort. Led by the brave Ḥujjat, they defended themselves against an enemy that was much stronger than they were. Again and again they put the enemy to flight. When, after a long struggle, very few of the Bábís were left, their enemy was able to overcome them by a trick. They were taken prisoner and nearly all cruelly put to death.

Fifty years later, Zanján was still a dangerous place for the Baháʼís. That is why ʻAbduʼl-Bahá, during the last pilgrimage, had advised Varqá not to keep his Baháʼí Writings and possessions in Zanján any longer. Varqá decided to take them to Teheran, the capital of Persia.

The evening before they were to leave, they went to see a good friend in the telegraph office in order to say goodbye. When they came out of the telegraph office they were seen by a mullah. He made sure that the governor of the city heard that that evening some Baháʼís had come out of the telegraph office. The governor became very angry at that. Why that should make him angry, no one knew. Perhaps he thought that they were making plans to murder him. He at once had a couple of Baháʼís from Zanján arrested and put in prison. Rúḥu'lláh and his father had already left the city, but the governor commanded his soldiers to follow them and bring them back. So they too ended up in prison.

There was one thing about which Rúḥu'lláh and his father

must have been very glad about: their Bahá'í possessions that 'Abdu'l-Bahá had advised them to take to a safe place were saved as if by a miracle. The animal that was carrying the two bags was not brought back by the soldiers. The bags later found their way into safe hands!

Rúḥu'lláh's father had a very hard time in that prison. The governor and the divines of Zanján went on trying in all kinds of ways to get Varqá to renounce his faith. But Varqá was a steadfast believer. Nothing whatever could persuade him to deny his faith in Bahá'u'lláh. Finally, the governor decided to send Varqá with Rúḥu'lláh and two other Bahá'ís, Mírzá Ḥusayn and Ḥájí Imán, to Teheran. Before the journey began, a heavy chain was placed around their necks and shackles round their ankles. Only Rúḥu'lláh's feet were free of shackles. But not for long!

In the first village where they stopped, they were brought again before the Muslim divines. Here again, the divines could not make Varqá budge. When they realised this, they began on Rúḥu'lláh. A boy of twelve, surely all of them together could manage him. Or so they thought! They soon found that they were no match for him either. He even made fun of them. Instead of honestly admitting their defeat, they were enraged. 'This child is insulting holy divines,' they cried. 'and why is he not fettered? Send for the carpenter.' The man came and fixed fetters to Rúḥu'lláh's feet.

In prison in Teheran they were equally badly treated. They often got nothing to eat. The prison guards even tried to get money from them. They placed an extra heavy chain around the Bahá'ís' necks and said it would only be taken off if they got money from them. But Rúḥu'lláh, his father and the two other Bahá'ís had no money. They had nothing to give the guards.

Yet the heavy chains stayed round their necks. Any of their possessions which they still had were also taken. There were some very valuable things among them. For instance, a white overgarment which had belonged to Bahá'u'lláh. Rúḥu'lláh's father begged the thief not to steal that garment from him. It was so unbelievably precious to him. But it was taken. And something much worse: to torment Rúḥu'lláh's father the thief himself put on the garment and walked around places where Varqá could see him from the prison!

Thus things were made difficult for the Bahá'ís in the prison in all kinds of ways. It was not looking good for them. Would all four of them ever come out of it alive?

# 19

## Rúhu'lláh (III)

At the same time as Rúhu'lláh and his father were in prison, preparations were being made in Persia for a magnificent feast. Náṣiri'd-Dín Sháh had been Shah of Persia for fifty years. The feast in honour of the Shah would be celebrated all over the country. Thousands of people came to the capital city to cheer and honour him.

On the day before the great feast the Shah proudly went to the mosque. It would all begin in the morning! Then thousands of people would cheer for him. How he was looking forward to it! But Náṣiri'd-Dín Sháh also had enemies. People who had suffered under his unjust rule. They hated him so much that they really wanted to murder him. When the Shah was in the mosque a follower of one of these enemies shot him through the heart. He died on the spot. And that was only one day before the festival during which he was to have been acclaimed by the whole population.

The news immediately spread like wildfire around the city and the country. Who could have done this? Many thought at once that the Bahá'ís could have done it. They had suffered so much under the Shah that they had now taken revenge.

The head of the prison, where Rúhu'lláh and his father were, also thought that the Bahá'ís had the murder on their conscience. He did not even take the trouble to find out if this was true. Then he would have known that the Bahá'ís had nothing to do with it. He felt that he had to avenge the murder

of the Shah. Angrily, he rushed into the prison. He stamped his foot and shouted and gave orders to make the chains even shorter and to check the locks. He placed soldiers everywhere with guns at the ready. The prisoners were terrified. What was in store for them now? They could not understand it since at that moment no one knew that the Shah had been assassinated.

The fury of the prison governor was, however, only directed at the Bahá'ís. Their chains were removed and they were dragged out of the prison. After that, Rúḥu'lláh and his father were taken through a long passage to another room.

Anxious and puzzled, Ḥájí Imán and Mírzá Ḥusayn remained behind. They heard voices and saw someone fetching the whip for the bastinado. A little while later they saw that one of the guards was washing blood off a dagger in a pond. Not long after that, they saw someone going away with Rúḥu'lláh's father's clothes. Then they knew that they had murdered Varqá.

Full of suspense, Ḥájí Imán and Mírzá Ḥusayn waited to see what would happen to themselves. The door opened, they were about to go through it but it was immediately closed again. A little later they saw the head of the prison running past in panic, calling, 'Bring these two back to the prison; I'll deal with them in the morning.'

So Ḥájí Imán and Mírzá Ḥusayn went back to their cell. They had no doubt that Varqá had been killed. And that they themselves were going to be killed the next day. But how had Varqá been put to death? And where was Rúḥu'lláh? What had happened to him? And why had the prison governor run away in panic? To find out, Ḥájí Imán and Mírzá Ḥusayn begged the prison guards to tell them what had happened. The guards were not all so cruel as their governor and some of them then told them how things had gone with Rúḥu'lláh and his father.

When Rúḥu'lláh's father stood before the prison governor, the latter began to berate him in a dreadful manner:

'Now you have finally done what you wanted to do,' he screamed. Varqá still did not know that the Shah had been murdered. He calmly replied that he was not aware that he had done anything wrong. This answer made the prison governor even angrier; it looked as if he might well go mad with rage. He pulled out his dagger and stuck it into the chest of Rúḥu'lláh's father, demanding, 'How do you feel now?'

'I feel better than you do.'

'Tell me,' said the prison governor, 'whom shall I kill first, you or your son?'

Calmly Varqá replied, 'It is all the same to me.'

Then the governor handed him over to the bullies. The four

of them attacked him and cut his body into pieces.

All this happened before Rúḥu'lláh's eyes. In tears, he cried, 'Oh dear father, dear father, take me with you, take me with you, take me with you!'

The prison head stepped up to him. 'Don't cry. I will take you away and make sure that you will get an allowance and work from the Shah.'

Bravely, Rúḥu'lláh replied, 'I don't want you. I don't want your money. I don't want any job you can get for me. I want to be with my father.' Then he began to weep again.

Disappointed because Rúḥu'lláh had turned down his offer, the head of the prison ordered his men to fetch a piece of rope and strangle the boy. But there was no rope and so the bullies took the whip they used for the bastinado to kill him with that. When he ceased to make any movement, they let his lifeless body fall to the ground. Delighted, the governor ordered his men to fetch the other two Bahá'ís. But the moment that they opened the door, the dead body of Rúḥu'lláh sprang up and fell back to the ground one yard away with a thud. The bloodthirsty governor got a dreadful fright. In total panic, he began running out, shouting back to his men that he would deal with the other two Bahá'ís the next day.

Ḥájí Imán and Mírzá Ḥusayn were brought back to their cell. After they heard what had happened to Rúḥu'lláh and his father, there was no comforting them. Mírzá Ḥusayn wept the whole night, until at last he fell asleep. Then he dreamed about Rúḥu'lláh. He looked so very happy. He came to Mírzá Ḥusayn then and said, 'Did you see how I rode on the neck of the Emperor?' Mírzá Ḥusayn knew at once what he meant, for he had often told him about that promise. When Rúḥu'lláh was saying goodbye to 'Abdu'l-Bahá at the end of his last pilgrimage, the Master had given him a clap on the shoulder and said, 'Should God will it, He can make Rúḥu'lláh ride on the neck of an emperor to proclaim the Cause of God.'

How did it go with Ḥájí Imán and Mírzá Ḥusayn? The prison governor had said he would deal with them the following day. But the next day nothing happened. Nor the days after that. Because their lives were spared, we now know how Rúḥu'lláh and his father died a martyr's death.

# 20

## The First Pilgrims from the West

In Persia, the Bahá'ís were persecuted and killed, like Rúḥu'lláh and his father, and many thousands of others. In 'Akká, in the Holy Land, 'Abdu'l-Bahá was a prisoner who for years had not been allowed to leave the city. He was also constantly being opposed by the Covenant-breakers, especially His half-brother Mírzá Muḥammad-'Alí. How could the Faith go on growing if there was so much opposition? Surely it was God's Plan that it should be spread throughout the whole world?

Yet in spite of everything, God's Plan just went on. In America, six thousand miles from Persia and from 'Akká, the Faith began to grow rapidly. Ibráhím Khayru'lláh was busy teaching it every day. After five years, there were already nearly fifteen hundred Bahá'ís there. He had taught them much about 'Abdu'l-Bahá. They wanted to meet Him. Since 'Abdu'l-Bahá could not travel as He was a prisoner, a small group of Bahá'ís decided to go to see Him. They had to be very careful so as not to make any difficulties for Him. For if His half-brother Mírzá Muḥammad-'Alí saw that a large group of pilgrims had arrived from America, he would immediately go to the authorities to stir up trouble. Therefore they travelled first to Egypt and then went in three small groups one after the other to the Holy Land. When one group reached Haifa, they waited in their hotel until it began to get dark in the evening. Only then did they go to 'Akká to the house of 'Abdu'l-Bahá. As unobtrusively as possible.

What was it like to be with 'Abdu'l-Bahá? Can you imagine

anything so special and impressive that you just have no words to tell anyone about it? This was the way with many pilgrims. Even though for some their visit may have lasted only three days, they would never forget those three days as long as they lived. One of them wrote that these three days were the most memorable of her whole life. It was the greatest privilege of her life to be allowed to meet 'Abdu'l-Bahá and to look upon His face. She had never met such a special person and would never meet another one.

One of the pilgrims was May Bolles. She lived in Paris and had been invited by the American pilgrims to go with them to meet 'Abdu'l-Bahá.

*Robert Turner*

She gladly accepted this. She had had a vision. In this she had seen a man in Eastern dress beckoning to her from the far side of the Mediterranean Sea. When she saw 'Abdu'l-Bahá for the first time she was really amazed – He was the man in her vision! She fell at once at His feet. He lifted her up and spoke to her in Persian in His gentle, kindly voice. She was completely overwhelmed by His saintliness and purity of heart.

Many pilgrims stayed a few days in the house of 'Abdu'l-Bahá. They experienced hospitality such as they had never known before. They could not have felt more at ease in their own homes. Munírih <u>Kh</u>ánum and her daughters did all they could to make their guests comfortable. They were even given their beds to sleep in. The Holy Family was always ready to help and they were always happy together. They often talked about their memories of Bahá'u'lláh.

Just like Abul-Qásim. He had been Bahá'u'lláh's gardener for many years. He too loved to speak of his memories of Bahá'u'lláh. He told the pilgrims his story about the locusts. One day, Abul-Qásim had seen a huge swarm of thousands of locusts flying towards the garden. They settled on the trees and began to strip them bare. The same trees under whose shade Bahá'u'lláh had so often sat. Abul-Qásim hurried to Bahá'u'lláh and begged Him to make the locusts go away: 'My Lord, the locusts have come, and are eating away the shade from above Thy blessed head.' Bahá'u'lláh smiled and said that the locusts also had to eat and that Abul-Qásim should leave them alone.

Disappointed, Abul-Qásim went back to the garden and saw that the trees were getting barer and barer. After a while he could not bear to look any more. He ventured to go back to Bahá'u'lláh and humbly begged Him to send the locusts away.

Then Bahá'u'lláh stood up, went into the garden and when He stood under the trees covered in locusts, He said, 'Abul-Qásim does not want you; God protect you.'

Bahá'u'lláh then lifted the hem of His robe and shook

it; immediately the thousands of locusts all rose together and took their leave.

The pilgrims learned a great deal about their new Faith which they had only heard of a few years previously. This they heard from the Bahá'ís who lived in the Holy Land. Of course they learned the most from 'Abdu'l-Bahá. They were with Him every day. He would eat with them, He would teach them the Faith and would visit the holy places with them. From him they learned what it meant to truly love each other. Like the time when it was arranged that they would go with 'Abdu'l-Bahá to Mount Carmel. Everyone was looking forward to it. But when the time came, one of the pilgrims was ill. What did the others think? What a pity that one of us cannot come but something so important as a visit to Mount Carmel must surely still go on. Is this what 'Abdu'l-Bahá said too? He said that there would be no meeting on Mount Carmel that day. 'We could not go and leave one of the beloved of God alone and sick. We could none of us be happy unless all the beloved were happy.'

'Abdu'l-Bahá also taught them how bad it is to speak ill of other people. When 'Abdu'l-Bahá was in the city one day, caring for the sick, one of the pilgrims had gossiped. That evening at the table she was not aware that anything was wrong. Until the moment when her eyes met those of 'Abdu'l-Bahá, when she suddenly realized what she had done. She burst into tears. At first no one at the table paid any attention to her. But after a little while 'Abdu'l-Bahá looked at her, He smiled at her and said her name several times as if He were calling her. His loving look had made her understand that she had been forgiven. Then she was able to dry her tears and be happy and joyful once again.

When they woke up on the last morning, they realized that in the afternoon they would be back on the boat and that every hour would be taking them farther away from 'Abdu'l-Bahá. Can you imagine that they had absolutely no wish to leave? But they knew that they could not stay any longer and that this would not be right either.

During their last visit to 'Abdu'l-Bahá some of them broke down and wept. He asked them not to cry any more and said He would only speak to them when all the tears had gone. His last talk was one they would remember all their lives. He encouraged and gave them confidence with these words:

' . . . I say unto you that anyone who will rise up in the Cause of God at this time shall be filled with the spirit of God, and that He will send His hosts from heaven to help you, and that nothing shall be impossible to you if you have faith.'

That afternoon they were on the boat and their return journey had begun. But their sorrow had turned to joy and gratitude. They knew that 'Abdu'l-Bahá would always be with them and that He would always help them. He had, after all, said, 'I am with you always, whether living or dead, I am with you to the end.'

The pilgrims knew what they had to do. They had to do their very best to tell as many people as possible that Bahá'u'lláh had come as the new Messenger from God. So God's Plan was still moving forward, even if the Bahá'ís in Persia were being persecuted and even if 'Abdu'l-Bahá was a prisoner and even though His own brothers were working against Him.

After the journey made by these pilgrims from America, the Faith was first spread in their own country and from there to the whole world.

# 21

# The Disloyal Pioneer

Do you remember who Ibráhím Khayru'lláh was?

Ibráhím Khayru'lláh was the pioneer who went to America and proclaimed the Bahá'í Faith there. He travelled to various cities and gave courses on the Faith. When his students had attended all thirteen lectures on the course, he introduced them to the Greatest Name. Then they could become Bahá'ís. Thanks to Khayru'lláh there were already fifteen hundred Bahá'ís in America at the end of five years. When a small group of Bahá'ís decided some years later to make a pilgrimage to meet 'Abdu'l-Bahá, he was invited to go with them.

In Haifa, 'Abdu'l-Bahá showered praises on Khayru'lláh. He had done so much to spread the Faith in America! 'Abdu'l-Bahá called him 'the Peter of Bahá', the 'second Columbus' and 'the conqueror of America'. 'Abdu'l-Bahá showed him the great honour of being the only one allowed to help in the laying of the first stone for the building of the Shrine of the Báb. And in honour of Khayru'lláh's visit, He decided that the period of mourning after the ascension of Bahá'u'lláh was now over. Then the building in which Bahá'u'lláh is buried was first opened to the believers so that they could go there to pray. This was six years after the ascension of Bahá'u'lláh.

One of the many things which Khayru'lláh had done was to write a book about the Bahá'í Faith. He had finished it quickly before going on pilgrimage. He asked one of his friends to translate it into Arabic so that 'Abdu'l-Bahá could also read it and approve it. When Khayru'lláh was with 'Abdu'l-Bahá, however, he discovered that not everything in his book was in accordance with the teachings of Bahá'u'lláh. This would have been a wonderful chance to have his book corrected by 'Abdu'l-Bahá. But Khayru'lláh did not want anything in his book to be changed. So 'Abdu'l-Bahá could not possibly give it His approval.

There were other problems, too. The pilgrims discovered that what 'Abdu'l-Bahá told them sometimes differed from what they had learned from Khayru'lláh in America. They had no doubt about who was right. 'Abdu'l-Bahá. And when they were all with 'Abdu'l-Bahá, Khayru'lláh sometimes began to argue with Him; he thought that he was right and that 'Abdu'l-Bahá was wrong. 'Abdu'l-Bahá did not want any disagreements at all. He said that Khayru'lláh was also correct. He would not allow the other pilgrims to start arguments with Khayru'lláh.

'Abdu'l-Bahá surrounded Khayru'lláh with the greatest possible love. Very patiently, He tried to make him realize that only He, 'Abdu'l-Bahá, could interpret the Writings of Bahá'u'lláh correctly. And there was no one else besides Him who could do that. Not even Khayru'lláh, even though he had done such a lot for the Faith.

When the pilgrims returned to their own country they were thankful and happy. 'Abdu'l-Bahá had told them that He would always be with them. And they also knew what they must do; they must do everything they could to proclaim the Faith.

There was one pilgrim who was not happy and joyful on the return journey. That was Khayru'lláh. He was worried. He had always been the leader. If the Bahá'ís in America did not understand something, they had asked him to explain it. Khayru'lláh knew that that would not be the same now. From now on they would put their questions to 'Abdu'l-Bahá. They would then get different answers to the ones he had given them. They would believe what 'Abdu'l-Bahá said and not what he said. He was afraid that they would no longer see him as their most important leader.

When Khayru'lláh was back in America, he was warmly welcomed by the Bahá'ís. Meetings were at once arranged because the Bahá'ís wanted to hear all about 'Abdu'l-Bahá. Khayru'lláh spoke enthusiastically about 'Abdu'l-Bahá and the Holy Family. He said that he had brought the Writings of Bahá'u'lláh back with him and promised to see that they would be translated into English. Khayru'lláh acted as if he were obeying 'Abdu'l-Bahá and recognized Him as the only head of the Faith. But deep in his heart he did not want 'Abdu'l-Bahá to be the leader; he wanted to be the leader of the American Bahá'ís himself.

Khayru'lláh knew what would happen if the other pilgrims spoke about 'Abdu'l-Bahá. The Bahá'ís in America would recognize 'Abdu'l-Bahá as the head of the Faith. So as not to lose his leadership, he said that some of the pilgrims had not really understood everything and that their intentions were not honourable either.

He especially criticized Edward and Lua Getsinger. They had spent five months with 'Abdu'l-Bahá. They had got to know Him very well and they had learned a great deal from Him. When they talked about their pilgrimage, it was soon clear to the Bahá'ís that they were honourable people. Besides, they had brought a photograph of 'Abdu'l-Bahá back with them. And a recording of the voice of 'Abdu'l-Bahá, so that the Bahá'ís in America could hear His voice. We would find this quite natural now, but at that time this was something very special.

No one doubted the honesty of Edward and Lua Getsinger any longer. But some Bahá'ís were beginning to have doubts now about Khayru'lláh. What did he actually want? It was becoming clearer all the time. He kept trying to become the leader of the American Bahá'ís. He wanted 'Abdu'l-Bahá to tell the Bahá'ís to listen to him and obey him. He wanted to read all the letters to 'Abdu'l-Bahá before they were posted and he wrote to the Bahá'ís asking them to let him know what answer 'Abdu'l-Bahá had given. He had one newspaper publish that he was the head of the Faith in America. And the book which had not been approved by 'Abdu'l-Bahá was published anyway.

These were difficult times for the American Bahá'ís. They became anxious. One of them went to 'Akká, to 'Abdu'l-Bahá, for advice. He returned with an answer that was clear to everyone: no one could expect to be appointed leader of the Bahá'ís. Not even Khayru'lláh.

To help Khayru'lláh to change his mind, 'Abdu'l-Bahá then sent some Persian Bahá'ís to America. One of these was 'Abdu'l-Karím, the man through whom Khayru'lláh had become a Bahá'í in Egypt.

For two whole weeks they talked. Then Khayru'lláh said that he had been wrong and that everyone must obey 'Abdu'l-Bahá. Alas, that did not last long and he soon changed back to his old position.

The Bahá'ís in America really wanted Khayru'lláh to remain loyal to the Faith. After all, they had him to thank that they had come into contact with it and had become Bahá'ís. They fervently hoped that he would still change his mind. Alas, it became steadily clearer that he would not accept 'Abdu'l-Bahá as the only leader of the Faith. One year after his return from pilgrimage, Khayru'lláh finally severed his connection with the Faith.

Ibráhím Khayru'lláh had done a great deal in his early years in America to spread the Faith. Now, because of his ambition for leadership, a lot of confusion was created among the American Bahá'ís. Through this, it was that same Khayru'lláh who was the cause that many Bahá'ís in America left the Faith. He himself formed a group and hoped that many would follow him. But that did not happen. It became a very small group that did not exist for long.

What a shame that this is how Khayru'lláh ended up. In the years when he was telling his students that 'Abdu'l-Bahá was the head of the Faith, hundreds had accepted the Faith through his lectures. In the thirty years that he lived after that, no one else accepted the Faith through him.

# 22

## 'Abdu'l-Bahá's Best Translator

Ali Kuli Khan was the son of a prominent Persian family. He led a life of pleasure. Nearly every evening he gave a party. He took alcohol and drugs and was not at all interested in religion.

He had many friends. Until they came into contact with the Faith. They became Bahá'ís and no longer came to those parties. That was a thorn in Ali's side and he wanted his friends back. He went with them to the Bahá'í meetings and he was going to make sure they would change their minds and give up their faith. This went on for months but his friends stayed loyal to the Faith. Then one evening he heard about the sufferings of the young Báb, and about the suffering that His followers had to undergo. And about Bahá'u'lláh and how His followers were still being persecuted. This changed him. He discovered that the teachings of Bahá'u'lláh were the only salvation for his country, even for the whole world. He became a Bahá'í. He was immensely glad, but at the same time in despair. He longed to be able to serve Bahá'u'lláh. But how? He also wanted to serve his country but that also came to nothing. How would he ever be able to serve? The Bahá'ís reassured him, telling him that he would surely succeed and that Bahá'u'lláh would help him.

Soon afterwards some Bahá'ís showed Ali a photograph of 'Abdu'l-Bahá. When he saw this noble face it made such a deep impression on him that he had only one more wish: he must go to 'Akká, to 'Abdu'l-Bahá. He knew that he must be careful. In Persia it was much too dangerous for Bahá'ís to say openly

95

that they wanted to make a pilgrimage to see 'Abdu'l-Bahá. It would have to happen without being noticed.

Therefore he travelled with a party to the east of Persia and hoped in this way to reach 'Akká via India. This did not work. Next he went to the west of Persia, but this way did not work either. Then he went travelling as a dervish, an indigent monk, and tried to get to 'Akká on foot. But even that failed and finally he found himself again in Teheran. He was no further on than he had been at the beginning.

Ali was not going to relinquish his plan. One evening, in the middle of winter when it was snowing and an icy wind whistled through the streets, he decided to try once more. Then and there. He did not even take the time to say goodbye to his family and friends. Ten friends went with him. In spite of the cold and snow, he kept on going, no effort was too much for him. At the Russian border he had to leave his friends behind; they had no passports. Ali himself had no passport either, but the governor was a Bahá'í and Ali whispered in his ear that he had to go to 'Akká to help 'Abdu'l-Bahá with translating. Ali was given a passport and travelled on to Tiflis, a port on the Black Sea. From there he could easily take a ship to 'Akká.

Again there was a setback. He had to wait because he had first to obtain permission from 'Abdu'l-Bahá to go to 'Akká. This had still not come. Was he now about to fail for the fourth time? Ali had lost all hope. Perhaps it was just not God's will that he should go to visit 'Abdu'l-Bahá. In a few days' time there was a caravan leaving with which he could go back to Persia. He began to make preparations for the return journey. Then suddenly a letter arrived from 'Abdu'l-Bahá's secretary; Ali was to leave at once for 'Akká. That same evening he began travelling on towards the Holy Land.

He arrived early in the morning. It was still dark. When he stepped out on land, he knelt and kissed the ground. He thanked God that his dearest wish had been granted. He went first to the house of one of the Bahá'ís in Haifa. They told him that 'Abdu'l-Bahá was in Haifa and when Ali realized that he would see Him very soon now, he became afraid and began to cry, saying, 'How can anyone like me, with so many shortcomings, be in the presence of Him before Whose eyes nothing is concealed?'

When he entered 'Abdu'l-Bahá's house, he was shaking all over his body, his heart was hammering in his chest. Then he saw 'Abdu'l-Bahá standing before him, tall, with His turban, in His robe and with a dark grey beard. Ali collapsed and fell to the ground.

'Abdu'l-Bahá helped him up, threw His arms around him and kissed him on both cheeks. He first had Ali taken to another room to drink something. A few minutes later He asked him in again and welcomed him in Persian, 'Marḥabá! Marḥabá!' and said to him, 'You have suffered much on your wanderings, but welcome! Praise be to God, you have reached here in safety.' 'Abdu'l-Bahá also told him that Bahá'u'lláh had promised Him that He would send people who would help Him to spread the Faith. The Faith had now reached America and many people in the West had been attracted to it. 'You, with your knowledge of English, are one of the souls promised me by Bahá'u'lláh. You have come to assist me by translating His sacred Writings as well as my letters to the friends in America and elsewhere in the West.'

Then 'Abdu'l-Bahá picked up a pile of letters, gave them to Ali and said,

'These are the answers that I have written to some of the American Bahá'ís. Go and translate them into English.' Ali opened the top letter. He had a shock. The letters were in Arabic!

'But my Master,' he cried, 'these are not in Persian! These are Arabic! I studied European languages, but not Arabic!'

Never had anyone looked at Ali so lovingly. The Master smiled. He went over to a table, took two handfuls of sugar lumps and told Ali to hold out both his hands. Then 'Abdu'l-Bahá said very solemnly and in a very particular way:

'Go, and eat this candy. Rest assured, the Blessed Perfection' – as 'Abdu'l-Bahá often called Bahá'u'lláh – 'will enable you to translate the Arabic into English. Rest assured that as time goes on you will be assisted to translate from the Arabic more easily than from the Persian.'

After this 'Abdu'l-Bahá showed him a room with a bed. He said to Ali that He Himself no longer needed that bed and that it was now his.

'This is your bed, sleep in it.'

Did Ali do that? Sleep in 'Abdu'l-Bahá's bed? Two years previously he had promised himself that he would only sleep in a bed again if he had attained the goal of his journey, i.e. 'Abdu'l-Bahá. All that time he had slept on the floor, even if he was offered a bed. And now that he had reached the goal of his journey, now he was allowed to sleep in a bed that had belonged to 'Abdu'l-Bahá! He dared not get into it and, as he was accustomed, went to sleep on the floor.

After three nights, one of 'Abdu'l-Bahá's servants came and asked if he knew that he was disobeying 'Abdu'l-Bahá. Ali was shocked when he heard this.

'What on earth do you mean?'

'I mean that you have not slept in the Master's bed, as He told you to do.'

'I did not intend to disobey Him,' stammered Ali. 'I simply

was not brave enough to sleep in a bed in which the Centre of Bahá'u'lláh's Covenant had slept.'

He promised the servant that he would now obey. But even so it was with fear and trembling that he finally went to sleep in the bed which had first belonged to 'Abdu'l-Bahá.

Ali's dearest wish had now been granted and he could now work every day for 'Abdu'l-Bahá. There was a great deal to do. More and more letters kept coming from America and the letters and replies to them all had to be translated. He began in the mornings at six o'clock and worked all day and all evening until midnight. Especially if there was a ship in the harbour which could take the mails with it, then as many letters as possible had to go out on that ship.

In a few months it was too much for Ali. He was exhausted. He lived near the sea but he was even too weak to walk to the seashore to bathe. Ali found it terrible to be so weak. He had taken so much trouble to travel to 'Abdu'l-Bahá in order to help Him. And instead of helping, now he was a burden. The doctors could do nothing for him. A miracle was needed to make him better.

'Abdu'l-Bahá knew how it was with Ali. One day, 'Abdu'l-Bahá was sharing out some grapes. Ali stood on one side by the wall and would also have liked to have some of the grapes. But he could not, as the doctor had said he was not allowed any fruit since it would only make him weaker. Then 'Abdu'l-Bahá beckoned to Ali to come and asked him if he would like a bunch of grapes too. Oh yes, please!

'Abdu'l-Bahá gave Ali a good big bunch and said, 'Eat these grapes and the blessings of Bahá'u'lláh will heal you.'

He ate the grapes and from that day on he was able to help 'Abdu'l-Bahá once more.

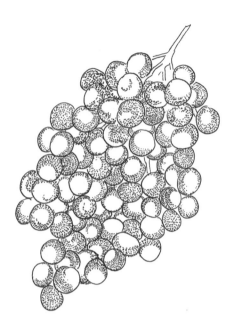

Ali also knew that 'Abdu'l-Bahá could read the thoughts of other people. You could hide nothing from Him. Once, Ali was taking a walk on Mount Carmel. All on his own. He was thinking about the past, his friends, and about the poems they used to recite to each other. After his walk he returned to 'Abdu'l-Bahá. 'Abdu'l-Bahá smiled at him and said, 'You have been thinking of your friends in Persia this afternoon. You have been lonely and reciting Persian poems.' Then 'Abdu'l-Bahá spoke the very words of the poem which Ali himself had recited as he was walking alone that afternoon.

'Abdu'l-Bahá often told Ali that he was His best translator. He also said that He was preparing him for a much greater task. After a couple of years he was sufficiently prepared for that task. Then Ali Kuli Khan travelled to America to help in spreading the Faith there.

# 23

## Thomas Breakwell

She had to stay in the city. Under no circumstances could she leave Paris. Why not? May Bolles did not know. 'Abdu'l-Bahá had given her this instruction. She had been with Him some years earlier; she belonged to the first group of pilgrims from the West who had visited Him in 'Akká. After that trip she wanted nothing more than to do what He asked of her. So now she stayed in Paris. It was not easy. She was supposed to be going with her mother and brother on holiday. Her mother kept urging her to come. But May held firm and finally they left without her.

Shortly afterwards, a young man came unexpectedly to her door. He had come from America and during the voyage had spoken often with a friend of May's. The latter thought that he ought to talk with the Bahá'ís and so she brought him to visit May. In their first conversation, the Bahá'í Faith was not mentioned. They talked of the things that interested him. In the afternoon he returned to his hotel. It was a fine summer day, without a breath of wind. Suddenly he felt a strong breeze blowing about him and an indescribably sweet and penetrating voice saying, 'Christ has come again! Christ has come again!'

The very next morning he appeared at May's door. Excitedly he told her what he had experienced the previous afternoon. When he had told her that the voice had said to him that Christ had come again, he said to May, 'You must think I am going crazy.'

'No,' replied May, 'You are just becoming sane.'

Then May began to speak to him. About the Báb and His short life and how the people had had Him killed. About His brave followers, the Bábís, who sacrificed their lives because they refused to deny their Faith. About Bahá'u'lláh Who had given mankind God's laws for this age. And about 'Abdu'l-Bahá. She told him about her pilgrimage and what it had been like to be with Him.

For three whole days they talked. Then Thomas Breakwell, as he was called, knew that he wished to become a Bahá'í. He sent a letter to 'Abdu'l-Bahá with these words: 'My Lord, I believe, forgive me, Thy servant Thomas Breakwell.'

That evening May went to collect her mail. With it there was a telegram from 'Abdu'l-Bahá. It said that she could now leave Paris. Now she understood why she had had to stay. How grateful she was that she had obeyed 'Abdu'l-Bahá, even though at the time she did not know why He had given her this instruction. The very next morning she went on holiday, to join her mother and brother. She took the telegram with her. When she gave it to her mother to read and told her about Thomas Breakwell, her mother burst into tears and said, 'You have, indeed, a wonderful Master.'

Thomas Breakwell had been planning to travel in Europe. Now he had only one desire: he wanted to meet 'Abdu'l-Bahá. He travelled to Egypt with another Bahá'í who was to make the pilgrimage. There, he received permission from 'Abdu'l-Bahá to come to 'Akká.

In 'Akká he went to the house of 'Abdu'l-Bahá. He was shown into a spacious room. Thomas Breakwell expected that 'Abdu'l-Bahá would be in that room. A group of men in oriental clothing stood at one end of the room. Thomas Breakwell looked at them but he could see no one who seemed special. He was afraid that he had failed to recognize his Lord. Suddenly he felt ill and weak. Disappointed, he went and sat at a small table. Was it for this that he had come all the way to this remote prison? Was it for this that he had changed all his plans to travel around Europe?

Then a door opened. It was as if the rising sun had appeared in the doorway. That was He! That was 'Abdu'l-Bahá! Thomas Breakwell sprang to his feet. In one second his disappointment and despair had changed into indescribable joy.

Thomas stayed in 'Akká for two days. To stay longer was not

possible because of the trouble that Mírzá Muḥammad-'Alí was causing. In one of his talks with 'Abdu'l-Bahá, Thomas told Him about his work. He had a well-paid job in a cotton mill in America. But there was something wrong there; children were employed in the mill who were much too young to be working. When he said this, there was a moment's silence. 'Abdu'l-Bahá looked at him and then said, 'Cable your resignation.' Relieved, Thomas sent off the telegram as soon as he could.

'Abdu'l-Bahá asked Thomas Breakwell not to return to America but to settle in Paris. There he did everything he could to teach the Faith. He rented a room in an out-of-the-way part of the city because this was cheaper. When he came to the meetings, he came on foot. The money he saved in this way he then gave to help spread the Faith.

Thomas Breakwell wanted to serve Bahá'u'lláh. That also meant serving his fellow men. People often came to him to discuss their problems. He would give them his advice and they left his house with shining eyes and heads held high. One day he was sitting with May Bolles in a bus. From the bus, he could see an old woman who was struggling to push a barrow of apples up a slope over a bridge. He excused himself to May, got off the bus and helped the old woman to push the barrow. To him, this was the most natural thing in the world.

After his visit to 'Abdu'l-Bahá, Thomas Breakwell had only a short time to live. He had tuberculosis and knew that he would not get better. But in spite of his poor health he stayed in Paris to serve the Faith just as long as he was able.

When Breakwell died, 'Abdu'l-Bahá knew immediately without having received any letter or telegram.

That evening 'Abdu'l-Bahá was in 'Akká, on His way home with His secretary. Suddenly, he said to his secretary, 'Have you heard?'

'No, Master,' replied the secretary.

'Breakwell has passed away. I am grieved, very grieved. I have written a prayer of visitation for him . . . twice I could not withhold my tears, when I was writing it.'

The Tablet begins with the words:

Grieve thou not over the ascension of my beloved Breakwell, for he hath risen unto a rose garden of splendours within the Abhá Paradise, sheltered by the mercy of his mighty Lord, and he is crying at the top of his voice: 'O that my people could know how graciously my Lord hath forgiven me, and made me to be of those who have attained His Presence! '

Through this Tablet 'Abdu'l-Bahá immortalized Thomas Breakwell. His name will never be forgotten.

# 24

## Years of Peril

It seemed as if it would never end. Mírzá Muḥammad-'Alí was again trying to oppose 'Abdu'l-Bahá. Now he had hatched another plan. He had sent Majdu'd-Dín, one of his henchmen, to Damascus. He was to tell the governor that, in 'Akká, 'Abdu'l-Bahá was organizing large meetings. He should also say that the Americans who were visiting were military advisers and that 'Abdu'l-Bahá was building a fortress on Mount Carmel in order to begin a rebellion against the government.

Do you know what a fortress is? A fortress is a solid building with thick, strong walls that an enemy would find difficult to conquer. Why would 'Abdu'l-Bahá need a fortress like that? He was building something very different on Mount Carmel. With His guidance, building had started on the Shrine of the Báb. On the very same spot which Bahá'u'lláh Himself had pointed out to 'Abdu'l-Bahá.

There was no truth at all in what Majdu'd-Dín was going to tell the governor in Damascus. But he did have money with him to offer him a bribe, as it is called. And for that money the governor would act as if Majdu'd-Dín's stories were true. He promised to help to put 'Abdu'l-Bahá off that land. He sent the reports on to the government in Istanbul. Feeling pleased with himself, Majdu'd-Dín went back to Mírzá Muḥammad-'Alí. This time they would surely get what they wanted.

A few days later, Mírzá Muḥammad-'Alí and Majdu'd-Dín were suddenly taken out of their house and brought as

prisoners to 'Akká. That was not quite what they had expected. What had gone wrong? When the Sultan in Istanbul had received the report, he decided that things would have to return to the way they were thirty years previously: the Holy Family and the Bahá'ís would all have to stay within the walls of 'Akká. None of them must leave the city. That meant Mírzá Muḥammad-'Alí and Majdu'd-Dín as well. They had fallen into the hole they had dug for someone else. In desperation, Mírzá Muḥammad-'Alí wrote letters to the governor of Damascus. After all, the governor had received a hefty sum as a bribe and he thought that he would help him. But there was no reply.

'Abdu'l-Bahá had to appear in court. For days He was examined. At the same time He tried to arrange for Mírzá Muḥammad-'Alí to have his freedom back. And what Muḥammad-'Alí himself had not managed to do, 'Abdu'l-Bahá succeeded in doing: Mírzá Muḥammad-'Alí and his hangers-on were allowed to leave the city again. 'Abdu'l-Bahá also saw to it that the Bahá'ís could go outside the city walls once more and carry on as usual with their work. He promised that He Himself would remain a prisoner inside the walls of 'Akká. This was an imprisonment that would last for seven years.

Thanks to 'Abdu'l-Bahá, Mírzá Muḥammad-'Alí and his henchmen had their freedom. Were they grateful to Him for this? And what did they do with their freedom? They missed no opportunity to make trouble for 'Abdu'l-Bahá. They even mocked Him because they were free and He was still a prisoner who could not leave 'Akká!

Three years later there were more difficulties. The governor of 'Akká was someone who had great respect for 'Abdu'l-Bahá. Through the machinations of Mírzá Muḥammad-'Alí, he was replaced by a governor who was hostile in his attitude to 'Abdu'l-Bahá. Mírzá Muḥammad-'Alí and his accomplices were again spreading evil rumours about 'Abdu'l-Bahá and inciting the people against Him. They bribed the officials with fine presents and large sums of money. Things became so bad that unfavourable articles about Him appeared in the newspapers. They also wrote reports containing false accusations which they sent to the government in Istanbul. Mírzá Muḥammad-'Alí hoped that the authorities would become alarmed and take measures to put 'Abdu'l-Bahá to death or banish Him to some remote spot. Mírzá Muḥammad-'Alí thought that he could then become the leader of the Faith. That was what his enmity had been all about from the start.

The government in Istanbul became uneasy and the Sultan sent a Commission of Investigation to 'Akká. Spies were placed around the house of 'Abdu'l-Bahá and they kept watch day and night to see who went in. It became very frightening. Many people were scared to go to visit Him. For the Bahá'ís, 'Akká was becoming too oppressive. At 'Abdu'l-Bahá's suggestion, they went for a time to Egypt. He could not receive any more pilgrims either.

'Abdu'l-Bahá had to appear before the Commission of Investigation. Unafraid, he denied all the accusations which had been made against Him. When they asked Him whether He wanted to overthrow the government, 'Abdu'l-Bahá showed the Commission the Writings of Bahá'u'lláh. He said that, if they read these, they would know that He, as the son and successor to Bahá'u'lláh, would never, ever entertain such plans.

Then the Commission brought out a flag on which was written 'Yá Bahá'u'l-Abhá'. This flag had been made by Mírzá Muḥammad-'Alí and sent to the authorities. Mírzá Muḥammad-'Alí said at the time that some of the Bahá'ís, under orders from 'Abdu'l-Bahá, had gone round the country with this flag in order to rally the people to rebel against the government. 'Abdu'l-Bahá replied to this that there were so many representatives of the government in the country and not one of these had ever mentioned having seen such a flag. What could the Commission say?

There was another accusation: 'Abdu'l-Bahá had bought large pieces of land in order to create a kingdom. To this He replied that this was nothing less than a miracle since He was a prisoner who was watched day and night by the Turkish authorities. How would He have any chance of creating a base for a kingdom? He offered to sell all those plots of land to the Commission for a small sum.

All the accusations were found to be false. The Commission tried once more. They said that He had subversive literature in

His possession and even that He had allowed this to be spread. The Commission had secretly bribed people who were willing to say they had witnessed this themselves. When the names of these people were revealed, 'Abdu'l-Bahá stood up. He declared emphatically that he did not possess any subversive literature and with great dignity walked out of the courtroom. Even though He was still a prisoner, He commanded so much respect that there was no one who dared to stop Him.

The investigation had totally failed. Mírzá Muḥammad-'Alí had suffered a great defeat. Yet he was still trying to have 'Abdu'l-Bahá banished or put to death. And He would succeed one more time in bringing 'Abdu'l-Bahá into great danger.

# 25

# The House of Worship in 'Ishqábád

Everything pointed to the fact that the sentence would be carried out: two men were to be hanged for having murdered a Bahá'í in 'Ishqábád. The gallows had already been erected and a huge crowd had converged on the place of execution.

'Ishqábád is a city in Russia, close to the border with Persia. Many Bahá'ís from Persia had fled there because they were still being persecuted in their own country. But there were others, too, from Persia who had gone to live in 'Ishqábád. Muslims, enemies of the Faith. They were jealous because there was great respect for the Bahá'ís there. They decided to kill certain prominent Bahá'ís. They hired two assassins and they, in broad daylight, in the middle of the street, stabbed Ḥájí Muḥammad-Riḍá to death.

The hired assassins and their clients had to appear in court. It had never happened that a Bahá'í had been murdered and that a judge had passed sentence. In Persia thousands of Bahá'ís had been killed but the murderer had never been punished. On the contrary, he was often even rewarded for it. And he thought that he had done a deed which was pleasing to God.

In 'Ishqábád it was different. The murderers were sentenced to death and those who had paid them were banished to Siberia. The mullahs in Persia were enraged. How could the Russian authorities sentence people to death because they had killed a Bahá'í? They did their best to have the death sentence changed to a lighter penalty. Even the Shah was involved. To no avail. The death sentence would be carried out.

Then the family of the assassins went to the Bahá'ís to ask if they would try to have the death sentence changed to a lighter penalty. The Bahá'ís consulted about what they should do and decided to go to the governor. There, they asked for the assassins to be released and if this was not possible to give them a lighter sentence. The governor was very impressed because the Bahá'ís showed so much forgiveness. He sent the request to the Czar and he would decide what should happen to the assassins.

But what did the Czar decide? No one knew. And on the day of the execution it looked as if the death sentence was still going to be carried out. The gallows on which the murderers would be hanged had already been erected, there was a grave dug for them and they were brought to the gallows wearing white garments. Only then, at the very last moment, the decision of the Czar was announced to the great crowd: through the intercession of the Bahá'ís the Czar had decided that the death sentence need not be carried out. Instead, the assassins were sent to Siberia. The sentence of those who had employed them, who had also been banished to Siberia, was halved.

Bahá'u'lláh was very pleased when He heard how the Bahá'ís of 'Ishqábád had acted toward the assassins. He wrote in the 'Tablet of the World' that He thanked God day and night that the friends had intervened with the highest authorities for the sake of their enemies and that their character and behaviour was acceptable in His eyes.

This event had important consequences for the Bahá'ís in 'Ishqábád. It was, of course, not long before the whole city knew that it was thanks to the Bahá'ís that the lives of the

murderers had been saved. Through this event, the Faith came to be highly esteemed in 'Ishqábád. The Russian government discovered that the Bahá'ís had no political intentions and would not oppose it. This helped the Faith to grow even more rapidly and the Bahá'ís received permission to build schools and to start a library. The most important result of this event was that the Bahá'ís received permission from the government to build a temple. It would become the first Bahá'í temple in the world. Bahá'u'lláh had indicated where the temple should be built. He knew that relatives of the Báb had bought plots of land in 'Ishqábád. Bahá'u'lláh then intimated that one of these plots must be used for the building of the temple. 'Abdu'l-Bahá made the design and architects worked upon that to produce the plans.

Ten years after the ascension of Bahá'u'lláh, 'Abdu'l-Bahá gave Ḥájí Mírzá Muḥammad Taqí instructions to begin on the construction of the temple. Ḥájí Mírzá Muḥammad Taqí was a cousin of the Báb. When he was still a child, the Báb had once stayed at his home. He had then seen how the Báb prayed and revealed the sacred texts. Ḥájí Mírzá Muḥammad Taqí's father doubted for a very long time whether the Báb was in fact a Messenger of God. Then Bahá'u'lláh revealed for him 'The Book of Certitude', the Kitáb-i-Íqán. Ḥájí Mírzá Muḥammad Taqí read it too, and like his father, then recognized the Báb as a Messenger of God. For the rest of his life he remained loyal to the Faith and everything he did was aimed at teaching the Faith. He treated everyone fairly and always kept his promises. Bahá'u'lláh was very pleased with him indeed. It was obvious to many that he would one day be given another important job.

This important job was the building of the temple in 'Ishqábád. Day and night He worked on this. He spent nearly all his money on it. The Bahá'ís of 'Ishqábád helped as much as they could. Through their joint efforts, the temple was built in eighteen years. But even after five years it was possible for people to go every week to pray there and for the Holy Days to be celebrated there.

The temple was built in the oriental style. It was surrounded by gardens. It was a nine-sided building with nine entrances. There was a pathway leading to each entrance. Beside the main entrance there were two minarets. On the site of the temple, a school, a hostel for pilgrims and a hospital were established.

For twenty years, the Bahá'ís and anyone who wished could visit the temple without any problem to pray there. But at that time much was changing in Russia. The Czar and his family were murdered and the country was then ruled by a Communist government. This gradually began to make things difficult for the Bahá'ís. They were not allowed their own schools any more and the temple was taken over by the government. The Bahá'ís were still allowed to rent the temple but they had to sign a contract that it was government property. The Bahá'ís had to pay not only the rent but all the expenses of the upkeep of the temple, even the insurance and taxes. It was a very unfair contract but the Bahá'ís wanted to keep the temple so much that they bore all the costs themselves and did their very best to keep it in good repair.

The Communist government, however, made things more and more difficult for the Bahá'ís. More than five hundred of them were imprisoned. Many of these died in prison or were sent to the coldest parts of Siberia. The Persian Bahá'ís who remained had now to flee back to Persia, or were sent back there. At last there were hardly any Bahá'ís left in 'Ishqábád. There was no one left to keep the temple in repair. The government had got its way. The temple was then used as an exhibition hall.

In 1948 there was an earthquake which cause serious damage to the temple. No one made any effort to repair it. It was at the mercy of wind and rain and it deteriorated more and more into a ruin. Fifteen years later it was so far gone that there was nothing to be done but to demolish it. The temple in 'Ishqábád had existed for less than sixty years.

But will it always be so? Will the day not come when building will again begin on a new temple in 'Ishqábád? What do you think?

# 26

## At Home with 'Abdu'l-Bahá

'My home is the home of peace. My home is the home of joy and delight. My home is the home of laughter and exultation. Whoever enters through the portals of this home must go out with gladsome heart.' These are the words of 'Abdu'l-Bahá. This is how He wanted it to be in His home. His home must be a home filled with laughter and delight.

If all goes well, if nothing goes wrong, it is not difficult to be happy and joyful. But if things don't go well? Or if you actually have to face severe setbacks? And you could say that is what the Holy Family had to do. The worst was past, they were no longer in the Most Great Prison. They could live in a house. But they were still prisoners and for years they were not allowed to leave 'Akká. In addition, it was extremely unjust that they were kept prisoner; none of them had done anything for which he or she should be punished. Sometimes their house was very closely watched and then they would see the guards walking

116

up and down in front of it. Another problem was that 'Akká was not a healthy city and because of this they often became ill. 'Abdu'l-Bahá and Munírih Khánum had nine children. Five of them died very young. Often there was very little money, so that they could only buy the most urgent essentials. Mírzá Muḥammad-'Alí and his accomplices often made their lives even more difficult. They kept sending bad reports about 'Abdu'l-Bahá to the authorities. Several times the threat was so great that no one in 'Akká dared to speak to the Holy Family.

If people have to live under those conditions, can they then be happy? Can such a house be a home where there is lots of laughter? Yet . . . in spite of all these difficulties, the Holy Family was a happy family. They loved each other and helped each other as much as they could. They had plenty of fun and always found something to make a joke about.

Every day they got up early in the morning to have prayers together. 'Abdu'l-Bahá was then already back from visiting the sick and going through His correspondence. His sister, the Greatest Holy Leaf, and his wife, Munírih Khánum and her daughters with their children, were all there. And also the people who lived with them in their house, like a Persian lady who had lost all her family through the persecutions in Persia. The children would sit by the door. Between the prayers, tea would be served and now and then the children would also chant prayers. Everyone listened attentively. The windows and

117

doors were open and sometimes the sparrows flew in to peck at the grains of sugar that the children threw for them.

Pilgrims were always a source of great joy to the Holy Family. When they arrived in 'Akká, they were lovingly greeted as if they were old friends the family had known for years. The family did everything to make their guests feel at home. Often, the pilgrims would be served at table by 'Abdu'l-Bahá Himself. The Holy Family wanted to know all about the Faith in the country from which the pilgrims came. They were prisoners themselves who could not go travelling to teach the Faith. But the pilgrims were the proof that the Faith had penetrated to faraway countries and was even growing stronger there. They were happy to hear every report of the progress of the Faith. When the first pilgrims from America and Europe came, they could not understand each other. They needed interpreters and these were hard to find. But the daughters of 'Abdu'l-Bahá asked the pilgrims to teach them English and they taught the pilgrims Persian in return. After a few years they could talk to each other and even wrote each other letters.

At 'Abdu'l-Bahá's table there were always conversations. 'Abdu'l-Bahá Himself often began to talk and give explanations. The pilgrims also had questions to ask. Like Laura Barney. She was an American and had a whole list of questions. She would ask them at the table, at least if there was time, for 'Abdu'l-Bahá always had so much to do. But whenever it was possible the question was discussed. 'Abdu'l-Bahá's answer was written down by one of His secretaries in Persian. This was checked by 'Abdu'l-Bahá and then translated into English. This is how the book *Some Answered Questions* came about.

Every day, 'Abdu'l-Bahá visited people who were in need.

Some of them were living in misery. This was noticed by Lua Getsinger, one of the American pilgrims. One day, 'Abdu'l-Bahá told her that He was too busy to go to visit a friend of His who was very poor and sick. He wanted her to go in His place. She must bring food for him and care for him as He Himself also did. He explained where she could find this man. Lua went off, happy and proud that 'Abdu'l-Bahá had entrusted her with this mission.

She returned quickly. 'Master,' she exclaimed, 'surely you cannot realize to what a terrible place you sent me. I almost fainted from the awful stench, the filthy rooms, the degrading condition of that man and his house. I fled lest I contract some terrible disease.'

Sadly and sternly 'Abdu'l-Bahá regarded her. 'Dost thou desire to serve God,' He said, 'serve thy fellow man for in him dost thou see the image and likeness of God.' He told her to go back to this man's house. If it is filthy she should clean it; if this brother of yours is dirty, bathe him; if he is hungry, feed him. Do not return until this is done. Many times had He done this for him and cannot she serve him once?

Lua obeyed 'Abdu'l-Bahá and did what He had asked her to do.

Another pilgrim was Florence <u>Kh</u>ánum. During her pilgrimage she sat nearly every day at the table with 'Abdu'l-Bahá. But she found she was never able to fix His face in her memory. On the last evening of their pilgrimage her husband called her to him.

'Do you remember', he asked, 'that 'Abdu'l-Bahá said that He would answer all the letters we brought to Him from America before we left?'

'Yes.'

'Come quickly, then. The Master is walking up and down in His room and He is answering the letters as if He knew the deepest secrets of those who wrote them. Yet He has never seen or met any of them.'

She went with him to another room. Through a passage they could see 'Abdu'l-Bahá still walking up and down past the doorway. Filled with admiration, she gazed at Him. She wished that he would stand still for a moment in the doorway so that she, being in the dark so that no one would notice, could see His face properly. At that same moment, 'Abdu'l-Bahá stopped in the doorway. She looked as long and attentively as she could. After a few moments 'Abdu'l-Bahá stepped back and went on dictating the letters.

A little later she hoped that 'Abdu'l-Bahá would stop in the doorway just once more. At once He stood there again, still, as if He were looking up at the stars. When she looked at Him, His whole face radiated a wonderful, golden light. The light became brighter and more intense but she could not take her eyes away. She began to be almost afraid, it was so beautiful. She said to herself, No matter how bright the light is, I will keep my eyes open! What a marvellous sight! What a magnificent opportunity!'

She kept gazing as long as she could. Just when she thought she could keep it up no longer, 'Abdu'l-Bahá went back in and continued dictating letters.

On rare occasions 'Abdu'l-Bahá would allow one of the Bahá'ís a glimpse of His splendour. This time Florence <u>Kh</u>ánum was the only one. Her husband was standing beside her. She asked him if he had seen anything unusual.

'No,' he said, 'I saw that the Master stopped twice in the doorway and that He looked magnificent. That was all.'

# 27

# Kay-Khusraw

From time to time 'Abdu'l-Bahá would go to Tiberias, a town in the Holy Land not far from 'Akká. There, He once heard a rabbi speaking to his Jewish flock in the synagogue.

> O Jews, you are in truth the people of God! All other races and religions are of the devil. God has created you the descendants of Abraham, and He has showered His blessings upon you . . . You are indeed the chosen people of God, you are above all the races of the earth! Therefore, all other races are abhorrent to God, and condemned by Him. In truth you will govern and subdue the world, and all men shall become your slaves . . . Do not profane yourselves by consorting with people who are not of your own religion, make not friends of such men.

The Jews believe that their religion is the true faith. They say that Moses is the last Messenger of God and that they are the chosen people of God. The Christians believe that Jesus is the last Messenger of God and that all who believe in Him will go to heaven. And the Muslims? They believe that Muhammad was the 'Seal of the Prophets'. They say that means that after Him a divine Messenger will never again appear on the earth. For them the Qur'án is the last holy book and after the Qur'án another holy book will never appear. Each one, the Jew, the Christian and the Muslim, is absolutely sure that he is right and that all the other religions are wrong.

They have forgotten one of the most important teachings of their faith: to love other people. Instead, the followers of one religion hate the followers of another religion. They sometimes show the greatest contempt for them, and regard them as unclean so that they do not even dare to touch them. If this should happen accidentally they at once go and wash so as to feel clean again. They have been known to set each others' houses on fire or kill each other. Or they even made war against each other, causing millions of people to be killed in the name of God. Each one thought he was killing an infidel and was defending the true religion. They even thought that God approved of that.

This enmity came about through blindly following what they were told. Everyone, Jew, Christian or Muslim, believed what their parents and the clergy had told them. They did not stop to consider whether it was true or not. If they had done that, they would have discovered that some things just cannot be true. But they did not take the trouble. They believed what they were told without thinking any more about it. This is how the divisions remained.

This division, this strife and all these wars will one day come to an end. It is God's plan that unity will come to the world. But how? Can the people themselves think of a plan, and carry this out, which would put an end to all this division and strife? No! Only a Messenger of God can bring unity among people. For this, Bahá'u'lláh came to the world: to establish unity. When the Jews, Muslims and Zoroastrians in Persia heard of the teachings of the Báb and Bahá'u'lláh and became their followers, they forgot their differences. Through Bahá'u'lláh they learned to investigate the truth for themselves and not to believe unthinkingly what others told them. Their hatred for each other changed to love. Instead of regarding each other as unclean, they embraced each other as the best of friends and if help was needed, they helped each other.

'Abdu'l-Bahá set the example. In 'Akká everyone could go to Him for help or advice. He made no distinction between Jews, Christians or Muslims, or between Arabs and Turks. He loved everyone equally. They all received the help they needed and everyone came away from Him content. At 'Abdu'l-Bahá's table, there were sometimes people from very different parts of the world. From oriental countries and from Europe and America. East and West were united in His home and at His table. That was just the beginning. Once, when guests from East and West sat at His table, 'Abdu'l-Bahá predicted that in future the East and West would become as one. They would be united like two lovers. East and West would reach out their hands to one another, like lovers, and embrace one another.

Again and again, 'Abdu'l-Bahá urged the Bahá'ís to travel to other countries. Especially the Bahá'ís from America. He asked them to go to India, Burma and Japan, to visit the Bahá'ís there and to spread the Faith. In this way, the Bahá'ís in those far countries would see that the Faith was for the whole world. After all, there were American Bahá'ís coming to visit them. And they all came together as equals and friends. They did not look down upon them as people from the West nearly always did on meeting those from the East.

Under 'Abdu'l-Bahá's guidance, the Bahá'ís from different countries and even from different continents learned to help one another. The Bahá'ís from America helped in Persia to establish schools; the Bahá'ís from Persia sent money to America for the building of the temple there; the Bahá'ís from Burma provided a marble sarcophagus in which the sacred remains of the Báb were placed. Because of their belief in

Bahá'u'lláh they would give anything for each other. If need be, even their lives. Like Kay-Khusraw from India.

One of the Americans who had gone to India at the request of 'Abdu'l-Bahá was Sydney Sprague. India is a hot country where in those days you could easily catch an infectious disease because of the unhygienic conditions. This happened to Sydney Sprague. In his enthusiasm, he stayed too long in the huge city of Calcutta. He caught cholera, a dangerous disease, from which many thousand people often died within a short time. Two Bahá'ís nursed him until they were not able to any longer.

Then one of the Bahá'ís asked Kay-Khusraw, a shopkeeper from Bombay, to look after him. Kay-Khusraw immediately shut his shop, made his will, said goodbye to his family and left. For four days he nursed Sydney Sprague. He was beginning to recover but was not really well again when Kay-Khusraw himself became ill. He had caught cholera, too. Within twenty-four hours he was dead.

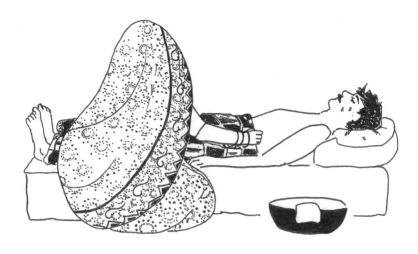

124

Afterwards, Sydney Sprague wanted to visit Kay-<u>Kh</u>usraw's family. He was dreading this and thought he hardly dared to look them in the face. But when he entered their home, they came to meet him with outstretched arms.

'Do not feel sad,' they said. 'It was right that Kay-<u>Kh</u>usraw should give his life for his brother. Besides, Mr Sprague, you are a great teacher and Kay-<u>Kh</u>usraw was a simple shopkeeper. He could never have taught the Faith like you.'

This is how great the difference is which the Faith of Bahá'u'lláh can bring about in people. Kay-<u>Kh</u>usraw sacrificed his life for someone from a very far country. His memory will always live on, as the first Bahá'í from the East who gave his life for a Bahá'í from the West.

# 28

## Birds of Dynamite

For centuries, the Ottoman Empire was great and powerful, respected in every country in the world. In 'Abdu'l-Bahá's time this was no longer the case. The empire had become so weak that it was being called the 'Sick Man of Europe'. Everywhere, rebellions were breaking out and it took Sultan 'Abdu'l-Ḥamíd all his time to keep his oppressed peoples under control.

Sultan 'Abdu'l-Ḥamíd was a cruel ruler. In some other countries he was known as 'The Great Assassin'. He had many enemies and was terrified that he himself would be murdered. He had secret pockets in his clothing and always had three revolvers on him. If there were people around him, no one was allowed to put his hand in his pocket. If documents were brought to him, they had to be handed to him at arm's length. He was even so afraid of spies that he would allow no electrical or telephone lines to be laid in Istanbul except in places which were always closely guarded. If anyone was suspected of rebelling against him, he was put to death, very often without any proper proof having been produced.

Mírzá Muḥammad-'Alí knew how dangerous it was for anyone to be suspected of rebellion. He sent, just as he had done before, reports to the authorities that 'Abdu'l-Bahá wanted to overthrow the government. He was supposed to have called on the people to oppose it and to be building a fortress on Mount Carmel. And exactly what Mírzá Muḥammad-'Alí had hoped, happened. The authorities again sent a Commission of Investigation to ʻAkká. The Commission was to investigate the same accusations as it had done four years previously. Then it had been found that the accusations had clearly been false. If the Commission did its work honestly, they would discover this soon enough, too.

But this Commission did not work honestly. The governor of ʻAkká, who thought well of ʻAbduʼl-Bahá, was dismissed. Spies were stationed around the house of ʻAbduʼl-Bahá. The post and telegraph office was closely guarded and all letters and telegrams were checked. The members of the Commission were great friends of Mírzá Muḥammad-ʻAlí. Some of the citizens of ʻAkká were forced to give false testimony against ʻAbduʼl-Bahá. A shopkeeper who refused to tell lies about Him was thrown into prison. The people of ʻAkká became so fearful that they did not even dare to go near His house. Even the very poorest no longer came on Friday mornings to receive alms from Him. The situation was beginning to look more and more dangerous. No one could imagine now that it could end well. There were even rumours going round that ʻAbduʼl-Bahá would be killed, or that they would send Him to Tripolitania, in the torrid African desert. He would surely not survive that.

Everyone was dreadfully worried. Except ʻAbduʼl-Bahá. He just went on with His work as if nothing at all was the matter. He wrote, as He had always done, letters to Baháʼís in the East and the West. He had repairs to the house carried out and He planted trees in His garden. When He also bought fuel for the winter, no one could understand it. Who would have his house repaired and buy fuel for the winter if he knew he was to be expelled from the city?

A few days before the Commission arrived, ʻAbduʼl-Bahá

told the Bahá'ís that He had dreamed that a ship had sailed into the Bay of Haifa and that birds that looked like sticks of dynamite were flying from the ship towards 'Akká. It looked very threatening and the residents of 'Akká were terrified. 'Abdu'l-Bahá stood very still and calm among the people, looking at the birds. The birds circled over His head and turned, without exploding, back to the ship. 'Abdu'l-Bahá said to the Bahá'ís, 'The meaning of the dream I dreamt is now clear and evident. Please God this dynamite will not explode.'

'Abdu'l-Bahá could have escaped if He had wanted to. There was an Italian ship in the harbour. In the middle of the night

an Italian friend came to Him and offered to take Him on the ship to a place of safety. 'Abdu'l-Bahá did not want to escape. He said that the Báb had sacrificed His life; how then could He run away?

'Abdu'l-Bahá stayed in 'Akká, even though the danger seemed to be increasing all the time. Mírzá Muḥammad-'Alí and his hangers-on were gloating. On previous occasions their plans to get 'Abdu'l-Bahá out of 'Akká had always failed. They were sure that this would now succeed. The Commission also visited the spot where the Shrine of the Báb was being built, on Mount Carmel. They wrote in their report about it that 'Abdu'l-Bahá was building a strong fortress on the mountain. Even though the Commission knew quite well that this was not true.

Then the Commission went on board the ship. One evening it began to sail in the direction of 'Akká. Everyone who saw it was sure that something was about to happen. 'Abdu'l-Bahá would be picked up and taken to the desert or some other remote place. The whole of Haifa and 'Akká held its breath. The Bahá'ís and members of 'Abdu'l-Bahá's family were in despair for fear that they would never see Him again.

When the ship drew near to 'Akká, something unexpected happened. It changed course and sailed off up the Mediterranean. The people watched in amazement. Slowly its lights disappeared into the distance. One of the most terrifying dangers which had ever threatened 'Abdu'l-Bahá had been averted. But had the danger now really gone away?

Shortly afterwards they heard that in the capital, Istanbul, an attempt had been made on Sultan 'Abdu'l-Ḥamíd's life. He had barely escaped. When the Commission submitted their report to the Sultan, he had no time for it; he was much too busy after the attempt on his life. The report was put aside. A few months later, the Young Turk revolution broke out. 'Abdu'l-Ḥamíd was forced to free all the religious and political prisoners. The authorities in 'Akká could not imagine that this would also apply to 'Abdu'l-Bahá. So they asked the authorities in Istanbul. Yes, was the answer. 'Abdu'l-Bahá is now free.

'Abdu'l-Bahá's dream had come true and the birds of dynamite had not exploded.

For fifty-six years 'Abdu'l-Bahá had been a prisoner. His imprisonment began when as a boy of 8 years old He travelled with His Father and family from Teheran to Baghdad. After that, the Holy Family was banished to Istanbul, Edirne, and finally to 'Akká. 'Abdu'l-Bahá was a young man of 24 when He arrived in 'Akká. For forty years he had remained an exile in 'Akká. Now that He was free, He was 64 and had grey hair and a grey beard.

What did He do with His freedom? He at once went to work to finish the important task which Bahá'u'lláh Himself had given Him, the building of the Shrine of the Báb.

# 29

# 'I was happy in My imprisonment'

'Abdu'l-Bahá was now free. Even though Sultan 'Abdu'l-Ḥamíd had ordered His everlasting imprisonment. When 'Abdu'l-Bahá heard that He had said, 'This is impossible! I shall not always be a prisoner. If 'Abdu'l-Ḥamíd were immortal, such a sentence might possibly be carried out. It is certain that one day I shall be free.' And so it came about. 'Abdu'l-Bahá was freed. Not long afterwards, Sultan 'Abdu'l-Ḥamíd was dethroned and put in prison. Until he died, he was a lonely, humiliated prisoner. Everyone despised him for what he had done.

It was very different with 'Abdu'l-Bahá when He was still in prison. He was happy in His imprisonment. He was not a criminal, no, He was a prisoner for the Cause of God. Every time He thought about that, He felt happy. No one who saw Him thought that they were dealing with a prisoner. He had many visitors and some of them even came from America and Europe! In 'Akká many people came to ask for His help, Jews, Christians and Muslims, who among themselves had a great dislike for each other, but they all knew how to find 'Abdu'l-Bahá. Even the governor of the city came to Him for advice.

'Abdu'l-Bahá always had a lot of work to do. Whether He was free or a prisoner, he did everything He could to serve His Father's Faith. When most people were in their beds at night, 'Abdu'l-Bahá was still at work. And in the morning, when nearly everyone was still asleep, the light was again burning in His room. From East and West piles of letters came with questions from the Bahá'ís. Not one letter was left unanswered. Sometimes He wrote up to ninety letters in one day.

He was also the great friend and helper of the poor. Every Friday morning at seven o'clock there was a long queue of about a hundred people at His door. These were the poor of 'Akká. They were blind, or very thin, walking on crutches or were so weak that they could hardly walk at all. Then 'Abdu'l-Bahá would come out and beckon the people to come to Him. If too many crowded forward, He would gently push them back. One by one, they were allowed to come to Him. They held out their hands and into every hand He put a few coins. He knew them all. With some, He had a little chat and spoke some words of encouragement to them. There were children too. At first they got nothing, but when all the adults had been and 'Abdu'l-Bahá was going back inside, He threw a handful of coins over His shoulder. The children fell eagerly upon them.

When people could not come because they were sick or too weak, 'Abdu'l-Bahá Himself would visit them and leave some money for them when He left. If the weather was beginning to get cold, He would take them to the shops and see that they had warm clothing and fuel for the winter. If they needed a doctor, He would pay the doctor. If something in their houses needed mending, He would send a carpenter.

Everyone could come to Him. Even if they were unfriendly or even acted in a hostile way towards Him. Like the man from Afghanistan who lived in 'Akká. He thought that 'Abdu'l-Bahá was a heretic and this man was setting others against Him. When there was a meeting, he bitterly accused Him, even in the mosque. If he met Him in the street, he would cover his eyes so that he did not have to see 'Abdu'l-Bahá. 'Abdu'l-Bahá was always kind to him and helped him whenever he needed it. If he had no food or clothing, 'Abdu'l-Bahá would provide them. The man accepted it all but never thanked Him. Once when he was sick and 'Abdu'l-Bahá was there when the doctor examined him, he again covered his eyes so that he did not need to see 'Abdu'l-Bahá.

This lasted for twenty-four years. All those years, 'Abdu'l-Bahá kept answering his enmity with kindness. Then one day, the man came to His door. Weeping, he fell at 'Abdu'l-Bahá's feet and begged for His forgiveness.

'Forgive me,' he said, 'for twenty-four years I have treated you badly and you have been good to me. Now I know that I was wrong.'

'Abdu'l-Bahá asked him to stand up, and from then on they were friends.

'Abdu'l-Bahá was happy in prison. But would He not rather have been a free man? Then He could have gone travelling to teach the Faith. Then He would not have had to direct the building of the Shrine of the Báb on Mount Carmel from 'Akká. He could have been there in person to see how the work was progressing. Then He could have gone to Bahjí, to pray at His Father's grave. That was not possible, and He missed it very much. So on the flat roof of His house in 'Akká, He had a wooden shed built, looking out towards Bahjí. Early in the morning He could be heard there chanting His prayers. When pilgrims came who could go to the Shrine of Bahá'u'lláh, He asked them to pray there on His behalf. How happy He was that He was now able to go! And that was the very first thing He did when he heard that He had been set free.

There was something else He had always wanted to do during all those years: work in the gardens surrounding the

Shrine of Bahá'u'lláh and water the plants. Now that could be done every Friday and Sunday again. Each time, He fetched sixty jars of water for the gardens. But that did not last very long. It was too great an effort for Him and after a while He became ill. The Bahá'ís noticed this and begged that they might be allowed to do this heavy work. 'Abdu'l-Bahá consented. But this went against the grain. In a few days it showed. He looked so sad that the Bahá'ís were sorry that they had asked Him if they could do it for Him. Two weeks later, He called them together. He told them that this work had always made Him very happy and brought peace to His heart. He asked them if it would be all right if He did it again Himself. They saw how happy this work made Him. How could they refuse Him?

# 30

## The Shrine of the Báb

Ḥájí Sulaymán Khán was in a hurry. Baháʾuʾlláh had told him to travel to Tabríz as quickly as he could. The life of the Báb was in great danger. Ḥájí Sulaymán Khán was an influential man. Perhaps there was still something he could do to save His life.

When he arrived in Tabríz it was, however, too late; two days earlier the Báb had been put to death by a firing squad. With His loyal follower, Mírzá Muḥammad-ʿAlíy-i-Zunúzí. It was he who had asked the Báb if he might sacrifice his life with Him. They had been fired upon by a regiment of 750 soldiers. Their badly mutilated bodies were left lying the whole day on the street. In the evening they were thrown outside the city gates, by the moat. Ten soldiers stood there on guard.

After two days, the bodies still lay there. When Ḥájí Sulaymán Khán heard that, he wanted to take them away at once and hide them in some safe place, even at the risk of his own life. The mayor of Tabríz advised him not to do it. He knew someone who could manage it. That person, along with some other men, collected the bodies in the middle of the night. They were wrapped in sheets and hidden in a factory belonging to one of the Báb's followers. A few days later, they were placed in a coffin and hidden in a safe place. Ḥájí Sulaymán Khán sent word to Baháʾuʾlláh that the bodies were safe and asked what should now be done with them. Baháʾuʾlláh replied that they should be taken to Teheran, the capital.

So began the long journey of the remains of the Báb. Care had to be taken all the way that it should not be discovered. At times it was hidden in a Muslim holy place. At others in the home of one of the Bábís. Once, a hole in the wall was made and the coffin was placed behind the wall for safety. The hole was closed up and nicely plastered over so that no one could suspect that anything was behind it. When danger again threatened that the coffin would be discovered, Bahá'u'lláh again asked for it to be moved to another place. In this way, the two bodies were hidden in Persia for fifty years in more than ten different places. Until 'Abdu'l-Bahá gave the order to bring them to the Holy Land. There, too, they had to remain hidden for another ten years before they found their final resting place. For sixty years, the Bahá'ís had faithfully followed the instructions of Bahá'u'lláh and 'Abdu'l-Bahá. Thanks to them, the body of the Báb was preserved in spite of all the dangers which had threatened it.

'Abdu'l-Bahá knew exactly where the Shrine for the Báb was to be built. Bahá'u'lláh Himself had pointed out to Him the spot on the slope of Mount Carmel. The construction began at the same time as the first pilgrims from Europe and America visited the Holy Land. 'Abdu'l-Bahá laid the first stone, together with Ibráhím Khayru'lláh, the pioneer who had proclaimed the Faith in America.

The building of the first part of the Shrine for the Báb took ten years. It was one of 'Abdu'l-Bahá's most important tasks and also one of the most difficult. The difficulties were mainly caused by the Covenant-breakers at the instigation of 'Abdu'l-Bahá's half-brother Mírzá Muḥammad-'Alí. When 'Abdu'l-Bahá tried to buy the site which Bahá'u'lláh had indicated, the Covenant-breakers went to the owner. They persuaded him not to sell it to Him. With great difficulty, 'Abdu'l-Bahá nevertheless succeeded in purchasing it, but then Mírzá Muḥammad-'Alí started again. He got certain people to go to the authorities and to say that they were the owners of the land. Six months later these claims were shown to be false. 'Abdu'l-Bahá could now begin the building work. However, the narrow road to the site was very difficult to negotiate. So 'Abdu'l-Bahá tried to buy another piece of land which would make it easier to reach the site. It should have been quite easy to do this. But the Covenant-breakers heard of the plans and went to the owner of the land and told him that he should ask a very high price for it.

The representative of the governor in Haifa also objected. He felt the place was not suitable and said that the Sultan in Istanbul would have to approve it. However, Sultan 'Abdu'l-Ḥamíd was already so suspicious and 'Abdu'l-Bahá knew this suspicion would now be increased. This would only mean more trouble. He went to speak to the representative and insisted on being told why he would not approve of the building. The man said that he did not dare to take upon himself the responsibility for approving the building. When they had spoken, 'Abdu'l-Bahá walked with him from his office to his home. When he arrived there, the man collapsed and died. The piece of extra land that 'Abdu'l-Bahá wished to buy was still not sold. The owner was making new conditions. First he said that he wanted to keep the trees on his land. That could be arranged. Then he said that there would have to be a boundary fence of barbed wire. 'Abdu'l-Bahá offered to build a wall for him, as high as he wanted it. Then there would have to be someone who could guarantee that his property was safe. It was agreed who that would be. When this was to be discussed, the owner did not appear. 'Abdu'l-Bahá was at the end of His tether. He could no longer eat or sleep. He then chanted a prayer of the Báb's over and over the whole night long. When He awoke the next morning He was told that two men from the German Consulate had been waiting a while to see Him. They had come to offer Him another piece of land.

'Abdu'l-Bahá overcame all the difficulties. Even when He could not go to Haifa to supervise the work Himself, because He was not allowed to leave 'Akká. And also when the Covenant-breakers reported to the government in Istanbul that 'Abdu'l-Bahá was building a fortress and wanted to rebel against the government. The building caused 'Abdu'l-Bahá so much trouble that He was often heard to say, 'Every stone of that building, every stone of the road leading to it, I have with infinite tears and at tremendous cost, raised and placed in position.'

Almost sixty years after the execution in Tabríz in Persia, the bodies of the Báb and His companion were entombed in their final resting place on God's holy mountain, Mount Carmel. In the morning, 'Abdu'l-Bahá had the marble sarcophagus brought up the mountain and placed in the tomb. This sarcophagus was a gift from the Bahá'ís of Rangoon, the capital of Burma. In the evening, the wooden coffin containing the two bodies was placed in the sarcophagus in the tomb. Only one lamp was burning and believers from both East and West were present. When the coffin had been placed in the sarcophagus, 'Abdu'l-Bahá removed His turban, took off His shoes, threw off His cloak and bowed low over the still open sarcophagus. His face transfigured and luminous, He rested His forehead on the side of the wooden coffin. Then He began to weep, so heartrendingly that all of those present wept with Him.

'Abdu'l-Bahá was responsible for the first phase of the construction of the Shrine. When the Báb was buried there, it was a rectangular building with a flat roof containing six rooms. Shoghi Effendi finished the construction. Three more rooms were added, it was surrounded by an ambulatory with pillars and crowned with a superstructure and golden dome. The Universal House of Justice was responsible for the construction of the stately buildings of the World Centre and for the terraces and their magnificent gardens: nine terraces between the foot of the mountain and the Shrine and nine terraces from the Shrine to the top of the mountain.

Things have turned out quite differently to what the Persian divines, who had the Báb put to death, had imagined. They not only put the Báb to death, but also thousands of His followers. They wanted no trace of His Faith to be left. God had a different Plan. The Báb was a Messenger of God and God will never allow one of His Messengers or His Revelation to be forgotten.

Now the Báb lies buried in a magnificent Shrine with a golden dome on Mount Carmel. Since time immemorial, Carmel has been a holy mountain. The Shrine is surrounded by beautiful gardens. In Haifa they already speak of it as the Eighth Wonder of the World. Its future is a glorious one. Hundreds of millions of pilgrims will visit the resting place of the Báb to pray and to honour Him. Even the kings and rulers of the world will come as humble pilgrims. They will hasten from the foot of the mountain to that Holy Spot. They will bring flowers. And when the kings reach the Shrine, they will lay aside their crowns and with deep respect and as humble worshippers enter there to pray.

No, none of the plans made by the divines who wanted the Báb to be forgotten had worked at all.

# 31

## A Sudden Departure

It seemed a day like any other day. In the afternoon 'Abdu'l-Bahá had been to visit some of the Bahá'ís in Haifa. They had sunk a well and 'Abdu'l-Bahá called in to taste the water. After this, He went up the mountain to the Shrine of the Báb. In the evening the Bahá'ís went to His house. This was their custom; every evening it was their privilege to be with Him. But how strange! 'Abdu'l-Bahá was not there! Then one of His sons-in-law arrived and told them that He had left on a ship bound for Egypt. Everyone was absolutely amazed. He had told no one of His plans. And no one had noticed anything out of the ordinary. He had suddenly departed. Desolate, the friends were left behind. How long would it be before they saw Him again?

'Abdu'l-Bahá was on his travels. After His release from captivity, the doctors had told Him this would be good for His health. He needed a change of air, they said. But was this why He had gone on a voyage? No! He went to make His Father's Faith known to the world. This is what He had longed to do during all those long years of imprisonment. The Báb and Bahá'u'lláh had never had the opportunity to go travelling. Now He had the chance. And even though He was now old, and His health was not good, so that His life might even be in danger, He went all the same. He went to tell the people that God had sent a new Messenger: Bahá'u'lláh.

Now he could travel, and not just because He was no longer a prisoner. There were other reasons. One of the most important tasks He had been given by Bahá'u'lláh had been completed: the building of the Shrine of the Báb. And the Báb's body was now buried there; after sixty years it was safe at last. As well as this, the Covenant-breakers under the influence of Mírzá Muḥammad-'Alí could do no more harm now. They could be troublesome from time to time but that was all. By being faithful to the Covenant the Bahá'ís were now so united that Mírzá Muḥammad-'Alí and his accomplices could never break that unity.

'Abdu'l-Bahá was intending to travel on as quickly as possible from Egypt to Europe. One month later, He departed on a ship but it then became obvious that He was much too weak for a long, tiring journey. He disembarked in Alexandria. It was not until a year later that He was strong enough to travel again. So he stayed in Egypt all this time.

This was to be an important year for Egypt. There was much hostility toward the Faith and it was often attacked in the newspapers. Some of them even said that measures ought to be taken against the Faith. So 'Abdu'l-Bahá was not very warmly welcomed. Things were written about Him in the papers which were totally wrong. There was even one journalist who said that 'Abdu'l-Bahá hated all religions and that His teachings were harmful to mankind.

Events in Egypt followed the same pattern as they had done forty years previously in 'Akká. There, the people had also been hostile to the Faith. But, through 'Abdu'l-Bahá, their hostility changed into friendliness. Now the same thing happened. 'Abdu'l-Bahá had only been there a short time before many people were coming to see Him. The learned and the wise came to learn from Him. The poor came to His door for help. A letter even arrived from a princess who wished to visit Him.

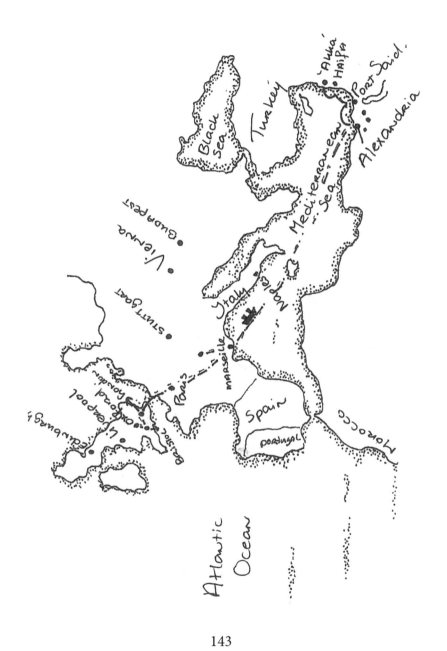

The journalists who had written hostile things about Him also came to see Him. When they got to know 'Abdu'l-Bahá they understood Him better. They came in as enemies and left as friends. The newspapers began to publish favourable articles about Him. Their prejudices melted away like snow in the sunshine. One of the most influential newspapers began to defend 'Abdu'l-Bahá and strongly reprimanded the other papers. It was their responsibility to give the facts instead of making false accusations. In six months, the attitude of the newspapers had completely changed. The difference was as night is to day.

After a year, 'Abdu'l-Bahá was strong enough to continue His journey to Europe. First He went to France, to Lake Geneva, for a short holiday. This was probably the first holiday of His life. He travelled about the countryside and enjoyed the magnificent mountains, forests and waterfalls. He took everything in: the lovely green fields, the spotless villages, a little village high in the mountains, a church tower rising above a cluster of houses, a pleasant, lonely spot on a mountain – He kept discovering beautiful things. Sometimes He and His companions went out by car, sometimes in a horse-drawn carriage. Once, when they had to climb a steep hill, 'Abdu'l-Bahá got out to make it easier for the horse. When they entered a village He had an immediate magnetic effect on the people. They came to stand around Him, took off their hats and called him 'Father'. Once one of the women ran into her house to fetch some bread and cheese. 'Take this, good Father,' she said to 'Abdu'l-Bahá.

Another time He and His companions wished to go into an inn to take some rest. A group of children approached Him. They crowded round Him and looked up at Him in wonderment. They had eyes only for 'Abdu'l-Bahá – it was as if they did not even see the other people who were with Him. They were selling little bunches of violets and were all trying to sell their flowers to Him. 'Abdu'l-Bahá took some money from his pocket and bought all the children's violets. A little later, the children came back to Him and tried to sell more violets to Him. One of the Bahá'ís wanted to send the children away.

'He would give away everything He has,' they whispered.

But 'Abdu'l-Bahá discovered a little girl who had not been there before. 'I haven't given anything to this little one,' he said. So she also got something.

A little later the group of children returned once again to Him. They held out their hands for more money. One of the Bahá'ís sent them away – they wanted to protect 'Abdu'l-Bahá from their covetousness. 'You have given them all something,' said one of the ladies.

One of the other Bahá'ís was called over.

'Have I given this boy anything?' asked 'Abdu'l-Bahá.

'I don't think so.'

So the boy also got something.

# 32

# 'Abdu'l-Bahá in London

'Abdu'l-Bahá's holiday was a short one. Soon, He was on His travels again. London and Paris were the two large cities which He visited on His first journey to Europe. He went first to London. This was a unique event. Never before had a leader of a world religion travelled from the East to a great city of the West. Never before had 'Abdu'l-Bahá had the opportunity as a free man to travel to proclaim the Faith. Never before had He stood before a large audience to give a talk.

There was already a small group of Bahá'ís in London then. They were able to make preparations for 'Abdu'l-Bahá's visit. Lady Blomfield placed her home at His disposal. This was a large and hospitable apartment. This was necessary, too, since many people from London and a wide surrounding area wished to visit Him. Articles about Him appeared in the newspapers. He was invited to give talks in two large churches in London. These were filled to the very last seat. 'Abdu'l-Bahá had never in His life spoken to such a large number of people and yet He appeared to be an experienced speaker. He spoke in Persian and an interpreter translated His words into English.

'Abdu'l-Bahá spoke in London of the unity of mankind and about peace. He forecast that a time would come when there would be no more wars between countries. The world would be a new world and the peoples of the earth would live together as brothers. By God's will, the Most Great Peace would come. When 'Abdu'l-Bahá spoke these words in London this was a very long way off. Especially in Europe, where war threatened all the time and troubles were constantly breaking out. Europe was like a huge arsenal full of arms. Only a tiny spark was needed to cause it to explode. More and more weapons of war were being manufactured and gradually every country was armed to the teeth. Three years later, in 1914, the First World War broke out. It was a terrible war in which nine million young men were needlessly sent to their deaths.

As if by a magnet, the people of London and round about were drawn to Him. From early morning to sometimes midnight, there was an endless stream of people of all classes and social backgrounds who wanted to see Him. Rich and poor, eminent people and ordinary working men. Bahá'ís from Persia came who could now at long last visit Him as a free man. On everyone to whom He spoke He made a deep, unforgettable impression. Whatever questions people brought to Him, they knew that 'Abdu'l-Bahá understood exactly what they meant. And everyone received the perfect answer to his questions.

'Abdu'l-Bahá was also aware of what was going on around Him, even if He was not present! One day, a lady arrived and asked if she could speak to 'Abdu'l-Bahá.

'Have you an appointment?' asked the Bahá'í who was arranging the meetings.

'Alas! no.'

'I'm sorry, He is speaking now to rather important people and cannot be disturbed.'

Deeply disappointed, the woman turned and went down the steps. She was an ordinary woman and did not dare to insist any further.

Then those in the house heard the voice of 'Abdu'l-Bahá, 'A heart has been hurt. Hasten, hasten, bring her to Me!'

147

One of the believers ran from the room and before the woman had reached the bottom of the steps he had caught up with her. Out of breath, he said, 'He wishes to see you, come back! He has told me to bring you to Him.'

Another time a tramp walked in.

'Is the lady of this house at home?' he asked one of the servants.

'Yes, but . . .'

'Oh please, I must see her!'

Lady Blomfield had heard this and went to the hall.

'Are you the hostess of 'Abdu'l-Bahá?' asked the tramp.

'Yes. Do you wish to see me?'

'I have walked thirty miles for that purpose.'

'Come in and rest. After some refreshment you will tell me?'

He went into the dining room. It is true that he looked like a tramp but when she spoke to him she soon found that he was not just an ordinary tramp. After a while the poor man began to tell his story. He had not always been such a scruffy-looking fellow. His father was a country clergyman and he had received a good education. He said that the previous evening he had intended to put an end to his useless life. He decided to take one last walk and happened to pass a newsagent's shop. In the window, he saw a photograph of 'Abdu'l-Bahá in a newspaper. When he looked at it, it seemed as if 'Abdu'l-Bahá spoke to him and called him to Him. The man said to himself, 'If such a personage exists on this earth, I shall take up again the burden of my life.'

He asked for the newspaper, read where he could find 'Abdu'l-Bahá and went to look for Lady Blomfield's house.

'Tell me, is He here? Will He see me? Even me?'

'Of course He will see you. Come to Him.'

When they knocked at His door, 'Abdu'l-Bahá Himself opened it. He stretched out His hands as if He were expecting a dear friend.

'Welcome! Most welcome! I am very much pleased that you have come. Be seated.' .

The pathetic man sank onto a low chair at 'Abdu'l-Bahá's feet.

'Be happy! Be happy!' said 'Abdu'l-Bahá, holding his hand and stroking his dishevelled hair tenderly. With a loving smile, He encouraged him, saying, 'Do not be filled with grief when humiliation overtaketh thee. The bounty and power of God is without limit for each and every soul in the world . . . though you are poor, you may be rich in the Kingdom of God.'

'Abdu'l-Bahá's love and warmth seemed to dissolve completely the cloud of misery which had hung about the poor tramp. A new look came into his eyes and his bowed head was held up straight. When he had sat for a while at 'Abdu'l-Bahá's feet, he stood up and said, 'Please write down His words for me. I have attained all I expected, and even more.'

Before he left, his hostess asked him what he was going to do now.

'I'm going to work in the fields. I can earn what I need for my simple wants. When I have saved enough, I shall take a little bit of land, build a tiny hut upon it in which to live, then I shall grow violets for the market. As He says, "Poverty is unimportant, work is worship."

'I need not say "thank you", need I?' he said to his hostess. Then he was gone, filled with confidence. The short visit to 'Abdu'l-Bahá had completely changed his life.

# 33

## Paris Talks

'Be kind to the strangers, whether they come from Turkey, Japan, Persia, Russia, China or any other country in the world. Help to make them feel at home; find out where they are staying, ask if you may render them any service; try to make their lives a little happier . . .When you meet a Persian or any other stranger, speak to him as to a friend.'

These words were spoken by 'Abdu'l-Bahá when, after visiting London, He went to Paris. As always, He Himself set the example for what He was teaching. In Paris He rented a large apartment. He said, 'This is my home and the home of my friends.' The room in which He received His guests was so big that there was space for between seventy-five and a hundred people. All visitors were welcome there, from whatever country they came or whatever religion they belonged to: Persian, English, German, French, American, Christian, Muslim or Hindu. And whether they were rich or poor did not matter either.

Often, He Himself went to visit the poor. Even in Paris. Many poor people lived in the great slums of Paris. Hardly anyone bothered about them or their children. They were supposed to look after themselves. Sometimes there were people who did their best to help them. Like Mr and Mrs Ponsonaille. When they became Bahá'ís they decided to look after poor children. Out of the little money they had, they bought food for them. They held children's classes and taught them passages from the

Writings of Bahá'u'lláh. There was so much interest in these classes that the churches wanted Mr and Mrs Ponsonaille to work for them. They did not want to do that. When the churches did not get what they wanted, they took away the car in which they had collected the children. The Ponsonailles did not give up and the Bahá'ís in Paris offered to help. They paid for timber and nails and the Ponsonailles used these to build another meeting place. 'Abdu'l-Bahá came to visit them there. He told the children that He loved them and that He was very happy to be with them. He had been in many beautiful houses but this one was the best, because it was filled with the spirit and love of Bahá'u'lláh. Even the most boisterous children were very quiet when 'Abdu'l-Bahá spoke. He said to Mr and Mrs Ponsonaille that the work they were doing made Him happy. For centuries, people would remember them. In future, people would not talk as much about kings and queens as they would about them.

When 'Abdu'l-Bahá wished to leave, He could hardly get to the door, since the children crowded around Him. They fell over each other to be allowed shake His hand. When He was bidding goodbye to Mr Ponsonaille outside, He slipped a good number of gold coins into his hand.

'Abdu'l-Bahá was usually happy and cheerful. But not always; sometimes He was sad about what was happening in the world. At that time a serious accident took place in France. A train fell into a river and twenty people lost their lives as a result. The newspapers were full of it and the manager of the railway was held responsible. 'Abdu'l-Bahá saw how the deaths of twenty people caused a great shock throughout the country. But at the same time there was a war being waged between Italy and Turkey. In North Africa there was also a huge campaign in which five thousand soldiers died. Hardly any attention had been paid to that. He was not only worried about the terrible things which were going on in the world. He was mainly sorrowful because people were so indifferent to the suffering of those in other countries.

Two days before His departure from Paris, a lady came hurrying in to the gathering. 'Oh, how glad I am to be in time! I must tell you the amazing reason of my hurried journey from America. One day, my little girl astonished me by saying, "Mummy, if dear Lord Jesus was in the world now, what would you do?"

"Darling, I would feel like getting on the first train and going to Him as fast as I could."

"Well, Mummy, He *is* in the world."'

The mother felt a great sense of awe as her small daughter said this.

'What do you mean, my precious? How do you know?'

'He told me Himself, so of course He *is* in the world.'

In amazement, the mother wondered: is this a message which is coming to me though my child? She prayed to God that it would be made clear to her. The next day the little girl began again, insistently: 'Mummy, why isn't you gone to see Lord Jesus? He's told me two times that He is really here, in the world.'

'Tiny love, Mummy doesn't know where He is, how could she find Him?'

'We see, Mummy, we see.'

In the afternoon they went for a walk. Suddenly the little girl stopped and cried, 'There He is! There He is!' She was trembling with excitement and pointing at the windows of a newsagent's where there was a picture of 'Abdu'l-Bahá.

The mother bought the paper, discovered where 'Abdu'l-

Bahá was to be found, and took the boat that same night. Fortunately, she arrived in Paris just in time.

This mother and her little daughter first thought that 'Abdu'l-Bahá was Christ, Who had returned after two thousand years to this earth. Many Bahá'ís in America and Europe also believed that and thought that 'Abdu'l-Bahá was a Messenger of God. But again and again, and very patiently, 'Abdu'l-Bahá explained that Bahá'u'lláh was the Messenger of God. And He, 'Abdu'l-Bahá, was the Servant of the Messenger of God, the Servant of Bahá'u'lláh.

'Abdu'l-Bahá gave talks every day. One of the Persian Bahá'ís who had travelled with Him translated His words into French. Lady Blomfield, 'Abdu'l-Bahá's hostess in London, had travelled with them to Paris. With her daughters and another Bahá'í they made notes of these talks. They put these into a book and sent this to 'Abdu'l-Bahá for His approval.

'Abdu'l-Bahá was very pleased with it and said that it should be published as soon as possible. This was done and within six months the book was finished. In this way, the book we know as *Paris Talks* came about. It is widely read and has now been translated into many different languages.

'Abdu'l-Bahá's journeys to France and England had taken over three months. The Bahá'ís in America were very eager that 'Abdu'l-Bahá should travel on from Europe directly to the States. He had, however, promised the Bahá'ís in the East that He would return to them. He first went back to Egypt and promised to come to America the following Spring instead.

# 34

# To America

If there was anything the American Bahá'ís really longed for, it was for 'Abdu'l-Bahá to come to the United States. When He was still a prisoner that was impossible. So some of them had then gone themselves to 'Akká to see Him. But now that He was free, He received countless letters begging Him to come to America.

'Abdu'l-Bahá said that America must be worthy to receive Him. What did He mean by that? That the American Bahá'ís should pay His travelling expenses? They had already collected quite a lot of money. When 'Abdu'l-Bahá received the first amount which had been sent to Him, He sent it back at once. He wrote that He had enough money to pay His own expenses, otherwise He would certainly not have accepted their invitation. He told them to give the money to the poor.

So 'Abdu'l-Bahá had meant something different when He said that America must be worthy to receive Him. He said that there must be love, unity and harmony among the American believers. In one of His letters He wrote that they were the fish of one sea, the birds of one rose-garden and the flowers of the same paradise. If disunity and differences of opinion were to disappear then He would be drawn as by a magnet to America.

Unity and love among the Bahá'ís. That made Him happy! Again and again, 'Abdu'l-Bahá wrote about this. When He was in Europe, one of the Bahá'ís suggested that He Himself should

come to America in order to unite the friends. Otherwise it would never happen, she thought. She received a clear reply: 'No, you must do that yourselves.'

After His journey to London and Paris, 'Abdu'l-Bahá spent the winter months in Egypt. There for a few months, He had the opportunity to regain His strength. Meanwhile, the invitations to America kept arriving. Even the clergy and the rabbis were asking Him to come and give a talk in their church or synagogue. The Bahá'ís of America were longing for Him to come to them. And 'Abdu'l-Bahá longed to be among them.

'Abdu'l-Bahá was intending to travel on the S.S.*Cedric* straight from Egypt to America. Many of the believers felt He should transfer to another ship, the *Titanic*. That was the largest, most luxurious and also the fastest passenger ship which had ever been built. It was so big and strong that people thought it could never sink. It was just about to make its maiden voyage from Europe to America. It could accommodate four thousand passengers and had a crew of almost a thousand. Travelling on the *Titanic* would be faster and less tiring. The extra cost for the voyage on this ship had already been collected by the Bahá'ís. When 'Abdu'l-Bahá heard about this invitation He reflected for a moment and then said, 'No, we will go direct, trusting in the assistance and protection of the Blessed Beauty. He is the true Protector and the divine Keeper.' How relieved the Bahá'ís were afterwards that 'Abdu'l-Bahá had not gone along with their suggestion. During that first voyage, the *Titanic* ran into an iceberg and sank in two-and-a-half hours. Fifteen hundred people were drowned in the icy water. It was the greatest disaster which had ever happened to a passenger ship.

When the *Cedric* departed from Egypt six Bahá'ís went with 'Abdu'l-Bahá. One of these was Shoghi Effendi, His eldest grandson. He was then 15 years old and would later become Guardian of the Faith. You can imagine how much a boy of 15 was looking forward to going to America on a big ship. But when the voyage had only just begun, problems arose.

The *Cedric* was an Italian ship, with an Italian ship's doctor. At that time there was a war between Italy and Turkey. The Holy Land was then still a Turkish possession. So the Italians regarded 'Abdu'l-Bahá and His companions as Turks and therefore as enemies. From the beginning of the voyage this had made things difficult. The ship's doctor found that one of 'Abdu'l-Bahá's party had an eye disease. With this condition, he would not be allowed to enter the United States. When the ship docked in Naples, a group of Italian doctors came on board to examine the eyes of the passengers. They said that the eyes of Shoghi Effendi and of two other Bahá'ís were infected. All three had to leave the ship. No matter how 'Abdu'l-Bahá and his companions pleaded, they were not allowed to continue the voyage. And if they did go, said the doctors, they would still not be allowed into America. 'Abdu'l-Bahá was very sad about this, especially because Shoghi Effendi could not come. He said they had been unjustly treated. Later this turned out to be true. At the end of the voyage, the doctor came to 'Abdu'l-Bahá. When He mentioned the name of Shoghi Effendi, the doctor admitted that he had not even examined his eyes. He begged 'Abdu'l-Bahá's forgiveness.

With the three remaining Persian Bahá'ís and six Western Bahá'ís who had come on board in Naples, 'Abdu'l-Bahá continued the journey. The other passengers wondered at the sight of these men in their long Oriental robes. They could not help looking at them. But they soon began to have great respect for 'Abdu'l-Bahá. They came to Him with questions and in His talks He told them about Bahá'u'lláh and His Teachings. Once, at the start of the voyage, the passengers had reserved the largest hall on the ship. Here, 'Abdu'l-Bahá gave a talk to over fifteen hundred people.

The voyage lasted seventeen days. When, in the morning, the ship sailed into New York harbour, a large group of Bahá'ís stood on the pier to greet Him. But He did not wish to be welcomed in that way. He asked one of the believers to come to Him. He returned with the message that they could go to the house where He would be staying that afternoon. There they could meet one another.

The Bahá'ís did what 'Abdu'l-Bahá had asked. Except for three ladies. Their longing to see Him was so great that they could not be patient for so long. They looked for somewhere on the docks where they could hide. They found a niche in the wall of a building near the ship. From there, they would be able to see Him without His knowing they were there. At least, that's what they thought!

A car arrived to collect 'Abdu'l-Bahá. Where did it stop? Just in front of the spot where the three ladies were hiding. Now they were trapped. To get away unnoticed was impossible now. Panic-stricken, they waited. They could see 'Abdu'l-Bahá walking towards them. Would He discover them? He walked to the car, was about to get in, but just before He did, He turned around for a moment and smiled at the ladies.

To hide from 'Abdu'l-Bahá was not as easy as they had thought!

160

# 35

## Arrival in New York

'What are you doing here?'

'Why have you come to America?'

'How can universal peace be achieved?'

The journalists in New York wanted to have the news of 'Abdu'l-Bahá's arrival in America in the newspapers as quickly as possible. They could not even wait until the *Cedric* had entered the harbour. When the ship lay at anchor before the harbour they hired a tugboat to take them to the vessel. All kinds of questions were then fired at 'Abdu'l-Bahá. 'Abdu'l-Bahá answered that it was His purpose to establish universal peace and the unity of mankind. He had already been to London and Paris. Now He had come to America to meet the people who were working for peace.

One of the journalists wrote a report which was sent to newspapers all over the world. 'Abdu'l-Bahá's arrival was announced in large bold type and photographs of Him appeared in the newspapers. They wrote that He had come to America to teach brotherly love, that he was teaching universal peace and was an apostle of peace. And that He had said that all religions were the same.

Not everything published in the newspapers was correct. One said that there were already twenty million Bahá'ís. Another that 'Abdu'l-Bahá had come as an ordinary tourist to the States to see interesting places. Although He had said very clearly that He had come to bring a message of universal peace and the unity of mankind. Others still, described Him as a prophet. 'Abdu'l-Bahá had Himself said that He was not a prophet but merely a servant of the servants of God. There was also a newspaper which had come to the conclusion that men could only become Bahá'ís if they let their beards grow.

In the afternoon, the Bahá'ís had gone to the home of the Kinney family. 'Abdu'l-Bahá had asked them to do this, when they came to meet Him in the morning at the docks. How happy the American Bahá'ís were now that they had Him in their midst! Their faces shone. For years they had longed for this day. They had written letters and collected signatures in order to invite Him. The great moment to which they had looked forward for years was now here. The house was thronged with visitors, standing almost on each other's toes. Everyone who was able to come was there.

'Abdu'l-Bahá Himself felt happy to be among the American believers. When He left Egypt, He knew it would be a tiring journey. But He had come anyway, because He had also longed to meet them and speak to them. He had had to overcome many difficulties to be able to make that long voyage. But that weariness and those difficulties disappeared and were forgotten when He saw the shining faces of the friends. He prayed that the love of Bahá'u'lláh would become visible in each one of those present. And that each one would become as a shining lamp of crystal whose beams would radiate the blessings of Bahá'u'lláh to every country in the world.

There were also friends of the Bahá'ís present. One of these was the Reverend Howard Colby Ives. He had been a seeker of truth for years. Nowhere could he find anything about which he could say, 'Yes, this is what I am looking for, this is what I need.' Shortly before 'Abdu'l-Bahá's visit to America, he had come into

contact with the Bahá'ís. One evening he was taking a walk with one of his Bahá'í friends. They were talking about what it would soon be like to see 'Abdu'l-Bahá in America. What would He look like? What effect would He have on the people?

Suddenly Howard Ives said to his friend, 'When 'Abdu'l-Bahá arrives I would like very much to have a talk with Him alone, without even an interpreter.'

'I am afraid that without an interpreter you will not get very far, for 'Abdu'l-Bahá speaks very little English and I think you speak even less Persian,' replied his friend.

Howard Colby Ives was not to be dissuaded. He said that he thought he would understand Him much better that way, even if no word was spoken.

The first afternoon that 'Abdu'l-Bahá was in America, Howard Ives was there. With great difficulty he was able to catch a glimpse of Him among the crowd of people. He felt that 'Abdu'l-Bahá was indeed a special person. But why were all these Bahá'ís so greatly impressed by Him? Why were they beaming with joy because He was amongst them? Howard Ives could not understand it. Yet he wanted to know. So he went at once the next morning to the hotel where 'Abdu'l-Bahá and his companions were staying.

In the hotel foyer he had no desire to speak to anyone. He went to stand by the window and looked out. He began to wonder what he was really doing there. He had no appointment and why should 'Abdu'l-Bahá pay any attention to him? As he stood there looking out, he heard the sound of voices in the hall. 'Abdu'l-Bahá came in. All eyes were upon Him, even the eyes of Howard Colby Ives. A few moments later 'Abdu'l-Bahá looked at the clergyman. He smiled and beckoned him to come to Him. Howard Ives could not believe that this was meant for him. He looked around – there must be someone else. But there was no one nearby. He looked again at 'Abdu'l-Bahá, who beckoned him again. Slowly, he went over to 'Abdu'l-Bahá. 'Abdu'l-Bahá extended both hands to him as if He had known him all his life. Then 'Abdu'l-Bahá motioned to everyone else to leave the room, even the interpreter. Now he was completely alone with 'Abdu'l-Bahá. He could scarcely believe it. The wish he had expressed some weeks previously had been granted as soon as they had looked at one another.

By the window there were two chairs. 'Abdu'l-Bahá brought him there, still holding him by the hand. Gently He said in English that he was His dear son. Howard Ives felt as if he were with his Father, but that Father was much more than an ordinary father. They sat down, knee to knee, eye to eye. 'Abdu'l-Bahá looked at him. It seemed to Howard Ives that until that moment there had been no one who had ever really seen him. He was filled with happiness. He had the feeling that he had come home. He was alone with his Father, who knew all about him. 'Abdu'l-Bahá did not speak. Nor was this necessary; His face spoke volumes. Even if He had spoken for an hour, He could not have said as much. Tears flowed down Howard Colby Ives' cheeks. With his thumbs, 'Abdu'l-Bahá wiped the tears from his face. Laughing, He said he should not cry, people should always be happy. The clergyman could not utter a word. But words were not necessary anyway. He knew this and he thanked God for it. They sat for a while together like this.

Suddenly, 'Abdu'l-Bahá leapt from His chair. He grasped Howard Colby Ives under the elbows, stood him up and threw both arms around him. He kissed him on both cheeks and hugged him so tightly that his ribs cracked. Then 'Abdu'l-Bahá placed His arm around his shoulders and accompanied him to the door.

That was Howard Colby Ives' first meeting with 'Abdu'l-Bahá. He had never told anyone that he had said one evening that he would like to be alone with 'Abdu'l-Bahá. His friend had never told anyone else either. Yet his wish had been granted, and that on the very first occasion that his eyes had met those of 'Abdu'l-Bahá. From that moment on, he took every opportunity to be with Him. Because of 'Abdu'l-Bahá, the life of the Reverend Howard Colby Ives was going to be entirely changed.

# 36

## The Down-and-outs of New York

As soon as 'Abdu'l-Bahá reached America, visitors thronged the house or hotel where He was staying. They were attracted to Him as if by a magnet. There were even those who followed Him in their cars from one meeting to another. Many invitations also came for Him to give talks. Even when He was in Egypt and during the voyage, the invitations had come. The clergy, in particular, asked Him to speak in their churches. The first Sunday that 'Abdu'l-Bahá was in America, He had been invited to give a talk in thirteen churches. It was, of course, impossible to accept all these invitations.

One of the invitations which 'Abdu'l-Bahá did accept was to give a talk for New York's poorest: the tramps and the homeless. Miss Juliet Thompson had arranged for this invitation. A few months earlier, she had given a talk in a shelter for the homeless in the Bowery, one of the poorest districts in New York. She had told them about 'Abdu'l-Bahá. How He had spent most of His life in prison. And that He was always full of love for everyone, no matter how cruelly He was treated. After

her talk, the person in charge of the shelter suggested inviting 'Abdu'l-Bahá when He came to the States. Whoever was in favour of the suggestion should stand up. All three hundred down-and-outs stood up.

When 'Abdu'l-Bahá came to visit the shelter, the hall was packed. He said to the homeless that He was very happy that evening. He had come here to meet friends. He went on to say, 'I consider you my relatives, my companions, and I am your comrade. You must be thankful to God that you are poor, for His Holiness Jesus Christ has said: "Blessed are the poor." He never said: blessed are the rich! . . . Jesus Himself was poor. He did not belong to the rich. He passed His time in the desert travelling among the poor and lived upon the herbs of the field. He had no place to lay His head – no home. He was exposed in the open to heat, cold and frost. Yet He chose this rather than riches . . . You will find many of the wealthy exposed to dangers and troubled by difficulties, and in their last moments upon the bed of death they must be separated from that to which their hearts are so attached.'

'Abdu'l-Bahá also told the tramps about Bahá'u'lláh. When He lived in Baghdad, He left the city and lived for two years among the poor. He ate with them, slept with them and felt it was an honour to be one of them. He even adopted the title of the poor and called Himself a dervish. Bahá'u'lláh has called everyone to be the servants and helpers of the poor. We must not forget their sorrow and troubles and go among them ourselves.

'Abdu'l-Bahá did not stop at words alone. Beforehand, He had given money to two of the Bahá'ís to take to the bank to have it changed into small coinage. They both returned with a bag containing about a thousand coins. When 'Abdu'l-Bahá had finished His talk, He went to stand by the door. The two believers with their bags of coins stood next to Him, one on each side. He shook the hand of each of the approximately five hundred down-and-outs and slipped each one some coins. Enough for one night's lodging somewhere, so no one had to sleep rough that night. 'Abdu'l-Bahá gave them much more than just a few coins. He treated them like friends and members of His family, as He had said in His talk. Not like tramps and outcasts, as nearly everyone else did. He gave them His divine love. He surrounded them with His love and was their friend – a friend such as they had never had before. Like the many who had met 'Abdu'l-Bahá, it was the same for them: this evening with 'Abdu'l-Bahá was one they would always remember.

When they returned to the hotel, 'Abdu'l-Bahá saw one of the chambermaids. She had earlier received a gift of roses from Him. 'Abdu'l-Bahá called her to Him, asked her to hold up her apron and emptied the coins that were left in the bag into her apron. He then went at once with his companions to His room. The girl was just able to stop one of the Bahá'ís to say to him, 'Oh, *see* what He has given me!'

He told her that 'Abdu'l-Bahá had been to see the homeless and had given each of them a few coins and treated them all most kindly. Then she said, 'I will do the same with this money. I will give away every cent of it.'

Later that evening 'Abdu'l-Bahá and the friends were talking about what had happened at the shelter for the homeless. One of them asked if charity was necessary. Laughingly, 'Abdu'l-Bahá replied, 'Assuredly, give to the poor. If you give them only words, when they put their hands into their pockets they will find themselves none the richer for you.'

Just at that moment there was a gentle knock on the door.

It was opened and there stood the chambermaid. It was if she could see no one else in the room. She went straight up to 'Abdu'l-Bahá and said, 'I wanted to say goodbye, Sir, and to thank you for all your goodness to me – I never expected such goodness – and to ask you . . . to pray for me.' Her voice failed and she began to sob, hid her face in her apron and ran out of the room.

# 37

# The House of Worship near Chicago

On His travels through America, 'Abdu'l-Bahá mainly visited the cities. First, he stayed a week in New York, then He went for a week to Washington, the capital. Next, He went to Chicago for one of the most important events of His journey: the laying of the foundation stone for the building of the first Bahá'í temple in America.

Ten years earlier, the Bahá'ís of Chicago had started with the preparations for this. They had received news of the building of the temple in 'Ishqábád in Russia. From a Persian Bahá'í they had received a report on the laying of the cornerstone. In his letter, he had encouraged them also to begin building a temple in America. The Chicago Bahá'ís consulted upon this and before long all its members were at one in support of this proposal. They asked 'Abdu'l-Bahá for His approval of the plan. He was absolutely delighted.

The group of Bahá'ís in Chicago was, however, much too small to attempt such a large project as the building of a temple. In a few years it became obvious to them that this must be a project for all the American Bahá'ís. When more than eight hundred Bahá'ís had signed a declaration of support for the construction, Mrs Corinne True and her husband affixed all the signatures to a roll of parchment and took this to 'Akká, to 'Abdu'l-Bahá. When she arrived and wanted to hand the roll to Him, He was there before her. Before she could say what was in the package, He took the roll, held it up and cried,

'Mashriqu'l-Adhkár! This . . . this is what gives me great joy. Go back . . . go back and work for the Temple; it is a great work, the best thing you could do, Mrs True.'

She asked what the temple should look like. 'Abdu'l-Bahá drew a plan and said that it should have nine sides, with nine entrances and nine paths leading to these. Between every path a pond should be constructed. 'Abdu'l-Bahá emphasized to Corinne True that she should devote herself to the construction of the temple. He said, 'Make a beginning, and all will come right.' At the end of this pilgrimage, He said once again to her that He wished her to devote herself to the construction of the temple.

Where should the temple be built? Some of the Bahá'ís thought in Chicago, close to the people. 'Abdu'l-Bahá, however, preferred a place where land was still cheap, preferably near Lake Michigan. Corinne True toured the area looking for a suitable place. She found it on the shores of Lake Michigan, near the little town of Wilmette. A national committee had now been appointed and it decided the temple should be built there. The committee sent a telegram to 'Akká with the news of this important decision. 'Abdu'l-Bahá received that telegram on the same day that the body of the Báb was interred in the mausoleum on Mount Carmel.

A good deal of money was needed to buy the land for the temple. The American Bahá'ís saved hard for this, sometimes with nickels, dimes and quarters. They got help from other countries; 'Abdu'l-Bahá encouraged the Bahá'ís in the East to contribute to the building fund. So money came not just from Western Europe but also from Egypt, Persia, India and South Africa. There were even contributions from 'Ishqábád, where the Bahá'ís themselves were building a temple. Such a thing had never happened before: Eastern countries contributing

171

to the building of a temple in America. Even the children in the children's classes were saving for this. When one of the pilgrims told this to 'Abdu'l-Bahá, He was very happy. If the children could only have seen how He glowed with joy and happiness! 'Very good, very good,' He said again and again.

Some Bahá'ís had very little money but still wanted to give something. Like Nettie Tobin. She was a widow and as a seamstress she could only just earn enough to keep herself and her two children. She was sorry she could give so little. She prayed that somehow she would have the chance to give something significant. Then in a dream she heard a voice telling her to look for a stone. She began searching at once and went to a building site near her home. The foreman allowed her to pick out a stone from the pile that the builders were not going to be able to use. She found one and went to a Persian Bahá'í friend to ask for help. Together they went with an old child's pram to the building site, hoisted the stone on to the pram and went with it to the tram. At first the conductor would not allow them on, but Nettie was able to persuade him to take them. It was a not an easy trip because they had to change twice on the way. The other passengers looked at them in amazement: who were these people getting on the tram with a large stone in an old pram? Nettie took no notice of this. Her goal was fixed; the stone had to go to the site where the temple was to be built. They got off the tram quite near their goal. But they could not go much farther; the pram collapsed. Nettie would not hear of giving up. She spied a boy with a barrow and asked him to help. They got to the temple land and wanted to take the stone right to the middle of the site. But this was not to be. The barrow bumped against something, overturned, and the stone fell on the ground. For two years, it stayed where it fell.

Until the day that 'Abdu'l-Bahá came to lay the first stone. A

tent had been put up for the ceremony, with room for about a hundred people, while outside the tent about another hundred stood. In His address, 'Abdu'l-Bahá predicted that in the future there would be temples built all over the world. The first temple was the one in 'Ishqábád. The Bahá'ís there had made great sacrifices for the construction of that. Around that temple there would be various other buildings, such as a hospital, a school for orphans and a home for those with disabilities. He expressed the hope that the same would happen at the temple in Chicago.

After 'Abdu'l-Bahá's speech, the company went outside. 'Abdu'l-Bahá asked them to bring Nettie Tobin's stone, which was still lying somewhere on the site. Meanwhile, He walked up and down and asked where the centre of the site was. When the stone was brought, one of the ladies handed Him a leather pouch containing a gold trowel. With this trowel, 'Abdu'l-Bahá tried to dig a hole in the ground at the spot which had been pointed out to Him as the centre of the site. It could not be done, the ground was too hard. So He asked for another tool. A young man ran to a nearby house and fetched a pickaxe. With a powerful stroke, 'Abdu'l-Bahá swung the pickaxe in the air. With a couple of swings He was through the sod. In the meantime, another boy had fetched a spade. 'Abdu'l-Bahá took the spade and then asked some of the ladies to begin the digging. Others joined in to dig – people of fifteen different nationalities from Asia, Africa, Europe and, of course, America. When the hole was big enough, 'Abdu'l-Bahá took a few handfuls of earth and distributed this among some of the bystanders. Then the stone was set in its place. 'Abdu'l-Bahá produced the gold trowel again and, with it, pressed the earth down firmly around the stone.

Then He said something very striking: 'The temple is already built.' Why did He say that? They had only bought a piece of land and the first stone was now laid. There was nothing more. They did not even know yet what the temple was going to look like. Only that it would have nine entrances and around it, nine gardens, each with a pool and a fountain, would be laid out. Architects had still to design it and many technical problems would have to be solved as well as a lot more money found to complete it. And yet 'Abdu'l-Bahá said, 'The temple is already built.' He was certain that the plan to build the temple would succeed. And it did. All the difficulties were overcome. Even when, during the construction, part of the building was damaged by fire. Forty years after 'Abdu'l-Bahá had laid the first stone, the temple was officially dedicated.

During the building work Nettie Tobin's stone could not remain where 'Abdu'l-Bahá had laid it. It was later found that the spot was not exactly in the centre of the site. The stone was carefully preserved. When the building was far enough advanced, it was concreted into the floor of the temple hall, on the exact spot where 'Abdu'l-Bahá had placed it.

Why should temples be built? Bahá'u'lláh ordained this in the Kitáb-i-Aqdas, the Most Holy Book. He wrote: 'O people of the world! Build ye houses of worship throughout the lands in the name of Him Who is the Lord of all religions.' The temple is a place in which to pray, the temple is dedicated to the praise of God. In the temple no talks are given; only prayers and passages from the holy books of all religions are read. 'Abdu'l-Bahá has explained that a temple is necessary for the proclamation of the unity of mankind. It is a place where different peoples and races, and the followers of all religions can come together to meet one another. This is how the Houses of Worship will lead to the oneness and brotherhood of the human race.

# 38

## The Children Go to Chicago

That Sunday morning, some children and their parents had been up since five o'clock. They were going on a trip. Not just any trip! No, they were going to meet 'Abdu'l-Bahá! He was expecting them at His hotel in Chicago. They were gathered together in a large room. The children sat in a circle, and their parents and other friends sat round this. 'Abdu'l-Bahá came in and everyone stood up.

'Abdu'l-Bahá sat down on a chair which had been placed ready for Him, and the children sang a song. After that, He called them one by one to Him. He took them on His knee, caressed them and patted their heads. He hugged and kissed the little ones. He put His arm around the older children. In English, He whispered to them to tell Him their names. Spontaneously, they all told Him their names. He gave each one an encouraging pat on the chest or on the back. He blessed them all. There was a benevolent silence. 'Abdu'l-Bahá had so much time for them. It was an unforgettable time. For the children, of course, but no less so for their parents. Perhaps they were thinking back to two thousand years ago when Christ was on earth. This was what it must have been like when the children came to Him.

Everyone was very happy. The joy and gladness was at its height when one of the little ones ran up to 'Abdu'l-Bahá. She threw herself right into His arms. When she was about to go back, she stopped a moment in front of 'Abdu'l-Bahá and suddenly burst out laughing. To the great amusement of everyone present.

After He had thus greeted all the children, 'Abdu'l-Bahá stood up and spoke to them:

You are the children of whom Christ has said, 'Of such is the kingdom of God'; and according to the words of Bahá'u'lláh you are the very lamps or candles of the world of humanity, for your hearts are exceedingly pure and your spirits most sensitive. You are near the source; you have not yet become contaminated. You are the lambs of the heavenly Shepherd. You are as polished mirrors reflecting pure light. My hope is that your parents may educate you spiritually and give you thorough moral training. May you develop so that each one of you shall become imbued with all the virtues of the human world. May you advance in all material and spiritual degrees. May you become learned in sciences, acquire the arts and crafts, prove to be useful members of human society and assist the progress of human civilization. May you be a cause of the manifestation of divine bestowals – each one of you a shining star radiating the light of the oneness of humanity toward the horizons of the East and West. May you be devoted to the love and unity of mankind, and through your efforts may the reality deposited in the human heart find its divine expression. I pray for you, asking the assistance and confirmation of God in your behalf.

You are all my children, my spiritual children. Spiritual children are dearer than physical children, for it is possible for physical children to turn away from the Spirit of God, but you are spiritual children and, therefore, you are most beloved. I wish for you progress in every degree of development. May God assist you. May you be surrounded by the beneficent light of His countenance, and may you attain maturity under His nurture and protection. You are all blessed.

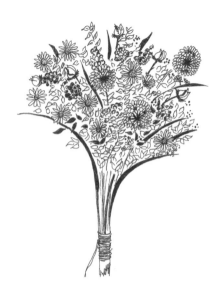

When He had finished speaking to the children, 'Abdu'l-Bahá took a bunch of flowers from a vase on the table and distributed these to the children. He also gave each one an envelope containing rose petals. He went round the circle once again and beaming at them, laid His hand on each little head and murmured a kind word to every child. The children thought that it was all over then. What a pity! They had so much wanted to stay with Him. But fortunately, 'Abdu'l-Bahá took them to the park and there they were all photographed with Him.

# 39

## The City of the Covenant

Every time a Prophet of God appears on earth, He promises that after Him another Prophet will come. Christ promised the coming of Muhammad, Muhammad that of the Báb, and the Báb prepared His followers for the coming of Bahá'u'lláh. Bahá'u'lláh Himself has promised that after one thousand years another divine Messenger will also appear. So each Prophet of God promises another Prophet will follow Him. This is called the Greater Covenant.

Bahá'u'lláh made a second Covenant with His followers: the Lesser Covenant. The Lesser Covenant means that immediately after the ascension of Bahá'u'lláh there would be someone to give guidance to His followers. Someone who could explain His Writings unerringly and who could tell the difference between truth and lies. Someone to whom they could go with all their questions and problems. What is remarkable is that Bahá'u'lláh wrote down clearly who would guide the believers after Him. For example, in His Will and Testament, and in the Most Holy Book, the Kitáb-i-Aqdas. When the Holy Family lived in Adrianople, He even revealed a Tablet specially, the Tablet of the Branch. In these Writings He appoints 'Abdu'l-Bahá as the Interpreter of His words and as the Centre of His Covenant. After Bahá'u'lláh's ascension, the Bahá'ís could bring their questions to 'Abdu'l-Bahá.

The Bahá'ís in the East knew what the station of 'Abdu'l-Bahá was. But those in the West? In New York, in any case,

they were not all agreed upon this. Some estimated His station too highly and claimed that He was the return of Christ. That amounted to thinking that 'Abdu'l-Bahá was a Messenger of God like the Báb and Bahá'u'lláh. Others did not estimate His station highly enough and claimed that He was just an ordinary person who through His hard work and service had earned this station.

When 'Abdu'l-Bahá was in New York, the time had come to explain to the Bahá'ís in the West what the Lesser Covenant was. And what it meant that 'Abdu'l-Bahá was the Interpreter of Bahá'u'lláh's Writings and the Centre of His Covenant. Therefore 'Abdu'l-Bahá had the Tablet of the Branch read to a group of about one hundred and twenty-five Bahá'ís. This Tablet had now, almost fifty years after Bahá'u'lláh had revealed it in Adrianople, been translated into English. In this Tablet, Bahá'u'lláh names 'Abdu'l-Bahá the Branch of Holiness, the Limb of the Law of God and the Trust of God amongst the people. Bahá'u'lláh also says, 'Whoso turneth towards Him hath turned towards God, and whoso turneth away from Him hath turned away from My Beauty, hath repudiated My Proof, and transgressed against Me.' That means that if anyone disobeys 'Abdu'l-Bahá, he is also disobeying Bahá'u'lláh and is then also disobedient to God.

Why is the Lesser Covenant so important? What would have happened if Bahá'u'lláh had not given His followers the Lesser Covenant? Then things would have happened in the

Bahá'í Faith just as they happened in the former religions. Differences of opinion would damage the Faith like raging storms. Divisions would dissipate its strength. In former religions there were divisions because the Prophet had not written down who, after Him, would guide the followers. There were always differences of opinion over the meaning of the teachings and over who should lead the Faith. There was no one that they knew would be able to answer their questions properly. Just because Bahá'u'lláh had written it down so clearly, it was clear to everyone that, after Him, 'Abdu'l-Bahá would lead the Faith. Through the Lesser Covenant, the unity of the Faith had been preserved. The time of division and disunity had now passed and the day of unity had dawned.

Bahá'u'lláh and 'Abdu'l-Bahá have ensured that the oneness of the Faith will always be preserved. As Bahá'u'lláh in His Will and Testament had appointed His son 'Abdu'l-Bahá, so 'Abdu'l-Bahá, in His Will and Testament, appointed His grandson Shoghi Effendi as the Guardian of the Faith. Shoghi Effendi did not make a Will in which he appointed a successor. But Bahá'u'lláh had also written that there would be a Universal House of Justice. And a few years after the passing of Shoghi Effendi, there were so many National Spiritual Assemblies that the Universal House of Justice could be elected. The Universal House now administers the Faith and protects it from division.

From the day that 'Abdu'l-Bahá announced that He was the Centre of the Covenant, New York became known as the City of the Covenant. To 'Abdu'l-Bahá, New York was an important city. Already in His first talk there, He expressed His hope that that city might become a city of love and that the divine fragrances would be spread from that city to every part of the world. He felt New York was so important that he kept coming back to it. More than one-third of the time He spent in America, He spent in New York. He Himself said that He had attended more meetings in New York than in all the other cities put together.

New York has now become a city in which much happens that is needed for the achievement of universal peace. The United Nations has its headquarters there. Almost every country is represented there so that they can discuss the problems of the world together. There, the political unity of mankind is becoming a reality. It is also the city where meetings of world leaders are often held.

Exactly eighty years after 'Abdu'l-Bahá's stay in America, a great event took place in the City of the Covenant: the second Bahá'í World Congress. This was in the Holy Year, a hundred years after the ascension of Bahá'u'lláh. The Congress was attended by about twenty-seven thousand people. They came from practically every country and territory in the world. All those different people, often in their traditional costumes – it was an ocean of races, colours and nationalities, full of harmony and love for each other. And full of love for Bahá'u'lláh. At nine other places, spread over every continent, Bahá'í congresses were also being held. At each one, there were visitors from different countries. The high point was on 26 November, the Day of the Covenant, the last day of the Congress. Via a satellite network, all the congresses were connected with one another and with the World Centre of the Faith on Mount Carmel. Each of the nine congresses sent a short message to the great Congress in New York. From Haifa, the message from the Universal House of Justice was read, which could be heard at all the congresses. At the same time this was on the television in many countries, and millions of people were able to see it. In many countries during these days articles appeared about the conferences and about the Faith.

Had not the wish, expressed by 'Abdu'l-Bahá on the first day He was in America, thus clearly been granted?

# 40

## The Herald of the Covenant

As soon as Mrs Lua Getsinger had become a Bahá'í, she began to teach the Faith. She started at home, with her own family. In order to be able to tell others about Bahá'u'lláh, she often went travelling. The more she could teach, the happier it made her.

But Lua's dearest wish was to be with 'Abdu'l-Bahá. With her husband, Edward Getsinger, she was

one of the first pilgrims from the West who visited 'Abdu'l-Bahá in 'Akká. After that, she was a pilgrim again several times in the Holy Land. Even once for longer than a year, in order to teach the Holy Family English. When 'Abdu'l-Bahá was in America, she never missed an opportunity to be in His presence. She was there in Chicago when 'Abdu'l-Bahá laid the first stone for the temple. He even asked her to be the first

184

to plunge the spade into the ground to start the digging. She was also there on that special day in New York, the day on which 'Abdu'l-Bahá announced to a group of the Bahá'ís that He was the Centre of the Covenant and New York the city of the Covenant.

In the afternoon of that same day, Lua and Juliet Thompson were with 'Abdu'l-Bahá. Juliet was an artist and 'Abdu'l-Bahá had asked her to paint a portrait of Him. Every few days he would sit for her for half an hour. That day, Juliet had just begun when 'Abdu'l-Bahá told her that it was making Him feel sleepy. Juliet replied that there was no objection if He wished to take a nap, that she would be able to go on with her work. But when He sat there, with eyes closed, radiating an immense sense of peace and calm, His majestic head so erect, Juliet discovered that she could not go on painting. She just could not do it.

At once, the peace and restfulness of 'Abdu'l-Bahá changed. Juliet described it in her diary like this. 'Suddenly, with a great flash like lightning He opened His eyes and the room seemed to rock like a ship in a storm with the Power released. The Master was *blazing*.' He then spoke some words in Persian to Lua. Lua understood Persian quite well, but 'Abdu'l-Bahá wanted to be sure she understood it all. One of the Persians was called to translate 'Abdu'l-Bahá's words:

'I appoint you, Lua, the Herald of the Covenant. And I AM THE COVENANT, appointed by Bahá'u'lláh. And no one can refute His Word. This is the Testament of Bahá'u'lláh. You will find it in the Holy Book of Aqdas. Go forth and proclaim, "This is THE COVENANT OF GOD in your midst."' For a very short time, 'Abdu'l-Bahá allowed His glory to be seen. Then He was once again just as He always was.

A herald is someone who announces important news. 'Abdu'l-Bahá had officially given Lua the task of announcing to the people that the Covenant of God was in their midst. Lua sprang up with joy. Her eyes sparkled. She looked like an angel with wings. 'Oh recreate me', she cried, 'that I may do this work for Thee!'

A few days later, 'Abdu'l-Bahá asked Lua to go to California to teach the Faith there. She would have to go travelling for Him. But then she would not be with Him every day, and she wanted nothing more than that. However, she also wanted to be obedient in every way. What should she do now? Lua was faced with a difficult decision.

She thought of a scheme to get 'Abdu'l-Bahá to change His mind. She sought out a spot where the poison ivy grew. This is a poisonous plant found in America. If you walk among the plants for a while, your ankles and feet will swell up. That's what Lua did, with the desired effect. Her feet were in a dreadful state. Now 'Abdu'l-Bahá could not send her travelling. The very next morning she sent Juliet out to tell 'Abdu'l-Bahá. He began to laugh, went over to the fruit bowl, took out an apple and a pomegranate and said that Lua must eat them. Lua ate them both up, even the seeds of the pomegranate. After all,

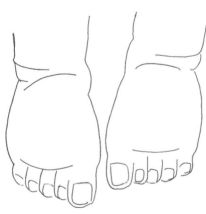

they had come from 'Abdu'l-Bahá! That afternoon He went to visit her. He lifted up the bedclothes and saw that Lua's feet were completely healed. Then He burst out laughing. 'See,' He said, 'I have cured Lua with an apple and a pomegranate.'

Lua tried again with another idea. She said that she could not go away because Juliet had to paint a portrait of her. 'Abdu'l-Bahá burst out laughing once again and said that the portrait could be painted later in New York. He also said that in a year's time she would be with Him in Egypt. Then Lua did what 'Abdu'l-Bahá wanted her to: she went to California.

One year later, Lua was with 'Abdu'l-Bahá in Egypt, as He had said she would be. There, He had a special mission for her. He wished her to go and teach the Faith in India. Lua thought that this would be much too difficult a task for her. 'Abdu'l-Bahá then told her that He had asked her to come from America specially for this. He also said that she should follow His example. He Himself had to deal with countless difficulties every day. He took no notice of these but continued on His way, looking neither to right nor left but straight ahead, way, way ahead. He told Lua that she, too, would have to possess unflinching determination. 'Abdu'l-Bahá gave her another specific instruction: in India she must take money from no one, not even if she needed it very badly.

In India Lua and Edward Getsinger went to work at once. They held talks for large groups and had discussions with all kinds of people about the Faith. They hoped that 'Abdu'l-Bahá Himself would come to India, as He had been to America. They regarded their work as a preparation for His coming to that country. The people here needed Him! In one of her letters, Lua wrote that if 'Abdu'l-Bahá were to spend one day in India, more would be achieved there than if they gave lectures for a whole year. They wrote to Bahá'í friends in America and suggested they should begin collecting money to make the journey possible. To Lua's great disappointment, it became evident some time later that 'Abdu'l-Bahá could not come to India.

From the very first day, life in India was difficult for Lua. It was hot, dreadfully hot. In December the temperature was still 40°C. Her health was not good and so the heat was even more burdensome for her. Even though she was often ill, if it was possible at all she would use the opportunity to teach. That was, after all, what 'Abdu'l-Bahá wanted and she did her utmost to act according to His wishes. Even when she was invited to go to the city of Agra. She knew that it was extremely hot there and that the uncomfortable train journey of two whole days in such heat would be really hard for her. Yet Lua went, since it gave her an opportunity to teach the Faith in a city where this had not so far happened. Agra was like an oven. Whenever she exerted herself even a tiny bit, perspiration broke out all over her. At night it was too hot to sleep. Once, when she had a visitor, it was too hot even to have a conversation. Another time, when her host had invited people to dinner, Lua hoped that the meal would consist of nothing but ice. One night, when a thunderstorm was raging, Lua went out in her nightdress to stand in the rain to be drenched in the cooling water.

There was another problem. Lua and Edward had very little money for their use in India. They had a small monthly income from which they had to meet all their expenses. And sometimes the money was late coming in. Having no money was very distressing for Lua. She was now in India to proclaim the Faith and could do nothing, not even travel, because there was no money. Her clothes were so worn that she could no longer appear on the street. But 'Abdu'l-Bahá had given strict instructions to accept money from no one. Before Lua and Edward Getsinger, there had been Bahá'ís going to India who had accepted money. Lua and Edward had to set a different example. Even if it was voluntarily given and even if they really needed it very badly for teaching the Faith, they did not accept it.

In spite of all the difficulties, Lua carried on. For a whole year! Then she had to give up because World War I made her work there practically impossible. Her husband Edward even left a few months before her. Lua returned to the Holy Land. Her dearest wish to be again with 'Abdu'l-Bahá had been granted. It was not, however, to be for long as because of the war, 'Abdu'l-Bahá could not offer her sufficient protection. She had to return to America. But she was not to see the land of her birth again. At the start of the journey she became ill and could no longer remain on the ship. So she found herself in Egypt once more. And even though her health continued to deteriorate, she kept on teaching the Faith. Until, very suddenly, she died. She was forty-four years old.

She was buried in the Bahá'í cemetery in Cairo, beside the famous Bahá'í scholar Mírzá 'Abu'l-Faḍl.

# 41

## 'Abdu'l-Bahá Gives a Unity Feast

Even during His journey through America, 'Abdu'l-Bahá was always very busy, from early morning to late at night. Sometimes He gave three or four talks in one day. And every day there was a constant stream of visitors who all wanted to speak to Him personally if they could. It was very tiring for Him. He was, after all, almost seventy. In addition, He had been a prisoner for over fifty years in an often unhealthy environment. This had seriously affected His health. The summer weather in New York made life even more difficult. So He went for nine days to a place where He would be able to get some rest. But before His departure, He gave the Bahá'ís another project.

'When I return, it is my wish to give a large feast of unity.' The believers were to look for a suitable place for this to be held. It should be out of doors, under the trees and far away from the noise of the city. It should be somewhere like a Persian garden and Persian food must be prepared. When they found a suitable place, they should let everyone know. All the friends must come and be His guests. It was to be a Unity Feast. All the guests were to be like the leaves and fruits of the same tree.

The Bahá'ís found a place to fit 'Abdu'l-Bahá's requirements. This was in the garden of the house of one of their number: a large lawn with a group of pine trees to give plenty of shade. Many friends were invited and everything was prepared. On the day of the feast, the guests sat in a large circle under the shade of the trees. The tables were set and flowers had been strewn on the lawn so that it looked like a beautifully patterned carpet. 'Abdu'l-Bahá Himself sat on the ground under one of the trees. He invited two ladies to come and sit with Him, one on each side. One was a rich, elegantly dressed lady and the other a wrinkled old woman, poorly dressed. Both ladies beamed with happiness at being allowed to sit with Him.

'Abdu'l-Bahá then gave a talk, too. He said that this was a marvellous gathering, that the guests had come because they were attracted to the divine Kingdom.

> This is a new Day, and this hour is a new Hour in which we have come together . . . The utmost love and unity will result; the favours of God will encompass us . . . Be happy and joyous because the bestowals of God are intended for you . . .
>
> Rejoice, for the angels of heaven are your assistants and helpers.
>
> Rejoice, for the glance of the Blessed Beauty, Bahá'u'lláh, is directed upon you.
>
> Rejoice, for Bahá'u'lláh is your Protector.
>
> Rejoice, for the eternal life is awaiting you.

'Abdu'l-Bahá told them that in past times many people longed for this illumined century. Often, they could not sleep at night, so strong was their desire to live in that time, even though it was only for an hour. Therefore, He told His guests, you must thank God with your hearts and souls that this favour has indeed been granted to you. Be, therefore, as the waves of one sea, as the stars of the same heaven, as fruits which adorn the same tree and as the roses of one garden. So that through you the unity of mankind will be established throughout the world.

After 'Abdu'l-Bahá's talk, the picnic was to begin. The tables were set out with dishes of Persian rice and fruit drinks. But at the moment when the meal had been announced, everything suddenly seemed to be going wrong. A stiff wind had begun to blow and it looked like a heavy shower of rain was on the way. Thunder and lightning could follow at any moment. Loud thunderclaps could be heard and dark clouds gathered in the sky. The first big drops of rain began to fall on the festive tables. What now? Picnicking in the pouring rain was, of course, out of the question.

Juliet Thompson was one of the Bahá'ís who attended this Unity Feast. She wrote in her diary what she saw that day with her own eyes. Calmly, 'Abdu'l-Bahá stood up and walked, followed by the Persian Bahá'ís, to the road and up to a crossroads. A chair had been placed there. 'Abdu'l-Bahá went to the chair and sat down on it. The Persian friends stood behind Him. This was quite a way from the place where the picnic was being held. Juliet saw how He lifted His face to the heavens. The thunder was still rumbling loudly and dark, threatening clouds were scudding through the sky. 'Abdu'l-Bahá remained sitting motionless, with His face still turned heavenwards. A strong wind rustled the leaves of the trees. The clouds soon began to disperse and blue patches appeared in the sky. The sun began to shine once more. Then 'Abdu'l-Bahá stood up and walked back to the picnic place.

The Unity Feast could now continue. The weather quickly improved; it was lovely to be out of doors. Everything was beautifully green and the scent of the pine trees filled the air. 'Abdu'l-Bahá's guests were delighted and relieved. The Bahá'ís served the guests with the rice and the fruit cordial, then went round with other delicacies that they had prepared. 'Abdu'l-Bahá Himself went round all His guests. He had little bottles of sweet-scented attar of roses, and dabbed a little on the forehead of each one. And what hardly ever happened, He then gave permission for photographs to be taken.

One of the guests had a question: 'What are the new teachings of this Cause which are not to be found in the other great religions?'

'Abdu'l-Bahá went to stand in the middle of the garden and called everyone to Him. While He walked backwards and forwards among the guests, He spoke about the unity of mankind and about equal rights for men and women. He also said that going to school must be compulsory for boys and girls and that all prejudices are harmful. He mentioned some more of the principles and explained each one in detail. During His talk, a car passed by. When the people in it saw 'Abdu'l-Bahá, they became so curious about what was happening there, that they got out and began to listen, too. They were pleasantly surprised and felt immediately drawn to these teachings.

In the evening, when darkness fell, there were still many

guests present. They stayed as long as they could; no one wanted to go home. They had clustered here and there on the lawn. They held burning tapers to keep away the mosquitoes. The light from the tapers fell upon the ladies' light-coloured dresses spread out on the grass. They looked like large moths. And the burning tips of the tapers were like dancing fireflies. It was a picture from a fairytale.

At the end of the evening, 'Abdu'l-Bahá went around the remaining guests and spoke to them. Then He departed. The last they heard from Him that evening was: 'Peace be with you. I shall pray for you.' Then He disappeared into the darkness.

For all the visitors it had been a special day, to be the guest of 'Abdu'l-Bahá. In His talk He had said that in the future hundreds of thousands of meetings like this would take place to commemorate this day. And that the same words that He had spoken to them at this meeting today would be repeated for centuries to come.

# 42

## Fred Mortensen's Journey

Many Americans made a long journey to be able to see 'Abdu'l-Bahá. One of these did so in a most unusual way. That was Fred Mortensen.

In his youth, Fred had got into bad ways. He had the wrong friends. In the evenings he often drifted about the streets and then things happened which should not have happened. If there was a fight anywhere, Fred was sure to be involved. Breaking into grocery shops to steal fruit and all kinds of other things was something he did not like to miss. He stopped at nothing. Once he was passing a shop with his friends. One of the boys saw some bananas hanging in the shop window and said, 'Look at that big bunch of bananas!'.

'Gee, I wish I had some,' said another.

'Do you?' said Fred.

They heard a dog barking in the shop and when they looked in they saw a large guard dog. Who would now dare to break in? Fred! He was not going to be frightened off by the bulldog, so he smashed the window, grabbed the bunch of bananas and shared them out among his friends.

Another mean thing that he and his pals did was to annoy the Jews. They stole their wine, broke the windows of their houses and made their life so much more difficult than it often already was. Fred cared nothing about God's commandments or the laws of the land.

Fred was a great sorrow to his mother. She did her very

best to get him on to the right road. With almost saintly patience, she kept praying that her son might find the path to righteousness and happiness. But things went from bad to worse with Fred. He kept going around with the wrong kind of friends. It seemed as if he would never change.

Once, of course, the police caught him. He went to prison but before he was sentenced, he managed to escape. For four years, he stayed out of the way of the police. Until the day he saw one of his friends being arrested. Fred wanted to help him get away but there were still a couple of police officers about. Fred began to run and, to get free of the police, climbed over a high wall. That was his mistake. He fell off and broke his leg.

Fred had to appear in court. He was defended by a lawyer who managed to get him off lightly. The lawyer did much more than that. He was a Bahá'í and told Fred about the love of God, about Bahá'u'lláh and 'Abdu'l-Bahá and their love for mankind. At first Fred was bewildered. Why did he keep going on about this? But he still went back each time to see his lawyer, whose words made more and more of an impression on him. Who would have thought that his character would ever change? Yet that is what happened. Fred became a new man.

Fred's lawyer also told him that 'Abdu'l-Bahá was in America. Fred truly longed to meet Him. When the rumour went around that 'Abdu'l-Bahá might soon be returning to the Holy Land, Fred at once made up his mind. He would go himself to see 'Abdu'l-Bahá. So he set off. On his way he attended a convention of printers. But he had not the patience to wait for the meeting to end. He wanted to get to 'Abdu'l-Bahá. In the night, before travelling any further, he had a dream. He dreamed that he was 'Abdu'l-Bahá's guest. He was sitting with many other people at a long table while 'Abdu'l-

Bahá walked back and forth, telling stories. Later, when he met 'Abdu'l-Bahá, it happened exactly as Fred had dreamed, and 'Abdu'l-Bahá looked exactly as He had seen Him in his dream.

But how was he to continue his journey? He had very little money and 'Abdu'l-Bahá was in Green Acre, a journey of hundreds of miles! Fred was not to be put off by that. He decided to travel as many tramps did in those days: sneaking underneath goods trains to 'ride the rails' and climbing on top of passenger trains. In this way, he travelled, sometimes

by night, from one city to the next. And he reached his goal! Exhausted and very dirty, but enormously happy, he finally arrived in Green Acre.

Next morning, he got up early so as to be at the hotel in time. When Fred was introduced to 'Abdu'l-Bahá, He looked at Fred, but all He said to him was: 'Ugh! Ugh!' 'Abdu'l-Bahá did not even shake hands with him. When 'Abdu'l-Bahá had greeted the other guests, he told Fred curtly to sit down and pointed to a chair. Fred had remained standing because there were some older ladies for whom there were no seats. But he had to sit down, what else could he do? He was rather confused at this reception. And also a bit rebellious. He had made such an effort and had such a difficult journey, and now he was being received like this! He did not know what to think.

A little later he was called to meet 'Abdu'l-Bahá in His room. 'Abdu'l-Bahá welcomed him with a smile and a warm hand-clasp and asked him to sit down. He Himself sat down opposite Fred and said: 'Welcome! Welcome! You are very welcome.'

Then He asked, 'Are you happy?' Three times 'Abdu'l-Bahá repeated this question.

Fred was surprised that He had asked it three times. Of course he was happy!

'Where did you come from?'

'From Minneapolis.'

'Do you know Mr. Hall?' Mr. Hall was the lawyer who had helped Fred with his court case.

'Yes, he told me about the Cause.'

'Did you have a pleasant journey?'

If there was one thing Fred had hoped, it was that 'Abdu'l-Bahá would not ask him about his journey. And now he had only just met Him and that was nearly the first thing He asked.

Fred looked at the floor; what now? But 'Abdu'l-Bahá asked him once again, 'Did you have a pleasant journey?'

Fred looked up and into the eyes of 'Abdu'l-Bahá. They were like two dark, sparkling jewels, looking right into the depths of his soul. Then he realized that 'Abdu'l-Bahá knew everything and he must tell Him all about it.

He replied, 'I didn't come as people generally do, who come to see you.'

'How did you come?'

Fred told Him that he had ridden under and on top of the railway trains.

'Explain how.'

Fred looked again into 'Abdu'l-Bahá's eyes and saw how they had changed and seemed to radiate a marvellous light. It was the light of love and Fred felt much happier. He explained how he had travelled by riding the rails under the goods trains and on top of the passenger trains. When he had finished his story, 'Abdu'l-Bahá kissed him on both cheeks and gave him lots of fruit to take with him. And He kissed the dirty cap which Fred had worn on his journey.

One week later 'Abdu'l-Bahá left Green Acre for another city. When He was saying goodbye to everyone, He suddenly told Fred to come and sit in His car and accompany Him. So he spent an extra week with 'Abdu'l-Bahá! And when he was going back home, he received enough money for the return journey from 'Abdu'l-Bahá.

These meetings with 'Abdu'l-Bahá remained deeply engraved in Fred's memory for the rest of his life. Every moment of them was a precious memory. Years later, Fred wrote of them, 'These events are engraved upon the tablet of my heart and I love every moment of them. The words of Bahá'u'lláh are my food, my drink and my life. I have no other aim than to be of service in His pathway and to be obedient to His Covenant. This is the Power of his Spirit, his love and his mercy to me.'

# 43

## The Fable of the Traveller in the Wilderness

At first glance, all seemed to be well with the Reverend Howard Colby Ives. He preached every Sunday about God and his congregation listened eagerly to his sermons. In various places, he was able to see that a new church was built. He believed in Jesus Christ and in His words. But was the Christian world where he lived really as Christ had intended? There were always more questions for which he had no answers. He read books, in fact a great many books. But nowhere could he find a clear answer about which he could say, 'Yes, that's what I'm looking for, that's what I need.' Even though he was a clergyman and he told people every Sunday about God, still he himself had the feeling that he was seeking God. He could not find God anywhere and no longer knew where he should seek Him. And what is worse than when people search for God, they do not know where they can find Him? The Reverend Colby Ives was very unhappy about it.

Through a friend he received an invitation to a meeting of the Baháʼís. He wondered whether or not he should go. There were so many of these movements from the East nowadays. Why should he? He was just about to throw the invitation into the wastepaper basket. But then he changed his mind. In order not to disappoint his friend, he would go anyway.

It was all so different from what he was used to in a church service. After the first time, he felt himself attracted by it and decided to go to these meetings more often. He got some Bahá'í books and when he read these his interest increased even more. He bought all the books he could lay his hands on and kept reading them. He could hardly think of anything else and for months he did not even allow himself the time to read the newspaper. When he heard that 'Abdu'l-Bahá was coming to America, he expressed the wish that he would like to be with Him alone on some occasion. And this happened, on the very day after 'Abdu'l-Bahá's arrival. Do you remember this from a previous chapter? And that 'Abdu'l-Bahá threw His arms around him so tightly that his ribs cracked?

After that first meeting, he went to as many of the meetings for 'Abdu'l-Bahá as he could. Especially on Sundays. In the morning he would preach in his church and in the afternoon he would listen to a talk given by 'Abdu'l-Bahá. He was more and more strongly attracted to the Faith. And no wonder, so many wonderful things happened to him when he was with 'Abdu'l-Bahá. Unimaginable worlds were revealed to him, new spiritual worlds he could never have dreamed of. Every visit was a special event. Like the time when people from very different countries had come together in the greatest harmony and love. People from France, Germany, England, Persia, India, Russia, Palestine, and black and white Americans: they all mingled together as the best of friends. Where else in the world could this possibly happen? Just being with 'Abdu'l-Bahá brought about a complete change in him, even if 'Abdu'l-Bahá had not said a single word. He then felt perfectly happy.

Each time, he tried to hold on to this feeling of overwhelming happiness for as long as he could. But again and again it escaped him. He sometimes became discouraged and considered not going any more to the Bahá'í meetings. His family and friends did not make things easier for him either. They thought it very strange that he was so interested in the Baháʾí Faith. They ridiculed him. One even said that he ought to see a doctor. He must be sick, to be interested in that. Yet he kept going to the Baháʾí meetings. He knew now that he could never stay away.

How could he explain this to other people? That at one moment he was overwhelmed by a joy that knew no bounds and that a little later his joyful feeling had altogether disappeared? Years later, in order to explain it to a friend who had gone through the same experience, Howard Colby Ives invented the 'Fable of the Traveller in the Wilderness'.

There was once a traveller who got lost in an impenetrable wilderness. It seemed to him that he had been wandering around for ages, alone and abandoned. There was no path. No sun shone by which he could work out his position. The thorny bushes tore at him and a relentless wind and rain beat mercilessly upon him. He had no home.

Then, suddenly, when he had given up all hope, he came to a mountainside overlooking a lovely valley and there he saw a heavenly palace, the true home of his dreams. With unspeakable joy, he hurried to it in order to enter. But he had scarcely set foot inside when a strong hand grasped him by the collar and . . . he was back in the horrible wilderness.

But now he had hope. He had seen his home. And with a courage he had never known before, he went again to look for it. He was more careful now. He paid attention to the signs along the way. And he tried to see the little rays of light through the thick canopy of leaves overhead. After an exhausting search, he saw his home again. He did not hurry to enter this time. He took good note of where it was. He got his bearings with the help of the sun. Carefully and reverently, he went in.

But the strong hand again wrenched him from that beloved house and he was back again in the huge wilderness. But this time he was not at all downcast. He now knew where it was! And with great joy went again in search of it. He carved marks on the trees so that he could find the path again.

The sky cleared and the sunbeams helped him to find the way. And soon, much more quickly than the previous time, he found his home again and went in. This time he felt more peaceful and assured and had no fear of the grasping hand. And when the hand came and took him, setting him down again in the wilderness, he hastened on firmer feet to begin his search once more.

The sun was now shining brightly. The song of the birds lifted his heart. Now he cleared a path for himself. He pulled up out of the ground the thick undergrowth which impeded him. He knew only too well that, as long as he was on this earth, he would have to tread this path many times again. But he had found his home and if the people's ridicule threw him into confusion, and darkness overcame him, he could find his way back home. Back to God.

Howard Colby Ives had found his path. The piles of books that he had read before he heard of the Faith had not helped him much on his way. In the Bahá'í books and the talks of 'Abdu'l-Bahá he found answers to his questions. Yet he still needed time to understand what it was really about. 'Abdu'l-Bahá had already left America some months earlier by the time it finally became clear to him that the Báb and Bahá'u'lláh were, just as Christ, Messengers of God. And that 'Abdu'l-Bahá was the Centre of the Covenant: He was the only one who could explain the Writings of Bahá'u'lláh correctly.

When he became a Bahá'í, he could no longer be a clergyman. He decided to devote his life from then on to telling people about Bahá'u'lláh. Together with his wife, he intended first to earn a good deal of money and when they had saved enough, they would go travelling to teach the Faith. They soon had to abandon this plan. How long would they have to work before they had saved enough? Much too long! They decided to do it another way. They found jobs as salespeople, for which they had to travel a lot. They sold all their possessions in order to be free to travel. It was not always easy to have no home of their own and to be always on the road. They had very little money. Once, all they had left was twenty-five cents. Only if they could sell something that afternoon would they be able to eat and stay in a hotel that night.

For years, they travelled in this way through America and in every place they came to they gave talks on the Faith. They told thousands of people about Bahá'u'lláh. And many of their listeners became followers of Bahá'u'lláh.

# 44

## Travelling to California

The Baháʼís of California were longing for ʻAbduʼl-Bahá to visit them too. It was not looking very likely. He was, of course, constantly travelling. From New York, where He had arrived off the ship, He went to Washington, the capital of the United States. From there to Chicago, where He laid the first stone for the Temple. Then He went back to New York and gave it the title of the City of the Covenant. He travelled to a place just outside New York where He gave a great Unity Feast one beautiful summer evening. He visited Green Acre, where Fred Mortensen came to see Him, and shortly after that He was in Canada. He had already covered thousands of miles. And now to go all the way to California, on the other side of America?

ʻAbduʼl-Bahá never planned His journeys long in advance. His companions hardly ever knew when they would have to pack their bags again and where they would be in a few days' time. Sometimes things seemed to go wrong, too. Once, they had to change trains but missed their connection. 'A pity,' they all said. But ʻAbduʼl-Bahá said, 'Oh, it matters not. There is a wisdom in this.' They took the next train and on the way saw that the train they had missed had been in an accident. ʻAbduʼl-Bahá then told them that Baháʼuʼlláh had protected them. Just as on the voyage to America, when He had decided not to travel on the *Titanic*.

At first ʻAbduʼl-Bahá was not intending to go to California. When the Baháʼís there heard this they were bitterly

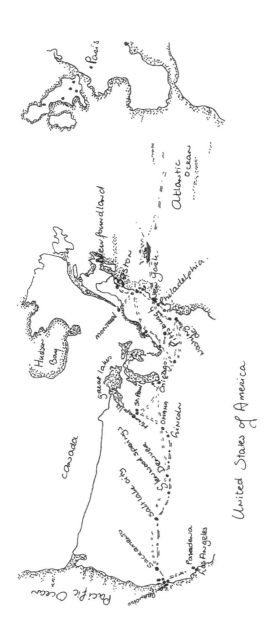

Paris

Atlantic
Ocean

Newfoundland

Hudson
Bay

Boston
New York
Philadelphia

Montreal

Great Lakes

St. Paul

Chicago
Omaha
Lincoln

Canada

Salt Lake City

Sacramento

Pasadena
Los Angeles

Pacific Ocean

United States of America

disappointed. They sent telegrams and letters and begged Him to come after all. Some of the ladies even travelled for days to New York to invite Him personally. And again they repeated how much they were longing to have Him there. Their wish was granted. 'Abdu'l-Bahá decided to go.

It was indeed very exhausting for Him. Travelling by train was not so comfortable in those days. You were usually pretty thoroughly shaken up by it. And it was several days' journey. Yet He went. After all, He had come to America to proclaim the Faith of Bahá'u'lláh. Sometimes there was just time for a little pause. For instance, when He was passing close to the Niagara Falls. When He stood looking and admiring the majestic waterfalls, He thought of Bahá'u'lláh. He related how, in His younger years, Bahá'u'lláh had often gone into the mountains near the city of His birth, Teheran. There were also cascades and then He would pitch His tent beside one of these waterfalls and camp for a while. 'Abdu'l-Bahá's companions suggested to Him that He should stay a few days at the Niagara Falls. But He said it was not possible. He had no time, not even half a day. He had to go on with His work.

It was not only the travelling that was burdensome for 'Abdu'l-Bahá. He also had worries and sorrows because of what the Covenant-breakers like Ibráhím Khayru'lláh were doing. Do you remember who he was? He was the Syrian who had brought the Faith to America. Hundreds of Americans had become Bahá'ís because of his classes. When he discovered that he could not become the leader of the Bahá'ís of America, he betrayed the Faith. He had remained in America. When he heard that 'Abdu'l-Bahá was in Chicago, he again sowed seeds of doubt and disunity. He wanted 'Abdu'l-Bahá to come and visit him as a sign of respect. To one of Khayru'lláh's employees 'Abdu'l-Bahá said that if K͟hayru'lláh's intentions were sincere, He would gladly receive him just like anyone else. But K͟hayru'lláh did not come.

'Abdu'l-Bahá often worried about Covenant-breakers. At times He looked sorrowful and downcast. In the train He once said that He had not slept the whole night. The Ark of God was being battered on all sides by storms. He wondered what would happen when He was no longer there. Would the Faith, just as after the ascension of Bahá'u'lláh, again have to suffer the attacks of the Covenant-breakers? 'Abdu'l-Bahá's mind was far from being easy about it.

In the company that travelled with Him through America there was also someone who made difficulties and caused Him much sorrow. This was Dr Faríd. He was a nephew of 'Abdu'l-Bahá's, his mother was a sister of Munírih K͟hánum. He had learned English and was often the translator for 'Abdu'l-Bahá's talks. Dr Faríd was looking for money. He saw that 'Abdu'l-Bahá would take no money from anyone in America to pay His travel expenses. He refused every offer. Behind 'Abdu'l-Bahá's back, however, Dr Faríd went to visit rich Bahá'ís and told them that He did need money. Only He would not ask if others were present. But if they were to give it to him, he would make sure that 'Abdu'l-Bahá received it. He asked other people for money to build a hospital on Mount Carmel. And in all kinds of other ways he worked against 'Abdu'l-Bahá. Even though 'Abdu'l-Bahá had educated him and had made it possible for him to study medicine.

On the way to California, 'Abdu'l-Bahá stopped in a number of cities like Minneapolis, Denver and Salt Lake City. Wherever He went He aroused great interest. In every city He visited, He went to see the Bahá'ís. Reporters were sometimes waiting for Him at the station so that they could write an article about Him

209

for their newspapers. Everywhere, He received invitations to give talks. Too many to be able to accept them all.

On all His travels in America, 'Abdu'l-Bahá only once took a day off. That was on the way to California, in Glenwood Springs, a beautiful resort in Colorado surrounded by high mountains whose sides were covered in green trees and colourful wild flowers. There were spas, fed by the hot springs. With His travelling companions He went bathing in these. In one building the hot water gushed from a cleft in the mountainside. It was so hot that you could not stay in it for more than fifteen minutes.

When they were going to have their meal, the hotel manager ordered a large table to be set for them outside. So they were able to enjoy their food out of doors. The other guests looked on with some curiosity at first. Just imagine, at a time when it was a rare event for gentlemen from the East to travel about America in long robes. Even in the hotel, people looked at them. But it was not long before the guests were greatly impressed by 'Abdu'l-Bahá. They said, 'How nice to dine in this way. This is obviously a very important person.' They wanted to know why He had come to America. That day, many of the guests heard about the Faith.

Even on His day off, 'Abdu'l-Bahá told people about Bahá'u'lláh!

# 45

## 'You are happy because you have seen 'Abdu'l-Bahá'

Just imagine if you had been young in the time of 'Abdu'l-Bahá. And that you went with your parents to a meeting to hear 'Abdu'l-Bahá. There were a lot of people and not nearly enough seats for everyone. Where would you sit?

Juanita Storch was seventeen when 'Abdu'l-Bahá visited California. Like all the other Bahá'ís, she had been looking forward for weeks to His arrival. She came to the very first meeting for 'Abdu'l-Bahá. The house was packed with visitors, where was she to sit? She sat on the floor, right at the front. It was the best spot you could wish for. She was sitting close to 'Abdu'l-Bahá and so she could see everything that happened. When 'Abdu'l-Bahá appeared in the doorway, everyone stood up. How happy she felt when she saw Him! He said 'Alláh-u-Abhá' several times. His voice sounded like spoken music. Those present replied 'Alláh-u-Abhá' also and then 'Abdu'l-Bahá gestured to everyone to be seated. Juanita had a good view of Him when He was speaking. In her diary she wrote that she had the feeling of always having known Him and that she had often seen Him before. She was sure this was true. 'Abdu'l-Bahá went round the room and shook everyone by the hand. Including Juanita. It was only a short moment but for Juanita it was as if He had held her hand for at least ten minutes. The loving look He bestowed on her she cherished in her memory ever afterwards.

Each time she entered a house where 'Abdu'l-Bahá was, she felt the marvellous spirit of harmony, peace and brotherhood. There were usually many flowers. The faces of those attending radiated joy. Each meeting with Him was a special event, dominated by a spirit of love and unity.

Once, Juanita spoke to Maḥmúd-i-Zarqání, one of the Persians who were travelling through America with 'Abdu'l-Bahá. He asked her, 'Are you happy?'

She knew she was really happy and said, 'Yes.'

Then Maḥmúd said, 'You are happy because you have seen 'Abdu'l-Bahá.'

Meeting 'Abdu'l-Bahá was a unique event in Juanita's life. As it was for many others.

'Abdu'l-Bahá's journey through America was full of unique events and meetings. He spoke to Bahá'ís who had come from Japan. He also held lectures for Japanese Christians. Was it not a historic event that someone from Persia should give a talk to Japanese people in America about the unity of the Prophets of God? That had never happened before. It was also quite difficult. 'Abdu'l-Bahá spoke in Persian; His words had to be translated first into English and then into Japanese.

Another unique event took place in California: 'Abdu'l-Bahá's talk in a synagogue in San Francisco. There, He told the Jews about Abraham and Moses. Prophets in whom the Jews themselves believe. 'Abdu'l-Bahá asked: how can you tell that they were Prophets of God? By the influence which they had on people. Through them, a new civilization was created and through them people were changed. Before Moses' time the Jewish people were poor and uneducated, a nation of slaves who were oppressed in Egypt. Moses taught them and brought them to the Holy Land. There, a new civilization was created and because they kept the laws of Moses, the Jews were the most civilized and educated nation of that time. They were so well-known for their learning that even the famous Greek philosopher Socrates travelled to the Holy Land to study under the Jewish scholars.

Then 'Abdu'l-Bahá spoke about Jesus and Muhammad. How can we tell that Jesus was a Messenger of God? Through Him a new civilization was created. Through Him, nations which had always been hostile to one another became friends who had a great love for one another. Muhammad did the same. Before He came, the Arabs were wild tribes who were always at war with each other. They were barbarians who even buried their own daughters alive. Muhammad welded them into one nation and because they kept to the teachings of Muhammad, the Arabs became the most civilized and advanced nation of their time. Can there be any clearer proof that Muhammad was a Prophet of God?

He also told them that Jesus and Muhammad taught that Moses was a Prophet of God and that the Old Testament, the holy book of the Jews, was the Book of God. Jesus and Muhammad taught Their followers that they must believe in Moses and the Old Testament. It was because of Christ that the teachings of the book of Moses became known throughout the world. In many countries still, there are people who bear the names of prophets and people from the Old Testament.

The Christians and the Muslims believe in Moses and accept Him as a Prophet of God. Is that any disadvantage to them? No, on the contrary, this is their blessing! Then 'Abdu'l-Bahá asked what harm could come if the Jews in their turn were to accept Christ and recognize Muhammad as a Messenger of God. If they did so then there would be no more wars in the

Promised Land and no more blood would be spilt. The earth would become a paradise and the Promised Day of God would dawn. 'Abdu'l-Bahá went on to speak of the prophecies in the Bible. There, it says that a time will come when the wolf and the lamb will drink from the same source, and the lion and the calf graze in the same meadow. Will this ever literally happen? No, we will always have to keep these different animals apart. These prophecies have quite a different meaning. They mean that the nations and races and the different religions of the world will come to agree. Hatred and conflict will disappear, all religions will be united and human brotherhood will become a reality.

There was absolute silence in the synagogue while 'Abdu'l-Bahá was speaking. He stood between two palm trees in the light of the sun coming in through the coloured glass of the windows. There were about two thousand Jews present; every seat was filled. It never happened that anyone spoke about Jesus or Muhammad as Prophets of God in the synagogue. The Jews did not want to hear such things. But 'Abdu'l-Bahá had done it and He spoke with so much conviction that no one contradicted Him and His listeners were greatly impressed. How had this come about? How could He do what for two thousand years had been impossible? 'Abdu'l-Bahá's answer to this was that it was possible through the help of Bahá'u'lláh.

At the corner of the street, almost opposite the synagogue where 'Abdu'l-Bahá had spoken, was a church. This church was about to be demolished and a new one was to be built on the same site. That meant that temporarily the members of that church had no building for their services. The religious leader of the synagogue, Rabbi Meyer, then did what 'Abdu'l-Bahá had said in His speech. He set all the prejudices, which had existed for centuries between the Jews and the Christians,

214

aside and invited the Christians to hold their services on Sundays in his synagogue. So for a while the Jews read on Friday evenings in their synagogue from the Old Testament. On Sundays the Christians in the same synagogue read from the Old and the New Testament.

'Abdu'l-Bahá heard about this later and praised Rabbi Meyer for his noble action. He said also that people would speak of his good intentions and generosity for centuries to come. When Rabbi Meyer heard how 'Abdu'l-Bahá had written about him in one of His Tablets, his face lit up with happiness.

# 46

## At the Grave of America's First Bahá'í

'Abdu'l-Bahá made the journey to California to meet the Bahá'ís there. They had been asking Him to so often and so urgently. One of them was Mr Thornton Chase, but he was not to see 'Abdu'l-Bahá again in this world.

'Abdu'l-Bahá called Thornton Chase the first American Bahá'í. He was not exactly the first. Perhaps the third or fourth. But he was the first who remained loyal to the Faith and served it for the rest of his life. He was not only the first Bahá'í of America, he was the first, too, of all the countries of the Western world.

From his early years, Thornton Chase had been interested in religion. He actually investigated everything. He read the books of every religion and every sect he heard of. There was not, however, a single faith that he could completely accept. But he was convinced that this time was the 'Day of God' and was determined to spare no effort to discover what God had brought to mankind. He kept on seeking for the truth. Thus he came into contact with Ibráhím Khayru'lláh. What Khayru'lláh told him about Bahá'u'lláh and 'Abdu'l-Bahá fitted in with the many prophecies which Thornton Chase had studied. He followed the lectures given by Khayru'lláh and became a Bahá'í.

Thornton Chase was always looking for opportunities to make the Faith known. He had a job for which he often had to travel. This was fortunate. In every city he visited, he sought out people who were interested in the Faith. If he later returned, he would continue to teach them. He held many lectures. There was then very little literature about the Faith. Therefore he himself wrote some pamphlets and a book.

In those early years, it was not always easy for the Bahá'ís in America. Especially when Khayru'lláh became a Covenant-breaker because he would not recognize 'Abdu'l-Bahá as the Centre of the Covenant. The difficulties which were then created caused many Bahá'ís to leave the Faith. Not Thornton Chase – 'Abdu'l-Bahá gave him the Persian name of Thábit, the Steadfast. To the end of his life, he was always ready to serve the Faith. He, too, hoped that 'Abdu'l-Bahá would come to California. But he passed away the day before 'Abdu'l-Bahá arrived there.

'Abdu'l-Bahá refused many invitations because He wished above all to visit the grave of Thornton Chase. He travelled to Los Angeles specially for this purpose. When He and His companions reached the cemetery, 'Abdu'l-Bahá walked straight to the grave. He had never been there before, no one had given Him directions, but yet He knew where to find it.

At the grave, He asked for flowers and arranged these most lovingly and carefully on the grave. Then He turned to face 'Akká and recited the Tablet of Visitation. In His talk at the graveside, 'Abdu'l-Bahá said that Thornton Chase was the first Bahá'í of America. He had served the Faith loyally. Now it was as yet unknown how valuable he had been but in the future this would become abundantly clear. He would always be remembered. 'Abdu'l-Bahá also said that in future his grave should be visited on His behalf every year. He bowed low over the grave of His beloved follower and kissed the gravestone. All those present followed His example.

After the visit to the grave of Thornton Chase, 'Abdu'l-Bahá
stayed another week in California. People kept seeking His
presence. All day long, from early morning to late in the
evening. Some seized every opportunity to be with Him. One
of these was Ramona Allen. She was then 23 years old. Later in
her life she wrote down her memories of 'Abdu'l-Bahá's visit.

Her first meeting with 'Abdu'l-Bahá would always remain
etched in her memory. He was exactly as she had expected
Him to be: an angel from Heaven. Ramona had come with
her parents and 'Abdu'l-Bahá came to meet them with
outstretched arms. 'Marhaba! Marhaba!', he said in Persian.
'Welcome! Welcome!' It was if the sun had suddenly shone out
in the soft, rosy glow of an early morning. There stood 'Abdu'l-
Bahá in His oriental dress, in His 'abá and with His turban on.
He was surrounded by a golden glow. The room seemed full
of sunshine. Everywhere there were lovely, fragrant flowers.
Ramona's heart overflowed with joy now He was there at last,
now that she could see Him with her own eyes and with her
own ears hear His voice. He took both her mother's hands and
said, 'Welcome, Mrs Allen, welcome, very welcome! You have
a very united family, a very united family, and you will all be
through all the worlds of God.' Ramona and her parents felt
very happy to hear these words. He shook all their hands and
bade them welcome once again. Ramona gave Him a little
bunch of flowers: yellow roses from their own garden. He
smiled when He thanked her. He knew that she gave the roses
out of love. When He looked into her eyes, His eyes seemed
to say that He understood what was in the depths of her heart
and that He knew all about her. She felt as if she had entered
another world. At that moment she decided to devote her life
to Him. After this, He Himself poured tea for them, in crystal
glasses. It was the most delicious tea that Ramona had ever

tasted. All too soon, they had to say goodbye, for others were waiting to be greeted by Him.

Ramona and her father were also invited again one evening to the house that 'Abdu'l-Bahá had rented. When she entered His room, He was sitting on His bed and leaning against the pillows. One of the Persians was engaged in massaging His feet. 'Abdu'l-Bahá told them that His feet were often very painful and that the massage helped to lessen the pain. It had begun when, as a young boy of eight, he had travelled from Teheran to Baghdad in the icy winter weather. His feet had been frozen. Now, in America, sixty years after that dreadful journey, His feet still hurt Him.

On the day that 'Abdu'l-Bahá left California, Ramona and some other Bahá'ís brought Him to the train. She and her friend got into the train so that they could be with Him for a few more minutes. Suddenly, the two girls looked at each other with the same thought: why don't we go along to Sacramento, too? That was the last city in California that 'Abdu'l-Bahá was going to visit. They were talking this over but before they could decide, the train began to move. They had to stay where they were! They no longer had any choice.

In Sacramento, 'Abdu'l-Bahá praised the people of California. They were noble people, unselfish and peace-loving. He hoped that the supporters of peace would daily increase in number and that their unselfish ideas would spread to every part of the world. And that the flag of universal peace would be hoisted for the first time in California. Ramona was there when 'Abdu'l-Bahá spoke these words.

Thirty-three years later, Ramona Allen Brown was present at another meeting in California, in San Francisco. It was just after World War II. It was a very important meeting: fifty-one countries had decided to form the United Nations. They wanted to make an end to wars which had now, twice in short succession, so dreadfully ravaged the world. The flags of all the countries taking part were displayed. Important statesmen made speeches. The moment for the signing of the Accord had arrived. At that thrilling, poignant moment, a new flag was carried onto the platform: it was the flag of the United Nations.

To her great amazement, Ramona saw that the wish expressed by 'Abdu'l-Bahá at the end of His visit to California, was being fulfilled thirty-three years later.

# 47

## The Black Rose

Shall I do it? Or perhaps better not? Pauline Hannen asked herself this question when she saw a black woman on the street. Her shoelaces were undone. The woman had both arms full of parcels and could not possibly tie her own laces. Should she help her to do them up? It was certainly very unusual for a white woman to kneel down in the middle of the street to tie a black woman's shoelaces.

Pauline had learned from an early age to be afraid of black people. She had heard bad things about them. If anything went wrong, it was always the fault of the blacks. From the Bahá'í Writings she had discovered that this was prejudice. When she saw this woman, she thought of one of the Hidden Words.

> Know ye not why We created you all from the same dust? That no one should exalt himself over the other. Ponder at all times in your hearts how ye were created. Since We have created you all from one same substance it is incumbent on you to be even as one soul, to walk with the same feet, eat with the same mouth and dwell in the same land . . .

These words from Bahá'u'lláh helped Pauline to get over her prejudices. She stopped the woman, knelt down in front of her and tied up her laces. In the snow, in the middle of the street. Everyone could see her! The woman was astonished and the passers-by were as well: a rich, white lady who knelt in the middle of the street to tie the shoelaces of a black woman. Surely this was not the 'done thing'? People stared at her as if she were mad. For Pauline it was an important turning point in her life: she decided to teach the Faith to the black people.

The black people of America were in a bad way. They had been taken out of Africa as slaves to work on the American plantations. They had had no rights. Fortunately, just as in other countries, slavery had now been abolished in America. The black people had become free. Alas, the abolition of slavery did not mean that black people were now treated as equals by the white people. They did not have the rights in their daily lives which they should have had according to the law. They were treated as inferior citizens and all too often even their lives were in danger. Thousands of blacks were simply murdered by the whites, who were not punished for this. Like the blacksmith. He had done good business with his smithy. With the money he had saved, he bought a horse and a mule. This was a sign of prosperity, a way of showing that he was doing well. The white people in that town thought that only they should own such things. One night they called him out of his house and shot him dead. It was touch and go that they did not murder his wife as well.

At first, the white Bahá'ís in America were no different to their countrymen. They also thought it natural that blacks and whites did not visit each others' homes. It never even occurred to them that this did not fit in with their new religion, of which the most important principle was the unity of mankind. When the first black people became Bahá'ís in Washington, the blacks and whites held separate meetings. 'Abdu'l-Bahá changed this. He wrote a letter ordering meetings and Nineteen Day Feasts to be held to which both white and black people were invited. By doing this, they could show that the teachings of the Faith were a good way to make prejudices between the races disappear. The first Nineteen Day Feast was held in the home of white Bahá'ís. There were thirty-five people present, one-third of whom were black. It was a blessed and happy Nineteen Day Feast.

When some years later, 'Abdu'l-Bahá came to America, He often spoke about unity and harmony between white and black. It always pleased Him if there were whites and blacks present if He gave a talk anywhere. He said once that, for God, there were neither blacks nor whites. The colour of the skin was not important. God did not look at colours. He looked at the hearts. If a heart was pure, it did not matter whether the skin was black, white or yellow.

'Abdu'l-Bahá Himself set the example in applying the principle of equality. He was once invited by one of the Bahá'ís to lunch. A good number of prominent people from New York were there. 'Abdu'l-Bahá Himself had asked Louis Gregory, one of the first black people in America to become a Bahá'í, to come too. When lunch was announced, the guests went to sit down. But not Louis Gregory; he held back and waited for an opportunity to leave the house without being noticed. When the guests were sitting down, 'Abdu'l-Bahá looked round and said to the host, 'Where is Mr Gregory? Bring Mr Gregory!'

It appeared that a place had not been set for him. After all, this was not the custom. The host fetched him. 'Abdu'l-Bahá moved cutlery and plates to one side and said that another place must be laid beside Him. Louis Gregory was given a seat on 'Abdu'l-Bahá's right, the place of honour!

'Abdu'l-Bahá did the same when he received a group of street children as His guests. One day, He was walking with the Persian Bahá'ís in the streets of New York. As usual, their oriental clothing attracted a lot of attention. Including from a group of cornerboys. They came up to the visitors and began shouting at them, and some even threw sticks at them. One of the ladies of the party could not bear seeing 'Abdu'l-Bahá being treated like this. She spoke to the boys and told them He was a holy man. He had been a very long time in prison because of His love for mankind. He was now on His way to give a talk to the down-and-outs of New York.

'Can't we go too?', one of the boys who seemed to be the leader asked her. That was not possible. 'But next Sunday He will be at my house and I will make sure that you can meet Him there too.' She gave the boys her address.

Twenty or thirty boys appeared the following Sunday at her door. They were so spruce and clean; they had all made a big effort to look their best. At the door of His room, 'Abdu'l-Bahá greeted each boy personally and talked and laughed so much that you would think He was one of the boys Himself. The boys immediately felt at ease in this rather grand house.

One of the last who entered was a black boy of about thirteen. He was the only black one of the group and it was clear that he was afraid he might not be welcome. After all, black people never came as guests to the house of a white person. A heavenly smile appeared on 'Abdu'l-Bahá's face when He saw the boy. He made a gesture as if He were welcoming a prince. He called out loudly so that everyone had to listen, that here was a black rose! It was suddenly quiet in the room. The boy's face began to glow with happiness. Who knows how often he had been called a black this or a black that – it was always something nasty. But a black rose – no one had ever called him that.

'Abdu'l-Bahá had a treat. He sent for a big box of assorted chocolates. Five pounds! These were unwrapped and He went round with the box. Each boy got a good handful of chocolates. When He had finished, He put down the almost empty box. He picked out one very dark chocolate, first examined it Himself and then showed it to the other boys. They wondered what He was going to do with it. 'Abdu'l-Bahá went over to where the black boy was sitting. With a smiling face, He held the chocolate up beside the boy's black cheek and laid his arm around his shoulders. He said nothing, but no words were needed to make His meaning clear. The boys all understood. There was silence

in the room. The boys looked at their friend as if they had never seen him before.

And the black boy himself? He did not seem to be aware of what was going on around him. He saw only 'Abdu'l-Bahá. His face lit up and he could not take his eyes off Him. One of the Bahá'ís present at the time later wrote that he had never seen a face with such a heavenly expression.

225

The American Bahá'ís had understood what 'Abdu'l-Bahá was teaching them. And they followed it too. This was quite difficult in a country where such strong prejudices against coloured people existed. One of the Bahá'ís was told he would have to leave his house. His landlord did not want to rent his house to someone who would have black people to visit.

During one of the final weeks of 'Abdu'l-Bahá's visit to America, the Bahá'ís wanted to hold a great banquet. The owner of the hotel did not want to allow any black people to attend it. The more the Bahá'ís insisted, the more stubbornly he refused. He just did not want any black people in his hotel. He was afraid that it would be bad for his business. He said that if even one coloured person was seen going into his hotel, respectable people would never set foot in it again. His business would then be ruined. He got his way and only white people were present at the banquet.

The white Bahá'ís did not leave it at that. They made sure that the following day a banquet was held for the black people. At one of the white people's homes. The black people were the guests at the table and they were served with love and respect by white ladies. It was a unique event. Had it ever happened in America that black people had been served by whites?

'Abdu'l-Bahá was extremely pleased by what had happened. He told the Bahá'ís that they were carrying out the laws of Bahá'u'lláh and acting in accordance with the teachings of the Supreme Pen. Behold what an influence and effect the words of Bahá'u'lláh have had, He said. People no longer hate one another or avoid each other. Prejudices have been done away with and you are serving one another with great sincerity.

# 48

## A Different Gift

'It is now more than two years that I have been far from the Holy Shrine of Bahá'u'lláh. Now I must return,' said 'Abdu'l-Bahá shortly before His departure from California. California was the farthest point of His journey. It was almost on the other side of the globe. He still had a long journey ahead of Him. First, by train to the eastern states, then by ship across the Atlantic. In Europe He would take the train again, visiting some other cities on the way, and finally return via Egypt to the Holy Land. It would be more than a year before He was back at that spot on this earth which was so dear to Him, the Shrine of Bahá'u'lláh in Bahjí.

There was another reason why 'Abdu'l-Bahá wished to return to the Holy Land, in fact had to return. He knew that within two years a dreadful war would break out. Would He then be able to return? In America He had already been confronted with war in Europe. Two Turks were sitting in the train. They told Him that they were on their way to Turkey to fight for their country. When 'Abdu'l-Bahá was back in New York, the newspapers were just then reporting on the war between Turkey and some of the Balkan countries. On the street, He and His companions in their long Eastern robes were often stared at suspiciously. Some hotels even refused to give them rooms because they thought that they must be Turkish.

In America 'Abdu'l-Bahá often warned of the war that was coming. More than once He mentioned Europe as a huge powder-keg. One tiny spark would be enough to set off an explosion. In one of His talks He said that for two thousand years now, war had been waged and blood shed. Let mankind now live in peace for a time. Look at history. The world of men had never had the blessing of universal peace. In past times, when there was war it cost perhaps ten, fifteen or twenty thousand people their lives. Now there were such weapons of war that a hundred thousand could die in a single day. We are all God's servants and every country is a part of the same earth. God is kind and just to all. He cares for all. He protects all. Why should we kill our fellow creatures?

In America, He had often called for the promotion of peace. He also spoke many times of the new principles which Bahá'u'lláh had revealed. Principles which had not been taught by any of the previous Messengers of God. Such as the unity of mankind, the need for a world government and a world auxiliary language. And that it is everyone's duty to investigate the truth for himself. These are teachings which are right for

mankind now that it is beginning to become mature and for the times in which we live. He expressed the wish that the American people would proclaim the unification and the oneness of mankind. So that peace would come and wars could be no more.

In spite of 'Abdu'l-Bahá's call to peace, war broke out in Europe. A large part of the world was involved in this, even the Holy Land. 'Abdu'l-Bahá Himself would be placed in great danger by it. He escaped being horribly put to death by only a hair's breadth. Only just in time, the British army was able to set Him free.

'Abdu'l-Bahá remained in New York for the last few weeks of His American tour. He again received many invitations to give lectures. But He did not accept these; he wanted now in particular to be with the Bahá'ís. They were all too eager to come, now they could be with Him and could still hear Him speak. Sometimes the house in which 'Abdu'l-Bahá was speaking was so full that people had to stand on the stairs. He taught them on every aspect of the Faith. Day and night, He was busy preparing them for the things which must be done and the sacrifices they would have to make. They became steadfast in the Covenant of God and a strong sense of unity and love grew up among the friends.

This was exactly what 'Abdu'l-Bahá wanted: unity among the friends and love for one another. This made Him happy and joyful and this was the greatest gift that they could give Him. The Bahá'ís thought that they should give Him other gifts. They had bought jewels for the members of the Holy Family. At first, He received these and said they were beautiful and most acceptable. But much better than these gifts were the gifts of the love of God which remain preserved in the treasuries of the heart. These gifts would remain forever throughout the worlds of God. But jewels have to be kept in boxes and vaults and will eventually perish. 'Abdu'l-Bahá said that in His house no diamond rings were worn, 'nor do we keep rubies. That house is sanctified above such adornments. I, however, have accepted your gifts; but I entrust them to you for you to sell and send the proceeds to the fund for the Mashriqu'l-Adhkár in Chicago.' The friends kept urging Him to take the gifts. However, 'Abdu'l-Bahá was quite immovable. He did not accept them.

Then came the inevitable day of 'Abdu'l-Bahá's departure. Many people came on board the ship in the New York dock to take their leave of Him. There was not even room for everyone in the large salon which He had at His disposal. Sobbing with tears in their eyes, they stood before Him. He comforted them. Before they had to leave the ship, He spoke to them one more time. He told them He had repeatedly encouraged them to serve the cause of world unity and the unity of mankind. They must put their hearts and souls into this so that through their efforts the light of universal peace would shine and the whole of mankind become as one family.

One by one, they came to say goodbye to 'Abdu'l-Bahá. Each one received a bunch of flowers. Sadly they left the ship. On the quayside they gazed up at Him with tears in their eyes. They stayed waving there until He had disappeared into the distance.

# 49

## The Onward March of the Faith

Sixty years before 'Abdu'l-Bahá visited America, He had been on another journey. With His parents, He had travelled from Teheran to Baghdad, because Bahá'u'lláh had been ordered to leave Persia. As a small group of unknown people they travelled in the winter through the mountains. There was only one town in which they were welcomed because the inhabitants had heard of the Báb. But apart from this, there was no village or town where Bábís lived who could greet them and make them welcome.

How that changed when 'Abdu'l-Bahá was in America! In practically every city He visited, Bahá'ís awaited Him and came to welcome Him. From every quarter there was great interest in meeting Him. Even during the voyage to America, the telegrams were already coming in with invitations for Him. Before He had set foot on the quay, there were journalists who came on board for an interview with Him. Everywhere He went, the newspapers reported this and He was invited to give lectures. In whatever hotel He stayed or whatever house He had rented, from early morning until late in the evening, crowds of visitors came to listen to Him or to speak personally to Him.

But even if interest in America was so great, yet the Faith was still known in only a small part of the world. Most of the believers lived in Persia. Bahá'ís also lived in the countries surrounding Persia and in the Holy Land. In America there were about a thousand Bahá'ís and in Europe some small groups had formed. But in large areas of the world no one had ever heard of the Faith.

That was about to change, too. In America 'Abdu'l-Bahá said that He hoped that from there the Faith would be spread further round the world. When He was back in the Holy Land, He wrote hundreds of letters to the American Bahá'ís and revealed the Tablets of the Divine Plan. He wished the Bahá'ís to travel to every part of world to give the message that Bahá'u'lláh had appeared. As He Himself had also done. Many Bahá'ís went travelling or gave money so that others could go. Later, Shoghi Effendi and the Universal House of Justice made systematic plans for the spread of the Faith. These plans were carried out by the Bahá'ís. The results were amazing. The Faith has now penetrated to every country in the world.

This was very clear in the Holy Year, a hundred years after the ascension of Bahá'u'lláh. In May 1992, Bahá'ís from 180 countries came to the World Centre of the Faith in the Holy Land. They visited the holy places and in the night of the Commemoration there were more than three thousand Bahá'ís gathered around the Qiblih, the place where Bahá'u'lláh is buried. That same night, the Bahá'ís everywhere in the world commemorated Bahá'u'lláh's ascension. In November, 27,000 friends from over 200 countries assembled in New York for the great Bahá'í World Congress. They came from every part of the world. On the last day, televised pictures of the Congress were sent round the world via eight satellites.

This is only the beginning of the progress of the Faith. It will go on for centuries to come. Shoghi Effendi has described how the Faith will unfold in the future. It must first become known to mankind. And even though the televised pictures went round the world from the World Congress, a great many people have still never heard of the Faith. Shoghi Effendi also wrote that when the time comes that the Faith is growing, there will be much opposition to it. Then a period will come when it will be accepted on a large scale and a great many people will declare their Faith in Bahá'u'lláh. After that again, the Faith will gradually become the state religion of more and more countries. Finally, the countries will become Bahá'í states. Then, the laws of these countries will be based on Bahá'u'lláh's book of laws: the Kitáb-i-Aqdas.

A hundred and fifty years after the Báb had revealed Himself to His first follower, the Bahá'í Faith had spread practically all over the world. That was eighty years after 'Abdu'l-Bahá's journey through America. Would the Faith have been able to grow so fast if 'Abdu'l-Bahá had not made that journey to America? And if He had not written those countless letters to the American friends? And if He had not urged them to cross every sea and travel to every part of the world to establish the Faith there?

One of the Bahá'ís from Egypt, Muḥammad Yazdí, was very certain that the journey through America had been a historic event. In a letter to the American friends he wrote that future historians would describe it as an event of major importance. And the time would come, he wrote, that the whole of America would commemorate the day on which 'Abdu'l-Bahá set foot upon that land. That day was 11 April 1912.

We are lucky that we know so much about 'Abdu'l-Bahá's journey round America. Many of His talks have been preserved. 'Abdu'l-Bahá spoke to people in Persian. The Persians who travelled with Him translated His words into English. The trans-lations were immediately written down by one of the American Bahá'ís. Over a hundred talks have been collected in a book called *The Promulgation of Universal Peace*.

There is also a wonderful book about 'Abdu'l-Bahá's travels in America. This is called *Maḥmúd's Diary*, written by Maḥmúd-i-Zarqání, one of the Persian Bahá'ís who accompanied Him. It is a splendid book. If you read it – now or later – it feels as if you yourself are there and travelling round America with 'Abdu'l-Bahá.

# 50

## I would love to see a big storm!

'Abdu'l-Bahá had begun His return journey. America now lay behind Him and He was on the way to Europe on board the *Celtic*. He often took a walk on deck and spoke to many of the passengers. He treated the attendants to little gifts of fruit and sweets. He gave the captain two bunches of roses. The captain came to Him once to tell Him what a pleasure it was to have Him on the voyage. In the course of one of His conversations, 'Abdu'l-Bahá said that in the future people would cross the ocean in airships. Do you think that anyone in those days could imagine what He meant by that?

Just as on the outward voyage, the sea was calm and quiet. The sky was clear. It was comfortable to be travelling like this. Quite different to stormy weather because that is something you really notice. The ship is rolling from side to side, heaving up and plunging down with the waves. You can't walk normally, you have to keep holding on to something. Sitting down as usual to meals is no longer possible and drinking without spilling anything is very difficult. If you want to sleep you have to strap yourself into your bunk or you will keep rolling out. Would you like to experience this? 'Abdu'l-Bahá said that He would just once like to experience a good storm. And in a few days' time, His wish was granted. The sky darkened and a storm came up which lasted for three days. 'Abdu'l-Bahá stood on deck looking at the waves and said, 'Look at that imperial

wave, how it mounts high and devours the smaller waves! It is a wonderful sight. This is the best day. I am enjoying it.'

After a voyage of eight days, the ship arrived in England. 'Abdu'l-Bahá visited various cities and even travelled farther to the North, to Edinburgh in Scotland. It was just like the previous visits: everywhere He went, He was asked to speak. Even on the day of His arrival in London, a group of reporters stood on the doorstep. People thronged to see Him and hear Him speak, or to talk to Him privately. They stood sometimes to one side of the queue, waiting patiently for their turn. Many newspapers wrote about Him and this brought more and more people to see Him.

He wanted to meet everyone who was searching for truth. He did not consider invitations from rich or prominent people. With one exception. In America He visited a very affluent person who gave large amounts of money to good causes. Visiting the poor, that was what was important to 'Abdu'l-Bahá. At Christmas, He went to the Salvation Army. There, the homeless and the down-and-outs of London were gathered.

People with no homes and no friends. As happened every year, they were given their Christmas dinner there. 'Abdu'l-Bahá spoke to them and talked about Christ. Jesus was born to an ordinary family. His apostles were also plain people and His followers were some of the poor. All the Prophets of God were poor. Moses was an ordinary shepherd. Bahá'u'lláh was poor. If riches were important then Christ would have wished them for Himself. Many of those present listened so attentively to Him that they forgot to eat. And this at a time when they did not often have such a good meal in front of them! Before He left, 'Abdu'l-Bahá gave the manager of the home some money so that the down-and-outs could come back at New Year for another meal. When they were told this, they stood up as one man and gave a great cheer as He departed.

He was always concerned for the poor. Even at that meeting where many prominent people were present, such as the Rector of a University, a Member of Parliament, a doctor, a famous writer and many others. They were busy discussing education, socialism, submarines and wireless telegraphy with each other. What was 'Abdu'l-Bahá busy doing? He sat at a bay window, in the afternoon sun, with a dishevelled boy beside him. He had His arm around the boy's shoulders. The boy had come to 'Abdu'l-Bahá to ask Him for sixpence for his money-box and for his sick mother. He was beaming with happiness, there beside 'Abdu'l-Bahá.

'Abdu'l-Bahá Himself also paid the expenses of His journeys and of the hotels. He would not allow others to pay for Him. Once, it looked as if He was accepting money. When He was offered a cheque to buy a car to travel around England and to other European countries, He said he would gratefully accept the offer, took the cheque in both hands, as if He were blessing it, gave it back and said He was giving it back to be used for giving to the poor.

Once, He actually accepted a gift. It seemed a very modest gift. 'Abdu'l-Bahá was sitting with a group of Bahá'ís at table. One of them had just arrived from Persia. He gave 'Abdu'l-Bahá a tightly knotted cotton handkerchief. 'Abdu'l-Bahá untied the knot. Inside, there was a piece of dried bread and a shrivelled apple. The Persian friend explained that on his way through Russia he had met a Bahá'í who was very poor, who came up to him and said, 'I hear that you are going to see our Beloved. I have nothing that I can send Him, but this is my dinner. I beg you to offer it to Him with my love and devotion.'

'Abdu'l-Bahá spread the handkerchief out in front of Him. He looked at it with so much love and with such joy and kindness on His face that the people who were there would never forget. The meal which had been set before Him, He left untouched. He ate some of the meal which had belonged to the old man. He broke off a piece of bread, had it distributed among the other guests and asked them to eat this gift with Him, which had been given with such great love.

# 51

## Home Again

'Abdu'l-Bahá was on His return journey from America to the Holy Land. He visited several other European countries. He had been in Great Britain and was now in Paris. There, some German Bahá'ís came to see Him. They asked Him if he would also make a visit to their country. One of the ladies fell on her knees before Him to beg Him to do so. 'Abdu'l-Bahá gave them the same answer that He had given the friends in America: if there was love, harmony and unity among the Bahá'ís, He would be drawn as by a magnet to them. He was also invited to a party for the children in the little town of Esslingen. But would He be able to come? Would His health allow Him to travel to Germany as well?

It was a great surprise for the Bahá'ís of Stuttgart. 'Abdu'l-Bahá came unannounced. But as soon as they heard, they came to see Him at His hotel. One of the ladies knelt at His feet, her eyes full of tears. 'Abdu'l-Bahá told her she must not cry – she should be happy. She was also very happy, her tears were tears of joy, she said. He said that she must open her mouth and teach the Faith of Bahá'u'lláh so that it would spread through the whole of Germany. Then He praised her for her steadfastness and asked how long she had known of the divine Teachings.

'Five years.'

To this 'Abdu'l-Bahá replied, 'One year being a Bahá'í is like having lived for more than a thousand years.'

'Abdu'l-Bahá also went to the children's party in Esslingen. The children were standing ready to receive Him with flowers. He went to each one of them to accept their flowers. He caressed the children and took each one by the hand. He said that they were His children and hoped that they would have a spiritual education. And of course He had brought some treats with Him and gave them sweets and chocolates. You would love to have been there, because when 'Abdu'l-Bahá had treats He was very generous.

After this, He travelled via Austria on to Budapest, the capital of Hungary. There He met the famous Professor Vambéry. Professor Vambéry was very clever; he spoke fifteen languages. He had travelled through many Eastern countries. During those journeys he had studied various religions. His knowledge did not just come from books. He studied Islám by spending some time living as a Muslim among the Muslims. In the same way, he studied Judaism and Christianity. He had discovered that the followers of the different religions did nothing but hate and curse one another. He had written to 'Abdu'l-Bahá that he hoped His work would produce results. Because that would bring everlasting prosperity to mankind and the world. In Budapest Professor Vambéry wanted to visit 'Abdu'l-Bahá at His hotel. This did not happen as 'Abdu'l-Bahá had not returned in time and the Professor was not well. But to Professor Vambéry's great delight, 'Abdu'l-Bahá, in spite of the cold weather, came Himself to visit him the next day. The Professor had met many important people in his travels. Yet he wrote of 'Abdu'l-Bahá that he had never met such an exalted person and that it would be impossible to find anyone like Him. He was greatly impressed by 'Abdu'l-Bahá's knowledge. Professor Vambéry was himself a very learned and famous professor, and yet he said that 'Abdu'l-Bahá was the centre of knowledge.

From Hungary, 'Abdu'l-Bahá went back to Stuttgart. He had become ill because of the cold in Hungary. The doctor was sent for and told Him that He must stay indoors that evening. He must talk as little as possible to save His voice. That was most unfortunate at the time. The Bahá'ís had hired a room and invited many of their friends and acquaintances. 'Abdu'l-Bahá was to give a talk. That was now, alas, impossible and He asked one of the friends to speak instead. Six hundred people were seated in the room that evening. They had all hoped to see 'Abdu'l-Bahá.

When some of the Bahá'ís saw how much interest had been created, they went to see 'Abdu'l-Bahá at His hotel. They thought He should know that so many people had come. They wanted to ask Him if He could possibly come. Even for a little while, so that they could at least be in His presence. They had provided a warm car for Him so that He need not be exposed to wind and weather. 'Abdu'l-Bahá replied, 'I have promised the doctor not to go out. But I would willingly give My health for the holy teachings, in the service of friends of Bahá'u'lláh.' So, to the great delight of everyone in the hall, He appeared.

Next day, the Bahá'ís went to visit Him at His hotel. How would He be feeling today? They were astonished. He was looking well. He even sat up in His chair and said, 'The meeting yesterday evening was the best medicine for Me.'

After His visit to Germany, He stayed another month in Paris. He was no longer able to do what He had done in America, and visit other cities to speak about the Faith. He was too tired and weak for that. He could accept only a very few invitations and sometimes He had to cancel even those engagements. Even when they were held at the home of one of the Paris Bahá'ís. He could still receive some visitors at His hotel and hold small meetings there.

Then He left to travel on to Egypt. The pilgrims in Haifa were invited to come to see Him there, as were also some members of the Holy Family. In Egypt, too, there were many people who wanted to speak with Him. So many, that there

was not room enough for them all in the hotel. So a tent was pitched on the roof of the hotel to allow 'Abdu'l-Bahá to receive His visitors there. Not only did many people want to see Him but there were also a great many letters coming in, especially from people who had met Him in America. They all had to be answered. Even though He was ill, He kept going. He sat up in bed to deal with His correspondence.

'Abdu'l-Bahá stayed in Egypt for about six months. His family and the Bahá'ís in the Holy Land were becoming insistent that He should return to Haifa. Especially His sister, Bahíyyih Khánum. Even though she did not know exactly when He would return, she was already making preparations. There were Persian pilgrims in Haifa who were good at sewing. Bahíyyih <u>Kh</u>ánum asked them to make new clothes for Him. She said that she herself would keep the clothes safely. For as soon as 'Abdu'l-Bahá knew that He had some extra clothes, He would give them away. She had so often gone to get clean clothes for Him from the cupboard to find that they had disappeared. He had given them to someone else.

The last bit of 'Abdu'l-Bahá's world trip lasted three days. That was the voyage from Egypt to Haifa. How happy the family and the Bahá'ís were that He was back! It was three years and four months since He had suddenly departed. He had then told no one of His plans. Thank goodness He was now back again with them. They were so happy to hear His voice again in their own house!

Can you remember what 'Abdu'l-Bahá said in America about why He was so anxious to get back to the Holy Land? To pray in Bahjí at the Shrine of His Father. The second day after He returned, He went to Bahjí. With the greatest reverence and devotion, He laid His head on the threshold of the Shrine of Bahá'u'lláh.

Now 'Abdu'l-Bahá was really home again!

# 52

# 'I have a lamp in My hand...'

'Abdu'l-Bahá was home again! He could go again to the Shrines of the Báb and of Bahá'u'lláh to pray. How He had longed to do this while on His travels. And how often had He longed to be back on Mount Carmel, with its panoramic view of the Mediterranean Sea and of 'Akká on the opposite side of the bay. During His travels He had been to places which were famous for their natural beauty. He had been by Lake Geneva and in view of the mighty Alps. In America He had seen Niagara Falls, travelled by train through the Rocky Mountains and He had been to the coast of California. Yet He had found no spot to compare with Mount Carmel. Now that He was back, He could enjoy the magnificent view. He praised Haifa and

'Akká too, because of their climate. It had a good effect on His health. When He returned He was so weak that some thought He might soon pass away. But He recovered. This could be seen in His handwriting which, after a few months, was as firm as it had been before.

How was 'Abdu'l-Bahá able to cope with such an exhausting journey? He was old and every day brought its problems regarding His physical health. Sometimes He was too tired even to eat or sleep. Yet He Himself said that His body could stand whatever came along. Like the time in London. He arrived home exhausted. The Bahá'ís were anxious about Him because there was again a flight of stairs He had to go up. Suddenly, to everyone's amazement, He ran straight up the stairs. When He reached the top, He said with a smile to the people who were behind him on the stairs, 'You are all very old! I am very young!' When He saw how surprised the friends were at this, He said, 'Through the power of Bahá'u'lláh all things can be done. I have just used that power.'

The help and support of Bahá'u'lláh. 'Abdu'l-Bahá often spoke of this. By this, He could do things He would otherwise never have been able to do. He once said that when He wanted to give a talk, He turned first to the Abhá Kingdom and for some minutes sought guidance from there. When He knew that the confirmations of Bahá'u'lláh were descending on that meeting, He would begin to speak.

In this way He could give talks which no one had thought possible. In the churches in America He had spoken about Muhammad. He had even been invited by clergymen to speak in their churches. In the synagogues He spoke about Christ and Muhammad. For two thousand years, the Jews would not hear a word spoken in the synagogues about the Prophets of God who had appeared after Moses. In the synagogue in San

Francisco, 'Abdu'l-Bahá spoke about Muhammad and Christ! Practically everyone was pleased by what He had said. It was one of the high points of His tour of America.

If He attracted full audiences, if the listeners were very enthusiastic about His talk, or if there were people from different countries meeting harmoniously, 'Abdu'l-Bahá always said that this was because of the help and support of Bahá'u'lláh. 'Abdu'l-Bahá never said that it had anything to do with Himself. Bahá'u'lláh had enabled Him to make this journey across the world. It would otherwise have been impossible, because of His poor health. It was a journey of something like 25,000 miles. He had reached as far as California on the west coast of the United States, almost at the other side of the world. When he arrived back in Haifa, He said that if you bored a hole straight through the earth in California, you would come out the other end in 'Akká.

Would 'Abdu'l-Bahá be able to make another journey like that? He ardently longed for the Bahá'ís to arise and do what He Himself had done: travel around the world to spread the Faith. He Himself was too old to go on long journeys now. He also knew that the war which was about to break out would make travel impossible. Besides, the people of Haifa, 'Akká and the surrounding country would need Him badly. He had often urged the friends to go travelling, just as He had, around the world. As He had asked them in one of His last talks in London. He called upon the Bahá'ís to establish the Faith and allow souls to gain admittance to the Kingdom of God. He said:

> Look at me. All my thoughts are centred around the proclamation of the Kingdom. I have a lamp in my hand searching throughout the lands and seas to find souls who can become

heralds of the Cause, who can raise their voices in meetings and assemblages, who can become the defenders of the Cause. Day and night I am engaged in this work.

What is a herald? Long ago, before there were any newspapers, radio or television, the kings had heralds. If the king wished to announce anything to his people, this was told to the herald. He would then travel around the country to give the king's message to the people.

This is how 'Abdu'l-Bahá had travelled. As the herald of Bahá'u'lláh. With a lamp in His hand he had searched lands and seas. Well, not literally, of course, you understand. He meant that He was doing His best to find people who would, like Himself, travel to proclaim that Bahá'u'lláh had appeared. People who, just like Himself, could become heralds of the Faith.

# 53

## Mírzá Abu'l-Faḍl (I)

Mírzá Abu'l-Faḍl could not understand it. He was still young, 30 years old, and already famous throughout the country for his scholarship. And now he stood before an ordinary blacksmith who could not even read or write. The latter had asked him a question to which he had no answer. And worse again, when he thought carefully over what the smith had said, then he must believe in two things which could not both be correct. What had happened?

Abu'l-Faḍl was taking a little ride out of the city with a group of mullahs. One of the donkeys lost a shoe. So they had to find a blacksmith to put a new shoe on the animal. While he stood waiting, Ustád Ḥusayn, the blacksmith, asked him a question: 'Mullah, I have heard of some holy traditions of the blessed Imams which I'm finding it difficult to understand. Can you help me?'

Abu'l-Faḍl agreed that he should ask him the question.

'I have heard from the mullahs of a holy tradition about the mercy of God falling with the rain. Every raindrop is entrusted to an angel who brings the drop to the earth. Is that true?'

'Yes.'

'And I have also heard of the ritual uncleanness of dogs. There is also a holy tradition that the angels do not descend on a house where a dog is kept. Is that true?'

'Yes,' said Abu'l-Faḍl again.

'Then it should not rain on the houses where a dog is kept.

How can that happen? If it rains, the rain falls on all the houses.'

Abu'l-Faḍl was perplexed. He was angry and at the same time ashamed. His friends tried to reassure him and said to him, 'Pay no attention to that trouble-maker. He is only a Bábí who has been misled.'

They did not even take the trouble to think carefully about the question themselves. Mírzá Abu'l-Faḍl was not happy about that. He kept on thinking about it.

The smith told his story to 'Abdu'l-Karím, who had a shop in Teheran that Abu'l-Faḍl sometimes visited. The smith also said that Abu'l-Faḍl's pride was offended and he would probably accept an invitation to talk with some Bahá'ís to show that he was still the cleverest. Abu'l-Faḍl accepted the invitation. He would show the Bahá'ís that they were wrong and had better give up their faith and return to Islám. He wanted the growth of the Bahá'í Faith to be stopped. The man he was then speaking to had, like the blacksmith, also had very little education. But in his heart he was a deeply religious person. Every question that Abu'l-Faḍl asked was clearly answered and every objection he made against the Faith was refuted in simple language. Abu'l-Faḍl then said that he would like to speak to a scholarly Bahá'í. 'Abdu'l-Karím, the shopkeeper, was a wise man. He knew that it would be better for Abu'l-Faḍl to talk first to Bahá'ís who were not highly educated, but who had a good understanding of the Writings of Bahá'u'lláh. Abu'l-Faḍl kept trying to convince them that what they believed could not be right. But these, too, who in his eyes were simple people, were able to refute his criticism. He was amazed that people who had never studied had such an understanding of the mysteries of the Qur'án and other holy books and could explain them so clearly. When, afterwards, he did have a conversation with a learned Bahá'í, he was completely dumbfounded by his knowledge.

This went on for months. Then he began to investigate the Faith and to study it. He prayed to God to show him the truth. He began to read the books of the Báb and Bahá'u'lláh. Including the Book of Certitude. He read this with his mind,

but not with his heart. He even said that he himself could certainly write a better book. The following morning a woman came to him. She had heard that he was an excellent writer, a master of eloquence. So she asked him to write a letter for her. But nothing happened, not one word appeared on the paper, no matter how hard he tried.

He scribbled on the corner of the page and drew some lines on his fingernail. The great scholar could no longer write even an ordinary letter. The woman became impatient and said mockingly, 'If you have forgotten how to write a simple letter, why don't you say so instead of keeping me here while you scrawl?'

Abu'l-Faḍl was ashamed. Then he suddenly remembered that the previous evening he had said that he could write a better book than the Book of Certitude. He was a man with a pure heart and knew then that what had happened was nothing more than a clear response to his haughty attitude in regard to that holy book. With his mind Abu'l-Faḍl could no longer reject the Faith. But his heart was not moved, he did not yet understand that Bahá'u'lláh was much more than a great

250

scholar. He had not yet seen that Bahá'u'lláh was a Messenger of God.

The Bahá'ís invited him to read with them the Tablets of Bahá'u'lláh. Never in his life had he read such magnificent writings. Yet he still did not realize that the words of Bahá'u'lláh were the Word of God. Then they read a passage about Sulṭán 'Abdu'l-'Azíz saying that the Sultan would be killed and his ministers dismissed. Abu'l-Faḍl was speechless for half an hour when he heard this. He could not imagine that anyone would predict that. In any case, Bahá'u'lláh was a prisoner and how dared a prisoner speak to the Sultan? He said to the Bahá'ís that the fulfilment of this prophesy would be the proof for him of the truth. And as long as that had not happened he wanted nothing to do with them.

Six months later, Abu'l-Faḍl was walking along the street. He saw two Bahá'ís standing there. Hoping they would not see him, he pulled his 'abá over his head and quickly crossed the street. But it was too late, they had caught sight of him and said to him, 'Now the proof of the Faith of God has been established for you. The news that Sulṭán 'Abdu'l-'Azíz has been dethroned has just been come in by telegraph.'

Abu'l-Faḍl did not want to know. He became angry and cried, 'It's nothing to do with me that the Sultan has been removed. He's no relation of mine.'

The Bahá'ís reminded Abu'l-Faḍl of his own words: 'Did you not make your acceptance of the truth of this Faith dependent on this event?' Abu'l-Faḍl almost choked with rage and strode away without saying goodbye. He knew that he was being put to the test. But first he could avoid taking a decision. Bahá'u'lláh had foretold that the Sultan would be murdered and that had not yet happened. In the meantime he

*Sulṭán ʻAbduʼl-ʻAzíz*

had discussions with scholars. They could not help him. He knew that only the Baháʼís could answer his questions.

A few days later, a telegram came saying that Sulṭán ʻAbduʼl-ʻAzíz had been murdered. Abuʼl-Faḍl was in a quandary. It was as if he had lost his mind. Day and night he wrestled with the problem and could think of nothing else. He could not sleep, he did not eat. He only drank tea, smoked a lot and wept and wept continuously.

Then he began to speak to himself: You've been arguing with the Baháʼís for a year now. They are not learned people and yet every time it seems you come out worst even though you consider yourself a learned man. It is as if they are being inspired by God and helped by Him or as if the Holy Spirit speaks through them. He had another thought: if this Faith is not true, God will be the first to oppose it. It will not be able to go on existing.

One evening, he took one of the Tablets of Bahá'u'lláh. With tears in his eyes and with deep devotion he turned to God and began to read. Then he heard the Voice of God. He understood that the words of Bahá'u'lláh were the Word of God. He became more and more attracted by the words of Bahá'u'lláh and his heart was filled with love for Him. He felt that night a joy and delight overwhelming him which he could never describe as long as he lived.

How thankful he was to the Bahá'ís who had taught him the Faith so patiently. Even if he were to serve them all his life, even if he were to sacrifice his life for them, he knew he could never properly repay them. Even before it began to get light, he went to the house of 'Abdu'l-Karím. He kissed the threshold at his door and threw himself at his feet. He humbled himself before 'Abdu'l-Karím, who was completely overcome. This was a very different Mírzá Abu'l-Faḍl from the one he had been used to.

Then 'Abdu'l-Karím said that this humble attitude towards himself was not justified. It is God Who guides the souls, not man!

# 54

## Mírzá Abu'l-Faḍl (II)

It was a thorn in the side for the Muslim clergy. Mírzá Abu'l-Faḍl had become a Bahá'í. And not only that, he spoke to his students at the Theological University openly about his Faith, although he was a professor who, with his great knowledge, was respected throughout the whole country. They tried to get rid of him even though he was the best professor they had. They managed to engineer it that he had to give up his position at the university. It did not stop there; he was even thrown into prison. When he was freed after five months, the clergy tried to persuade him not to speak openly of the Bahá'í Faith but to act as if he were a Muslim. Would Abu'l-Faḍl want that? To stop telling people about Bahá'u'lláh? He could never do that! Even though he knew that it would get him into trouble.

In Abu'l-Faḍl's life many things changed after he became a Bahá'í. He had not only lost his job as a professor. Before becoming a Bahá'í, even when a young man he enjoyed much respect and was widely noted as one of the greatest scholars in the country. Now he was humiliated and scorned. He came of a family famous for their learning. Now his family wanted nothing more to do with him. They disinherited him too, so that he had absolutely no property now. He earned a little money by writing letters for other people and by copying out the Writings of the Báb and Bahá'u'lláh for the Bahá'ís.

Abu'l-Faḍl continued to teach the Faith. The Bahá'ís in Persia were still being persecuted for their faith. Sometimes the persecutions were so bad that people did not dare to mention the names of Bahá'ís out loud. And to speak well of them was really dangerous. Wherever he was, Abu'l-Faḍl let nothing deter him from openly speaking about the Faith. Especially when he actually received a letter from Bahá'u'lláh in which He wrote that he should invite people to tell them of this new Revelation. When fresh persecutions broke out again, Abu'l-Faḍl, with other Bahá'ís, found himself in prison once more.

In the beginning, it was very difficult for the believers who had been imprisoned. The opponents of the Faith wanted them killed. Many Bahá'ís were killed too, and the prisoners knew that any day they might be dragged out of the prison and cruelly put to death. These opponents did everything they could to discredit Abu'l-Faḍl and his fellow prisoners in the eyes of the Shah. But they could not convince the Shah that they were guilty. He therefore refused to allow them to be put to death. He decided, however, that they must stay in prison. This imprisonment lasted nearly two years. Only when the Shah could be convinced that the Bahá'ís had done nothing against the law did he give the order to release them.

Something else changed in the life of Abu'l-Faḍl. He was unusually intelligent. In his youth he had studied several sciences at the same time. He was cleverer than anyone else. Once a new Arabic dictionary was published, a very fat book of 1,400 pages. Abu'l-Faḍl took it home one afternoon and brought it back next morning. In that short time he had checked through the whole book. He had discovered two mistakes in it and could point them out exactly. Then some other learned men reviewed it; they took months to come to the conclusion that in the dictionary the two mistakes found in less than one day by Abu'l-Faḍl were the only ones in it.

Abu'l-Faḍl's knowledge excelled everyone else's. Until he discovered that he could not equal the Baháʼís. Even illiterate Baháʼís could answer questions he could not handle. This was because their minds were enlightened by the teachings of Baháʼuʼlláh. Now that he was a Baháʼí, Abu'l-Faḍl's mind was also enlightened by the words of Baháʼuʼlláh. His great knowledge and insight were from then on renewed and enhanced and he was freed from useless superstitions. Such as the superstition that every raindrop was carried by an angel to the earth. He not only understood the holy writings much better, he could also explain the most complicated matters very clearly. Abu'l-Faḍl did not think that this was his own doing. It came from a prayer that Baháʼuʼlláh had revealed for him. In this, Baháʼuʼlláh implored God to enable Abdu'l-Faḍl to teach His truth and to explain with wisdom what lay hidden in the ocean of God's knowledge. Before he was a Baháʼí, Abu'l-Faḍl could not answer the questions the Baháʼís asked him. Now it was the other way round, now the believers were asking him to explain the passages which they did not understand themselves. They even asked him to write books.

Abu'l-Faḍl did not want to do this. In spite of his great learning he was a humble man. He knew how high the station of Baháʼuʼlláh was. He did not feel worthy even to make a pilgrimage to see Baháʼuʼlláh. He also felt that – as long as Baháʼuʼlláh was on this earth – he could write no books. For, said Abu'l-Faḍl, 'in the days in which the Supreme pen was moving, its sound would be heard in all regions'. He felt it was presumptuous of people if they also wished to write. Until he once received a visit from Varqá, the poet, the father of Rúḥuʼlláh. He told him that during his pilgrimage to ʻAkká he had heard from Baháʼuʼlláh about the Báb's injunction that the believers should write books about Baháʼuʼlláh. Abu'l-

Faḍl asked Varqá whether Bahá'u'lláh thought that he too should serve the Faith in that way. Bahá'u'lláh had answered that such people must devote themselves to writing and to producing proofs. Because the Báb had advised it. When he heard this from Varqá, Abu'l-Faḍl began to write books. He knew a great deal about other religions. He could explain the old prophecies better than anyone before him had done. He found the solutions to centuries-old puzzles.

There was yet another change in the life of Abu'l-Faḍl. He began to make long journeys. He preferred to spend all his time in study and writing, but he submitted his own will to that of Bahá'u'lláh. So when Bahá'u'lláh asked him to travel round Persia to teach the Faith, he did that. After that, he travelled through Eastern Europe and Asia. He even went as far as Moscow and close to the Chinese border. After the ascension of Bahá'u'lláh, 'Abdu'l-Bahá asked him to come to the Holy Land. There Abu'l-Faḍl discovered that his knowledge was as nothing compared with the knowledge of 'Abdu'l-Bahá. He said of 'Abdu'l-Bahá that He was an ocean of knowledge. Compared with this he himself was like a pebble upon the shore of that ocean.

'Abdu'l-Bahá asked Abu'l-Faḍl to go to Egypt. Naturally, to teach the Faith there too. 'Abdu'l-Bahá gave him a special mission: he was not to speak at first about the Faith and not to say that he was a Bahá'í. At the famous University of Cairo, Abu'l-Faḍl very soon became known for his great learning. They were always ready to listen to his lectures and the manner in which he could solve complicated problems. When Islám was unfairly attacked by Christians, he was able to defend Islám better than anyone. Only when he had become very well known was it discovered that he was a Bahá'í. Many then

wanted to know more about it and became believers. Many more than if 'Abu'l-Faḍl had spoken about the Faith from the start.

Afterwards, at the request of 'Abdu'l-Bahá, Abu'l-Faḍl went travelling once again – this time to America. Because of Ibráhím Khayru'lláh, there were a quite a number of American Bahá'ís. But there were still very few Bahá'í books and what they had been taught by Khayru'lláh was not always correct. Therefore 'Abdu'l-Bahá felt it necessary to send Abu'l-Faḍl to America. This was a great sacrifice for him. He would miss the university, he did not speak the language, the climate in America was very different to what he was used to and he had to get used to very different food. Yet he did what 'Abdu'l-Bahá asked of him. 'Abdu'l-Bahá felt this trip to America was so important that He sent His own best translator, Ali Kuli Khan, with Abu'l-Faḍl, even though He Himself badly needed him. For nearly four years he taught the American Bahá'ís. Also at 'Abdu'l-Bahá's request, he wrote a book for the believers in America. Then he returned to Egypt. There he remained until the end of his life.

'Abdu'l-Bahá was very fond of Abu'l-Faḍl. He was inconsolable for days when He heard of his passing. He had been a great support to Him. He had often sent the friends with their questions to Abu'l-Faḍl. When 'Abdu'l-Bahá was in Egypt on the last stage of His journeying, He made sure that Abu'l-Faḍl would live somewhere close to Him. And if He felt discouraged, He would go to visit Abu'l-Faḍl. Then all His gloom would immediately disappear.

His whole life long, Mírzá Abu'l-Faḍl had studied and written a great deal. His room was often strewn with books. When he was studying, he did not like to be disturbed.

Once, there were a couple of ladies who wished to visit him. They knocked at his door but got no answer. They knocked again.

Still no answer. They tried it once more; they knew he was at home.

Then a voice was heard from inside the door saying, 'Abu'l-Faḍl is not here.'

The ladies burst out laughing. Inside the door someone else was having a good laugh. You have guessed, of course, who that was.

# 55

# The First World War

Happily, 'Abdu'l-Bahá began to recover from the weariness which had followed His long journeys. It was especially noticeable from His handwriting which was just as vigorous now as it had been before. He began again to visit His friends and the poor of 'Akká. How they had missed Him! They greeted Him and each other warmly but asked Him, 'Where did you go and leave us without a friend and brother? Did you not know you mean everything to us?' He had brought presents from Europe for them and warm overcoats for the poor old men of 'Akká. In a few months He was back working every day, from morning until late at night. Piles of letters came in from the countries which He had visited. The Bahá'ís came often with their questions to Him. Then there were the sick and poor who needed His help. And many pilgrims came to visit Him too.

When 'Abdu'l-Bahá had been back in Haifa six months, what He had so often warned of during his travels happened. Only one spark was needed to set off the powder-keg that was Europe. That spark was the murder of the Archduke Francis Ferdinand, the successor to the throne of the Austro-Hungarian Empire. He and his wife were shot on the streets of Sarajevo. It was not long before many European countries declared war on each other and invaded each others' countries. The First World War had begun. Millions of young men were sent to the war. They were told that it could only last a short time. Then they would return to their own countries and be welcomed back as heroes. But the war was to last for four years. A great many would not return but die at the front. Nine million solders were killed and many millions of others would feel the effects for the rest of their lives.

After the assassination of Francis Ferdinand, the very next day 'Abdu'l-Bahá told all the pilgrims in Haifa to return to their own countries. It was not long before the wisdom of this decision became clear. In the past, about fifteen ships had used to call at the port of Haifa every week. Soon after the outbreak of the war there was only one still calling. Hardly anyone could now leave Haifa.

Soon the war became more real in another way in Haifa. The people were beginning to panic. The government had made an order that all men between the ages of eighteen and forty-five must make themselves available for military service. They must be prepared to leave at any moment. This was announced on big red posters on the walls in the city. The whole city was in a state of commotion and everywhere there were people on the streets excitedly talking to one another. At night hardly anyone could sleep a wink. The women in particular complained bitterly. What would happen to the men and boys? Would they ever come home again? Who would look after them and their children when the men were away? They would have to fend for themselves for they received hardly any money from the authorities. And soon, prices began to shoot up.

It was an uncertain and anxious time for the people. Very little had to happen before great unrest was created. They knew that a couple of warships with their cannons could completely devastate their city in a very short time. One day when the sea was dead calm and so clear that they could see the rocks beneath the water, they thought these must be battleships. When they saw a small dot moving on the sea in the distance, they went looking for binoculars to see whether warships were coming. They lived in continual fear. Their fears were not without foundation. Haifa was also continually threatened with bombing. The threat and uncertainty became so great that 'Abdu'l-Bahá decided to take His family and the Bahá'ís over to Abú-Sinán, a village at the foot of the mountains of Galilee. He Himself and a servant remained in Haifa. Except for a few minor bomb attacks, Haifa was spared. When, six months later, the danger had subsided, the Bahá'ís came back.

Life seemed to go on as usual. In the surrounding villages food was being grown so that people had enough to eat. They were back in their homes in 'Akká and Haifa. There, they again had a view of the sea. In the evening, if the sky was clear, they could watch the sun go down in magnificent red, pink and orange colours on the western horizon. Sometimes beautiful banks of cloud hung over the sea. One of the pilgrims described these as castles of gold suspended between heaven and earth.

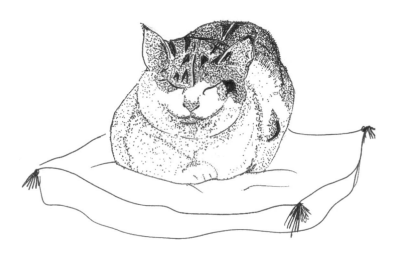

Attention was paid once more to the ordinary things of life. If a cat sat purring contentedly beside 'Abdu'l-Bahá's chair, He enjoyed that. This cat, He would say then, is so joyful, so carefree and free of fear. He often spoke about His travels. Like the time He visited the Zoo in Paris. There He saw a polar bear. People were staring at the bear, and the bear was staring back, as if he wanted to ask, 'How did I get entangled with these folk?' 'Abdu'l-Bahá's sense of humour never deserted Him.

Yet, wartime was a really difficult time for Him. Knowing that in Europe millions of young men were being killed in a terrible way. He said that during all His years of imprisonment He had never felt so sorrowful as now. He had warned so often about this. The war would not have been necessary if the European countries had been prepared to settle their differences with each other around the table. But they were not willing to do this.

The persecutions of the Bahá'ís in Persia which kept flaring up also gave Him much pain. Their possessions were plundered, they were driven from their homes and hunted into the mountains or the desert. Sometimes news came that one or more of the believers had been killed. 'Abdu'l-Bahá would then be so sad that He might not speak a word for a long time.

The most difficult thing for Him was perhaps that during the war there was no contact with the Bahá'ís in the rest of the world. Pilgrims no longer came and He missed their shining faces. When the war had been going on for some time, there were even no letters or telegrams coming in any more. He had no news of how the Faith was progressing. These had been reports which always made Him very happy. He once said that He wished He had gone to India. They had implored Him to come. Now He was doomed to do nothing. This had a serious effect on His health. But very soon things began to happen which made His presence in Haifa and 'Akká essential.

The country was hit by a dreadful disaster, a plague of locusts. In great, dense swarms they arrived. The swarms were so dense that they almost shut out the light of the sun. The insects ate up every bit of green there was. Except for a few fields of wheat, the country was eaten completely bare – not a leaf was left on any tree. There was no food left for the people. Famine resulted. Day and night, people came to 'Abdu'l-Bahá's door. For many, He was their only hope.

'Abdu'l-Bahá not only had known that war would break out, He also knew that then there would not be enough food. Even before He went to Europe and America, He had taught the believers to grow grain. In the years that they lived in the Holy Land, the Bahá'ís had bought various pieces of land. In the neighbourhood of 'Akká and Haifa, but also further east, near the city of Tiberias and in the Jordan valley. It was fertile land on which crops could be grown. Now and then, 'Abdu'l-

Bahá went there to see how the work was progressing. He had also taught the Bahá'ís to store the grain in such a way that it would keep for a long time. Two thousand years before, the Holy Land had been occupied by the Romans. They had dug pits in which grain could be kept for a long time. These had not been used for centuries. 'Abdu'l-Bahá had them repaired and the Bahá'ís stored their grain in them. The pits also had an unexpected advantage. Occasionally, bands of Arab robbers invaded the countryside. They took everything they could use. Sometimes even the doors were taken off the houses. But the grain stored in the pits was safely hidden from them. They never discovered it.

With this grain from 'Abdu'l-Bahá many people survived the war. But was He also safe Himself? To one of the pilgrims at the time, He said that it was as if He were seated just underneath a sword that could fall at any moment. He also said that He was not worried for Himself, but for the people who would then be left without His help. He hoped that He would be spared for their sake.

# 56

## Danger Averted

Major Tudor Pole worked in Egypt with the Intelligence Service of the British Army. He had first been a soldier and had to go into battle. In one battle round Jerusalem he was hit by a bullet. Seriously wounded, he lay unconscious underneath the body of another soldier who had been killed trying to help him. When daylight came, he recovered consciousness. He lifted his head, which was the only movement he could make. He saw that the Turkish soldiers were going though the battlefield and killing all the wounded British soldiers. Then Major Tudor Pole felt that an invisible protector was kneeling beside him. He was told to keep his head down. He obeyed. When the Turkish soldiers reached him, they passed quickly by because they thought he was dead. A little later he tried, in spite of his wounds and the pain, to crawl back to the British lines. He did not know which way he should go but again he felt that he was being led by this invisible protector. The doctor who treated him said that the bullet had gone straight through his body. It was a miracle that he was still alive. Through this extraordinary experience with his unseen protector, Major Tudor Pole started to believe that there must be a reason why he had come through it alive. He came to the conclusion that he was going to be needed for some other work in later life.

Now that he could no longer fight, he was transferred to the British Intelligence Service. There, he had to try to discover as much as possible about what the enemy was doing. He had

only just started work there when he discovered a report which gave him a great shock: if the Turkish Army was forced to leave Haifa, 'Abdu'l-Bahá and his family would be crucified on Mount Carmel before they left. Major Tudor Pole had met 'Abdu'l-Bahá in Egypt and in London before the war. In London He had even read out a talk given by 'Abdu'l-Bahá which had been translated into English. Now he was reading the news that 'Abdu'l-Bahá was in great danger. What could Major Tudor Pole do to save Him? He tried to warn his superiors, but none of them knew who 'Abdu'l-Bahá was. So no action was taken.

Why was 'Abdu'l-Bahá in danger? He was being threatened by Jamál Páshá, one of the three most powerful men in the Turkish Empire. It was, in fact, very strange that he should threaten 'Abdu'l-Bahá. 'Abdu'l-Bahá had once paid him a visit. Jamál Páshá was much impressed by 'Abdu'l-Bahá and

267

showed Him great respect. When the visit was at an end, he escorted 'Abdu'l-Bahá to the bottom of the steps to his house. This was very unusual, for the arrogant Jamál Páshá seldom showed respect for others. You would expect that he would now always treat 'Abdu'l-Bahá well.

But Jamál Páshá was an unpredictable ruler. And the Turkish Empire had many opponents, especially from peoples who had for centuries been oppressed. They wanted to be free of the Turkish yoke and uprisings were a regular occurrence. Many were killed just because the Turkish government thought that they were opposing it. In a country like that it was not difficult for suspicion to fall on anyone. Mírzá Muḥammad-'Alí, the half-brother of 'Abdu'l-Bahá, used this. For years he had hardly been able to do much mischief. But now, during the war, he did what he had tried so often in the past: get 'Abdu'l-Bahá into the Turkish authorities' bad books. He told Jamál Páshá that 'Abdu'l-Bahá was hostile to the Turkish government. And he gave presents to Jamál Páshá as bribes. Jamál Páshá's suspicions were aroused. He said that he would have 'Abdu'l-Bahá and His family crucified on Mount Carmel and have the Tomb of Bahá'u'lláh levelled to the ground. First, he and his army had to get the British out of Egypt. If after that he returned as the victor, he would carry out his evil plan. However, Jamál Páshá did not come back victorious. On the contrary, it soon looked as if he and his army would be ousted from the Holy Land by the British. Mírzá Muḥammad-'Alí had achieved his goal. 'Abdu'l-Bahá was indeed in grave danger. It was well known that Jamál Páshá had already had many innocent people put to death.

Meanwhile, the news which British Intelligence was receiving about the danger which threatened 'Abdu'l-Bahá became more and more alarming. And the Turkish army was losing more and more ground. What should Tudor Pole do? None of his superior officers showed any interest at all. He decided to do something that was strictly forbidden in the British Army. He secretly gave a letter to one of his friends who was going to London. Both knew the risk they were running. If this was discovered, they would have to appear before a British court-martial. They felt their message was so important that they would take the risk anyway.

The message reached the right people in Britain. It was for Lady Blomfield who, both times that 'Abdu'l-Bahá was in London, had placed her home at His disposal. She understood how serious the situation was and immediately got in touch with someone with influence in the government. That person wrote to the head of the Foreign Office. The news of the danger threatening 'Abdu'l-Bahá also reached Mrs Whyte in Scotland. She informed her son who was a Member of Parliament and he also wrote to the head of the Foreign Office. Both letters arrived there on the same day. The British government at once sent a telegram to General Allenby in the Holy Land with the order to 'extend every protection and consideration to 'Abdu'l-Bahá, His family and His friends.'

The British could, of course, do very little as long as Haifa was in the hands of the Turkish army. But they did allow news to leak through to the Turks that a heavy price would be paid if anything should happen to 'Abdu'l-Bahá. In addition, the British were given orders, as soon as Haifa was taken, to place guards on the house of 'Abdu'l-Bahá.

General Allenby had many problems to solve before he could liberate Haifa. His experienced soldiers had been recalled to Europe. In their place, troops from India had been sent who first had to be trained. And he must ensure by every means

that the Turks did not find out first that he was planning to seize Haifa.

Everyone had expected that it would be very difficult to take Haifa. Cannons were ranged to fire on the city. The Bahá'ís who lived in the city were very worried. What would that achieve? They went to 'Abdu'l-Bahá. He calmed down His excited followers and called upon them to pray. He reassured them and said that the cannons in Haifa would not do any damage and that no one would be killed. The Bahá'ís and the family of 'Abdu'l-Bahá were most concerned about Him. The British were coming and the Turkish army would soon have to leave Haifa. Could Jamál Páshá's plans still be carried out before their departure? Everyone was very worried. Except 'Abdu'l-Bahá. He was calmness itself and reassured all those around Him.

Haifa was surprisingly quickly taken by the British. Days before anyone had thought this possible. The city was undamaged.

The cannons were not well aimed and shot right over the city so that the shells landed in the sea. The British immediately asked where 'Abdu'l-Bahá lived. Indian army soldiers were placed on guard at His house. Jamál Páshá's evil plan could no longer be carried out. General Allenby at once sent a telegram to London that 'Abdu'l-Bahá was safe. The message was quickly sent on to the Bahá'ís in other countries. How glad they were to hear that, after all those years of silence, He was all right!

However, it was not yet entirely safe for 'Abdu'l-Bahá. It was quite possible that there were still Turkish snipers hiding in Haifa. They knew about Jamál Páshá's plan and they also knew that they would gain his favour if they carried out his plan. He was, after all, one of the most powerful men in the land. Therefore 'Abdu'l-Bahá's house would still be guarded by the Indian army soldiers for the present. After a while that danger had also passed.

Thus the centuries-old Turkish dominion over the Holy Land came to an end. The First World War would also soon be over. This was the last time that Mírzá Muḥammad-'Alí succeeded in putting 'Abdu'l-Bahá in danger. His behaviour had caused much fear and unease. But just like all his other misdeeds, this time, too, it had come to nothing. How he and his accomplices must have despaired!

# 57

## The Tablets of the Divine Plan

The Holy Land was liberated. 'Abdu'l-Bahá was safe. Jamál Páshá had not been able to carry out his evil plan to crucify Him and His family on Mount Carmel. Correspondence with the believers in other countries was again restored. Pilgrims were coming again. The dark years had passed.

During those dark years 'Abdu'l-Bahá had thought constantly about His friends in other parts of the world. He wished them to carry on His work. The time was near when He would no longer be able to do it Himself. He was now nearly 75 years old. They must do what He Himself had done: go into the world to teach the Faith. The Faith of Bahá'u'lláh was, after all, intended for the whole of mankind! No place in the world should be deprived of it. In those years when He had been isolated from the rest of the world and a terrible war had been fought in Europe, 'Abdu'l-Bahá had made a plan. A plan to make known worldwide the peace-loving Message of Bahá'u'lláh. The plan is explained in fourteen letters which 'Abdu'l-Bahá wrote to the Bahá'ís of the United States and Canada. Some of these letters had already been sent to the United States even during the war. Others had to be kept and stored in the room underneath the Shrine of the Báb. These were not taken to America until after the war by one of the Bahá'ís. Later, the fourteen letters were brought together in a book entitled *Tablets of the Divine Plan*.

'Abdu'l-Bahá wrote in one of the first letters about how He Himself, in spite of His weakness, had travelled through many countries in Europe and America. A person must forget the need for rest, comfort and attachment to this material world. He discusses the difference between human beings and animals and then talks about the cow and the little bird in the freedom of nature.

No matter how much man gains wealth, riches and opulence in this world, he will not become as independent as a cow. For these fattened cows roam freely over the vast tableland. All the prairies and meadows are theirs for grazing, and all the springs and rivers are theirs for drinking! No matter how much they graze, the fields will not be exhausted! It is evident that they have earned these material bounties with the utmost facility.

Still more ideal than this life is the life of the bird. A bird, on the summit of a mountain, on the high, waving branches, has built for itself a nest more beautiful than the palaces of the kings! The air is in the utmost purity, the water cool and clear as crystal, the panorama charming and enchanting. In such glorious surroundings, he expends his numbered days. All the harvests of the plain are his possessions, having earned all this wealth without the least labour . . . Thus it becomes evident that in the matters of this world, however much man may strive . . . he will be unable to earn the abundance, the freedom and the

independent life of a small bird. This proves and establishes the fact that man is not created for the life of this ephemeral world
. . .

'Abdu'l-Bahá explains that man is created for acquiring perfections. What use are riches and attachment to this world? He must aspire to eternal life and the exaltation of the world of humanity. He must wish for the promotion of the Word of God, the guidance of the inhabitants of the globe, the spread of universal peace and the proclamation of the oneness of the world of humanity. This must be done! If people occupy themselves only with the requirements of this life, they should walk the earth on all fours like the animals, says 'Abdu'l-Bahá.

When 'Abdu'l-Bahá wrote these letters, there were about 35 countries where Bahá'ís lived. This was already many more than immediately after the ascension of Bahá'u'lláh, when there were not even ten. But the Faith must be brought to every country and territory of all five continents. To the densely populated lands of Europe, but also to vast and thinly populated places like Siberia. To the Eskimo in Greenland, to the North American Indians, the original inhabitants of that continent, and also to the inhabitants of the many islands of the great oceans. To China, Japan, Australia, Africa, Alaska and elsewhere. 'Abdu'l-Bahá named 120 countries and territories in His letters to which the American and Canadian Bahá'ís must travel to proclaim the Faith. And Bahá'ís must also establish themselves in those cities and areas of their own country where there were as yet no Bahá'ís living.

Would 'Abdu'l-Bahá not have wanted to go travelling again Himself? Of course He would! He wanted it very much. In one letter He wrote:

O that I could travel, even though on foot and in the utmost poverty, to these regions, and, raising the call of 'Yá Bahá'u'l-Abhá' in cities, villages, mountains, deserts and oceans, promote the Divine teachings! This, alas, I cannot do. How intensely I deplore it! Please God, ye may achieve it.

After the war, the American Bahá'ís wanted Him to return once again to the United States. The news that He was safe had only just arrived when they sent Him an invitation. With over a thousand signatures of Bahá'ís from all over America. 'Abdu'l-Bahá Himself had planned a journey round the world. He wanted first to visit India, then South-east Asia and Japan, and later the Hawaiian islands in the Pacific. From there He wanted to travel right across America, visit some other European countries and finally via Egypt return to the Holy Land. It was a journey that would last between four and five years. It was not to be. Instead of going round the world and visiting the Bahá'ís in America, 'Abdu'l-Bahá urged the American believers themselves to go out into the world.

In the Tablets of the Divine Plan, 'Abdu'l-Bahá reminds the Bahá'ís of what Christ said to His disciples. They must travel to every corner of the world. Wherever they went they must bring the glad tidings of the coming of the Kingdom of God. Almost two thousand years later, the Báb gave the same mission to His first followers, the Letters of the Living. They were to go just like the disciples of Christ and spread the message of the new Faith. Now the Bahá'ís of America and Canada were given the same mission.

'Abdu'l-Bahá's master plan formed the basis for the later plans to take the Faith to every part of the world. Such as the Ten Year Crusade, a plan which Shoghi Effendi launched forty years later. This called upon the believers all over the world to arise and go to those places mentioned by 'Abdu'l-Bahá in these letters and where as yet no Bahá'ís lived. The Bahá'ís who answered this call and established themselves as the first believers in one of these places are called the Knights of Bahá'u'lláh. The Universal House of Justice now bases its plans upon 'Abdu'l-Bahá's Tablets of the Divine Plan. All over the world, the believers are working together on these plans.

'Abdu'l-Bahá did not just ask the Bahá'ís to leave their houses and homes and travel to unknown places. He wrote that they would always be in His thoughts, He would never forget them. And that day and night He was always engaged in thinking of the friends. He prayed for them from the depths of His heart. He told them that anyone who arose to travel to spread the Faith could be assured of God's help. In one of the prayers He revealed in the Tablets of the Divine Plan, 'Abdu'l-Bahá speaks of God's confirmations, which alone can change 'a gnat into an eagle, a drop of water into rivers and seas, and an atom into lights and suns'. Divine confirmations would surround them on every side.

The Tablets of the Divine Plan were not without results. Many a Bahá'í packed his or her bags and went out into the world. One of them even travelled four times around the world.

# 58

## 'Abdu'l-Bahá's Ambassadress

The war was over. The Tablets of the Divine Plan had been taken to America by one of the Bahá'ís from Haifa. They formed the central focus of the consultations at the first Convention of the Bahá'ís of the United States and Canada after the war. Each of the fourteen letters was read out and discussed. Some of the believers were quick to respond to the call of 'Abdu'l-Bahá. They left their homes and went travelling, or settled in another part of the world, such as Japan, Hawaii or Australia.

One of these was Martha Root. She wanted to leave immediately after the Convention. They even say that at the end of the Convention, everyone was wondering where she was. No one could find her. Until they looked in her room. There she was, busy packing her trunks to go away at once. This is, however, a story which may be true but we have no definite record. It is true, however, that Martha Root was the first to answer the call of 'Abdu'l-Bahá. She did not wait for anyone else to tell her. She wanted to do what 'Abdu'l-Bahá Himself could no longer do. To the end of her life she kept travelling to teach the Faith. She went around the world four times and visited practically every country. Russia was the only large country where she did not go.

When Martha had made a plan, she stuck to it. This she did on one of her first journeys to South America. She was in Argentina and wanted to go to Chile, on the other side of the Andes mountains. It was winter and the journey

through the mountains would be extremely difficult and dangerous. Everyone advised her not to go. She was treated to stories of frostbitten fingers and toes. Why not postpone her trip until the summer? Martha would not hear of it. She felt not a day should be wasted. 'Abdu'l-Bahá had after all mentioned those countries in His Tablets of the Divine Plan! Martha went! On the back of a mule, into the high mountains, through ice and snow, along deep ravines, through dark tunnels littered with boulders and over very narrow and slippery paths. She had dressed herself very warmly but she was dreadfully cold. Part of the journey was too dangerous to make on the back of the mule so the travellers walked hand in hand through the snow as they descended the slopes. High in the mountains, where the air was so thin, they had to stop every few minutes to catch their breath. At last they reached the other side in safety.

After such a hard journey you would say a few days' rest would be needed. Not for Martha! There, too, she immediately set to work to teach the Faith. Then she travelled on to Panama. Panama was a meeting-point for communications and had been mentioned by 'Abdu'l-Bahá as one of the countries where Bahá'ís should go to teach.

In whatever country Martha found herself, she always approached the press. She was a journalist by profession. She nearly always succeeded in getting the articles which she herself had written about the Faith published in the newspapers. She had learned Esperanto and in many places she told Esperantists about the Faith. Even if she was only passing through and spending just a few hours in that place, Martha went into that town. She always had suitcases full of books and pamphlets on the Faith with her. If there was a library, she visited it to present Bahá'í books. She distributed books and pamphlets to thousands of people. When possible, she held meetings, sometimes several in one day. Even if she was on board ship she was telling her fellow passengers about the Faith. And even if there was a storm and the ship was rolling to and fro. Once, she had to hold on to a pillar to remain standing. In this way she gave her talk.

She was genuinely interested in everyone she met. She knew that if you love people, they listen to you. Wherever she went she made friends. And through those friends she made more new friends, whom she could also tell about the Faith. If she needed help with anything there was very often someone who was glad to oblige. She advised a friend to make every meeting special. 'Give something always, if only a flower, some candy, or fruit. Pray', said Martha to her friend, 'that they will accept from you the Greater Gift.'

Martha was not deterred from approaching those in high places. She offered books and pamphlets to professors, ministers, presidents and even to royalty. Including to Queen Marie of Romania. She received the book *Bahá'u'lláh and the New Era*. Queen Marie was at once so taken with this that she kept on reading until three o'clock in the morning. The next day she sent Martha an invitation. As soon as she had welcomed Martha to her palace, she immediately said, 'These teachings are the solution for the world's problems.' Queen Marie wrote magnificent testimonies to the Faith which were published in nearly two hundred newspapers in Canada and the United States. These were later translated and published

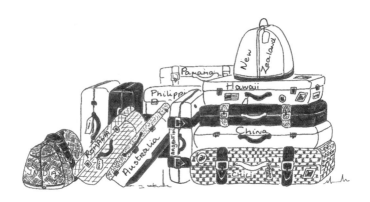

in Europe, China, Japan, Australia, the Near East and islands in every sea. Queen Marie of Romania was the first monarch in the world to recognize Bahá'u'lláh as God's Messenger for this time.

Again and again, Martha went travelling. Not only on her journey through the Andes had she been exposed to great dangers. On one journey through Central America she found herself in the midst of a revolution. On one of her last trips she was in China when Japan declared war on that country. Shanghai was bombed by the Japanese and the building in which Martha was could have been hit by a bomb at any time. She could then do nothing more for the Faith in China and with great difficulty she succeeded in leaving the country on an American ship. She had to leave nearly all her luggage behind. Her typewriter was one of the few things she could take with her. The ship took her to the Philippines, away from the dangers of war. She had only just arrived when another danger presented itself. The ground, and the building in which she was, began to shudder violently and to shake. It was one of the most powerful earthquakes the Philippines had had in a hundred years. It was followed by some smaller quakes and a typhoon. Even now, Martha was unscathed. And fortunately she was able to get back the luggage she had been forced to leave in China.

Travelling was seldom easy for Martha. She was often ill and had bad headaches. More than once she had to remain lying ill for days in her hotel room. As she grew older her health got worse. On her last journey she was sometimes in such pain that she was not even able to open her own suitcases. She would not see a doctor. She knew that they would say she should give up travelling – a piece of advice she would not take anyway. After her visit to the Philippines she travelled for another fifteen months through India. After that, she went to Australia and New Zealand. She was seriously ill when she decided to go back to her own country. When the ship called at Hawaii, she was too ill to continue the voyage. She was no longer able even to hold a glass of water in her hand. She had to stay behind and would never see her own country again. Lovingly, she was cared for during her last months in Hawaii by friends until she died peacefully there.

Then Martha Root had started on another journey. She did not need her twenty-two suitcases any more. Nor her little portable stove for cooking meals on her way. Her sick body, which had been giving her more and more pain, she could leave behind as well. She had begun her most exciting journey ever.

During her lifetime, Martha Root travelled over the eastern and the western hemispheres of the earth. She was buried in Hawaii, the island in the middle of the Pacific Ocean. Between the eastern and western hemispheres.

# 59

# The Tablet to The Hague

'This must never happen again!' At least the countries were all agreed about that. The First World War had cost the lives of millions of young men and caused enormous devastation. Even before the war international peace conferences had been held. They were not able to prevent World War I. Countries could want peace, but how could they achieve it? They must make agreements with each other about this. But what agreements? And what were the principles on which such agreements should be based? And how could anyone be sure that the agreements were kept? While the war was still going on, the Central Organization for a Durable Peace in The Hague had written several times to 'Abdu'l-Bahá. Only one letter had reached Him and that one had taken three years and ten months to get there. You can see how war can lead to chaos in the world! 'Abdu'l-Bahá replied at once to the letter. This is the letter we call 'Abdu'l-Bahá's Tablet to The Hague. He describes in it the principles mankind needs to apply in order to make universal peace possible.

You can compare the establishment of universal peace to the building of a house. You need all kinds of materials for it: blocks, timber, glass and paint for example. You could also call the principles which 'Abdu'l-Bahá lists in His letter building blocks for peace. What do these building blocks for peace look like? What are those principles? Let us imagine we are going on a journey. A journey through a world in which

282

the principles which 'Abdu'l-Bahá mentions in this Tablet are being applied. The principles which bring peace.

It is easy to go travelling. You do not need first to learn foreign languages to be able to understand people. Wherever you go, everyone has learned, as well as their mother tongue, the same world auxiliary language. Everywhere you go you can talk to people. You will be safe everywhere too, you need not be afraid that you will find yourself in the midst of a war. Of course, it can still happen that countries have differences of opinion. In the past, they then went to war with each other. Whichever nation was the strongest got its way, it did not matter much whether it was right or wrong. Now they bring their differences to a Supreme Tribunal of Justice. You could also call it a Universal Tribunal. This Tribunal comes to a just decision and the countries abide by that.

The differences between rich and poor are no longer so great as before. No one lives in slums now and no one goes hungry. Everywhere people have good houses, enough to eat and decent clothes to wear. Sometimes people may get into difficulties but then the rich will voluntarily share with them. Everywhere in the world, children go to school and learn to read and write. Because of this everyone can independently investigate the truth. No one blindly follows the beliefs of his parents. People have first thought about it properly. And they no longer hate others because they belong to a different religion.

People have laid aside their prejudices. Men and women treat each other as equals and it does not matter what colour your skin is. Everyone is treated equally. You meet friendship and love everywhere. Population groups in countries that used always to be at war with each other now live side by side in peace and as good friends. Justice reigns. No people

or country is oppressed by another. On our journey we come across differences everywhere. These differences are no longer a source of disunity. The world is only the more beautiful for them.

This is how the world will look in future. How can this world be brought about? That, too, is just like building a house. If people build a house it is not enough to have timber and blocks and all kinds of materials. A good plan is also needed and that is made by an architect. Just imagine if the builders were each to start working on his own plan! They would be having arguments all the time. The work would not progress and it might turn into a very strange house in the end. A house no one would want to live in. Only if the builders are agreed about what they are doing will it succeed.

So unity is also needed for the establishment of universal

peace. The countries must unitedly stand on the principles which make universal peace possible. They must also be united about the way in which these principles are adhered to.

'Abdu'l-Bahá has described in the Tablet to The Hague how the Supreme Tribunal should be brought about. Each country must choose a number of its best citizens to represent it. People who are well-informed about the problems of mankind and what the world needs. The whole country, the people, government, even the monarch or the president, will all stand behind their chosen representatives. Then these representatives of every country must elect the members of the Supreme Tribunal. The decisions of the judges so elected to the Supreme Tribunal will be binding. If any country does not obey the decision then all the other countries should together compel it to obey.

After the First World War, the League of Nations was set up by fifty countries. That was an important step. But the League of Nations could not keep the peace. Some countries took no notice of its decisions and another war began. After the Second World War the United Nations, the successor to the League of Nations, was founded. The United Nations has not been able to prevent war either. The League of Nations and the United Nations have been too restricted. They could not compel countries to keep to their decisions. The principles mentioned by 'Abdu'l-Bahá in the Tablet to the Hague cannot yet be fully applied. There is not yet enough unity and agreement.

Yet you can see that a great deal in the world has changed. Countries have become aware that they are jointly responsible for peace in the world. And that together they must ensure the security of all nations. The principles described by 'Abdu'l-Bahá in the Tablet to the Hague are becoming better known all the time. They are being supported by more and more people.

The sooner these principles are applied, the sooner the Lesser Peace will come. Then there will be no more war anywhere in the world.

# 60

## Sir 'Abdu'l-Bahá 'Abbás

Isfandíyár stood looking on with a sorrowful face. For years, 'Abdu'l-Bahá had needed him. If He had to go somewhere, it was Isfandíyár who would take Him there. With his mule and carriage. And now, just now when something very important was going to happen today, a large, beautiful motor car had arrived to collect 'Abdu'l-Bahá. 'I'm no longer needed,' thought Isfandíyár. He did not need to harness his mule to the carriage to take 'Abdu'l-Bahá to the ceremony, and such an important ceremony it was.

This ceremonial had been organized by the British government. They had not forgotten what 'Abdu'l-Bahá had done during the war. He had grown corn and had it stored. Even before the war He had begun to make preparations. When famine came during wartime, 'Abdu'l-Bahá was able to feed the people. And not only that. The British Army had taken Haifa after a rapid advance. Because of the rapidity of their advance, not enough food for the British soldiers could be brought to Haifa. The military commander spoke to 'Abdu'l-Bahá about this. He had enough corn so that there would be food for the soldiers too.

The British government decided to honour Him for this by giving Him a knighthood. This meant that He was then a member of the British nobility. That was a great honour which was only conferred on those who had performed outstanding services. It was to be a ceremonial occasion. Employees of the

287

British government had been sent specially from Jerusalem to Haifa for it. And they had sent an elegant and expensive car to call for 'Abdu'l-Bahá at His house.

When the car drew up in front of the door, they went to find 'Abdu'l-Bahá. Where was He, though? He could not be found anywhere. But . . . arriving in a big, posh car, was that really 'Abdu'l-Bahá's style? He had given Isfandíyár a nod: You go and harness up your carriage. That did not take long! And while the people who were attending the ceremony stood looking out for the car with 'Abdu'l-Bahá, He came calmly walking in from quite a different direction.

Representatives of the British government, prominent people in the country and leaders of other faiths were present at the ceremony together with Bahá'ís from various countries.

While the British soldiers saluted and military music was played, the gold medal was presented to 'Abdu'l-Bahá which had been awarded to Him by the King of England. He was now Sir 'Abdu'l-Bahá 'Abbás.

'Abdu'l-Bahá never used His title. Did He Himself think this distinction was so important? The British government wished to honour Him and show its appreciation. In turn, 'Abdu'l-Bahá was paying homage to the British government by accepting this honour. In the future, the British government will be honoured for having awarded this knighthood to 'Abdu'l-Bahá.

Even now, 'Abdu'l-Bahá went on with His work for the people. In spite of His advanced age. A society had been formed in Haifa for the purpose of improving conditions in the city and surrounding area. Muslims, Jews, Christians and Bahá'ís together wished to change things for the better for everyone living there. Regardless of race, religion or party. Everyone felt that 'Abdu'l-Bahá should be the President of this society. The people of Haifa were proud of having such a fellow-citizen as 'Abdu'l-Bahá. They were all delighted when He agreed to become President of the society.

He also encouraged others to help those who needed help. An international fund was set up for children living in desperate circumstances. In central and eastern Europe especially there were many children who were in great need after the war. They had no fathers or mothers now and there was no one to look after them, they had no homes, no food and no clothing. He praised their benefactors and called upon the people to be generous in their help for these orphaned children.

He was still working day and night. It was His custom to go to bed at nine o'clock in the evening. Then He would get up about midnight to pray and meditate for part of the night and to work on His correspondence. In the morning, He got up at six o'clock and began again reading letters and replying to them. After lunch He would take a brief afternoon nap. His daily relaxation was an afternoon walk or a short carriage ride. But then He was usually accompanied by one or more pilgrims and He would speak to them on spiritual matters. Or He would go to visit some of the poor to help them. All day long He was ready to help those who most needed His help. In the evenings He called the friends together in His room for the usual evening meeting.

There were nearly always guests in the house. Often, pilgrims stayed with Him and His family. It was one of His greatest pleasures to invite people of various races, colours, nationalities and religions to His table. There had been times when guests of five different faiths and from seven different countries were seated around His table. Lighthearted jokes would be told but there were also serious discussions on all kinds of subjects. 'Abdu'l-Bahá wanted everyone to feel at home in His house. 'My home is the home of laughter and mirth,' He said.

Isfandíyár was happy that 'Abdu'l-Bahá still needed him. But it would not be for very long now that he would be able to serve Him. 'Abdu'l-Bahá's strength was steadily failing. His life on earth was coming to its end.

# 61

## Bahíyyih Khánum – The Greatest Holy Leaf (I)

Anxiously, she sat hunched in a corner of the little room. She had thrown her arms around her little 4-year-old brother. They were alone. Their mother and older brother had gone into town. Would they come back? It was dangerous for them. If the people on the street found out that they were Bábís, they could be killed just like that on the spot. But they had to go. They wanted to know how their Father was. He was in a prison and every day one of the Bábís was taken out and cruelly put to death. And every day it could be their Father. What news would they have to bring home? Was their Father still alive?

This is one of the earliest memories of Bahíyyih Khánum. She was the sister of 'Abdu'l-Bahá, two years younger than He. As a girl she was called Fáṭimih. She once told the story of her life to one of the pilgrims. It was one of the few times she had spoken about her own life. She described the lovely house with the big garden where they had lived when she was only a little girl. And spoke about the terrible day when everything changed and they had to flee from their own home. About the fears she endured when her Father was locked up in the Síyáh-Chál. When He was released from that dreadful prison they also feared for His health. But there was something special about Him, they saw something new, a new radiance seemed to enfold Him. At first, Fáṭimih and 'Abbás – as 'Abdu'l-Bahá was called as a child – did not understand what it was. Later it became clear to them: their Father was Bahá'u'lláh, the Messenger of God that the Báb had foretold would soon be revealed by God. When they were both very young Fáṭimih and 'Abbás decided to devote the rest of their lives to His service.

Bahá'u'lláh had to leave Persia and be exiled to Baghdad. His family went with Him. They also went with Him when He was banished to Istanbul and Edirne. Bahíyyih Khánum said she was often frightened that she would be separated from Him. That was the worst thing that could happen to her. In Edirne it almost happened. Mírzá Yaḥyá, her uncle, who had already made so much trouble for Bahá'u'lláh, was again causing problems. He kept on complaining to the authorities. The authorities in Istanbul were so tired of this that they decided to split up the group of refugees. Bahá'u'lláh with His two brothers would be banished to 'Akká, Mírzá Yaḥyá had to go to Cyprus and all the others to Istanbul. For quite a while Bahíyyih Khánum lived in uncertainty; would she be going with her Father or be banished to some other place? Until Bahá'u'lláh Himself intervened and managed to arrange that they could all stay with Him. Only Mírzá Yaḥyá and three others were sent to Cyprus. Bahíyyih Khánum was happy that she could go with Bahá'u'lláh. Even though Bahá'u'lláh warned everyone who came that things would be very difficult for them.

It was a dreadfully difficult time. The journey itself: ten days packed tightly on a ship, without enough to eat or enough to drink. Then on the last day, for eight whole hours Bahíyyih Khánum sat with the others in the burning sun in an open boat sailing from Haifa to 'Akká. With nothing to drink. When they walked through the streets of 'Akká, they were booed and

hissed at by the people. And by then Bahíyyih <u>Kh</u>ánum was completely exhausted. At last she got to the prison. Would she and the others get some food and drink there?

Just imagine a young woman of twenty-two after such an exhausting journey. She would have to climb the stairway but must first pass though a courtyard which was indescribably dirty and where the stench was unbearable. She stood up to her ankles in filth. It was too much for Bahíyyih <u>Kh</u>ánum and she fainted. They could not lay her on the ground, it was much too dirty. Someone found a mat and she was laid on that. With a little of the dirty water they tried to revive her. She swallowed a little, vomited and fainted again. They threw some of the dirty water on her face. Then she came to and was able to go up the stairway.

There followed a miserable night. Everyone was terribly thirsty and they begged for water. Only after waiting for ages did they get some water. But it was far too dirty to drink. The bread they were given was not fit to eat. It was not long before they all became ill. Three of them died. Through the patient and wise actions of 'Abdu'l-Bahá the situation of the prisoners gradually improved.

Two years after their arrival in 'Akká an accident took place in the prison. Mírzá Mihdí fell through a skylight and died the following day. He was Bahíyyih Khánum's youngest brother, with whom she as a little girl of 6 used to stay alone in their home, her arms protectively around him. He was 22 when he died.

These are only some of the events in the life of Bahíyyih Khánum. Her whole life was full of difficulties. That was not the only thing. She also saw every day how Bahá'u'lláh had to suffer. How much sorrow that must have given her! Like the time when He became seriously ill because His half-brother Mírzá Yahyá had put poison into his teacup. Not a day of His life was passed without some tribulation. Bahíyyih Khánum saw this, day after day.

Just as did 'Abdu'l-Bahá. Their lives were closely linked together. If you read a book about 'Abdu'l-Bahá, then you will know a good deal about the life of Bahíyyih Khánum. They both had the same aim in life: to serve Bahá'u'lláh. During the lifetime of Bahá'u'lláh, but also after His ascension. Then the leadership of the Faith passed to 'Abdu'l-Bahá. He was faced with huge problems.

There was one on whose loyalty and support He could depend through thick and thin.

# 62

# Bahíyyih Khánum – The Greatest Holy Leaf (II)

In Bahá'u'lláh's Will and Testament, 'Abdu'l-Bahá was designated to lead the Faith forward. It was very soon obvious that some members of the family were not willing to obey Bahá'u'lláh's Will. Out of jealousy, they sowed disunity and worked against 'Abdu'l-Bahá. His half-brother Mírzá Muḥammad-'Alí in particular. Bahíyyih Khánum supported 'Abdu'l-Bahá through it all. He was her brother. She knew that He was also much more than her brother. Just as Bahá'u'lláh was much more than an ordinary father. Her brother had been appointed by Bahá'u'lláh in His Will and Testament as the Centre of the Covenant. He was the only one who could interpret the words of Bahá'u'lláh perfectly. If the Bahá'ís had questions, they must ask 'Abdu'l-Bahá. Bahíyyih Khánum understood that this also applied to her. No one knew better than she that obedience to 'Abdu'l-Bahá meant obedience to Bahá'u'lláh. To serve 'Abdu'l-Bahá was from now on her highest aspiration.

'Abdu'l-Bahá could entrust her with the greatest secrets. When the coffin containing the remains of the Báb arrived in the Holy Land, the Shrine for the Báb had still to be built. It was ten years before the Báb could be interred there. For some of that time the coffin was kept in Bahíyyih Khánum's room.

She it was who helped 'Abdu'l-Bahá during the war to

distribute the corn, which He had had grown, fairly among the people. She was also the hostess when pilgrims came to visit. Wherever they came from, they felt as much at ease as if they were in their own homes. Thus she served 'Abdu'l-Bahá with complete dedication, year in, year out, every single day until the end of His life.

As Bahá'u'lláh had done, 'Abdu'l-Bahá had also written His Will and Testament. This also indicated who was to lead the Faith after Him: Shoghi Effendi, His eldest grandson. Shoghi Effendi was only 24 when 'Abdu'l-Bahá passed away.

He was studying at Oxford. The sudden death of his beloved Grandfather was an incredibly great blow to him. He was called back to the Holy Land, since the Will and Testament could only be read if he was present. This said that he was to be the Head of the Faith. He had never expected this. It was a fearfully heavy burden to be placed on his young shoulders. The burden became even heavier because some members of his own family did not want to obey the Will. Just as had happened on the ascension of Bahá'u'lláh. It was so difficult for Shoghi Effendi that for three short periods he had to hand over the leadership of the Faith to someone else. Bahíyyih Khánum, his 75-year-old great-aunt, was the only one on whom he could rely. During those periods when he had to go away to Switzerland to regain his health, she acted as Head of the Faith. She wrote letters calling upon the Bahá'ís to be united and to be obedient to the Will and Testament of 'Abdu'l-Bahá. Everywhere, the Bahá'ís, with only a few exceptions, remained loyal to the Covenant. They accepted Shoghi Effendi as Guardian of the Faith.

Bahíyyih Khánum was the only member of the Holy Family who had remained faithful in every respect to the Will and Testament of 'Abdu'l-Bahá. She was always a great support to Shoghi Effendi. All the difficult decisions he had to make were first discussed with her. Her support for him was unconditional. After all, that was the will of 'Abdu'l-Bahá.

Bahíyyih Khánum lived to a great age – 86 years old. In every Faith there is a woman who stands out above all other women. For the Faith of the Báb this was Ṭáhirih. Bahá'u'lláh conferred on Bahíyyih Khánum this highest station among Bahá'í women. He gave her the title 'Greatest Holy Leaf'. Shoghi Effendi called her the most remarkable and impressive heroine of the Faith.

When you speak of a heroine, you think of someone who has done brave and noble deeds. She is famous and admired by many people. Bahíyyih Khánum was a heroine in a different way. There are very few who have suffered as much as she did. She nearly always kept herself in the background. She was always ready to help others who needed it. She comforted those who wanted comforting. For most of her life she was a refugee and could not act freely. She did not live in a fine palace and wore no expensive clothes, as queens do. Nor had she any hosts of servants around her. She was the one who served.

But in future, when all those queens in their fine palaces and expensive clothes have long been forgotten, Bahíyyih Khánum will live on in people's memories. For centuries, millions will flock in reverence to her grave on Mount Carmel, close by the Seat of the Universal House of Justice. And millions will take her way of life as the example for their own lives.

What did Bahíyyih Khánum herself think of the life she had had? She told the story of her life to Lady Blomfield. When she spoke about her mother, how she had to suffer on the journey from Teheran to Baghdad, the tears sprang to Lady Blomfield's eyes. Bahíyyih Khánum said, 'This time is very sad, Laydee, I shall make you grieve if I tell of it.'

'Oh, I want to be with you in my heart through all your sadness, dearest Khánum,' said Lady Blomfield.

Bahíyyih Khánum replied that her life had been all sorrow. But she said at once, 'But sorrow is really joy, when suffered in the path of God!'

That is what Bahíyyih Khánum herself said about her life.

# 63

## 'Abdu'l-Bahá's Last Days

'I seemed', said 'Abdu'l-Bahá when He was telling His family about the dream, 'to be standing within a great mosque, in the inmost shrine, facing the Qiblih, in the place of the Imám himself. I became aware that a large number of people were flocking into the mosque. More and yet more crowded in, taking their places in rows behind Me, until there was a vast multitude. As I stood I raised loudly the call to prayer. Suddenly

the thought came to Me to go forth from the mosque. When I found Myself outside I said within Myself, "For what reason came I forth, not having led the prayer? But it matters not; now that I have uttered the Call to prayer, the vast multitude will of themselves chant the prayer." '

He had another dream which was a little like the previous one. He had a room for Himself in the garden. He dreamed that Bahá'u'lláh had come to Him and said that He must destroy this room. The family were glad when they heard about this dream. Now at least He would sleep in the house which they had been trying to get Him to do for a while. They said, 'Yes, Master, we think your dream means that you should leave that room and come into the house.' When 'Abdu'l-Bahá heard that He smiled as if He did not agree with the family's interpretation of His dream. He did not explain the dream either, for which He had His own reasons, of course.

'Abdu'l-Bahá was weary. He knew that His end was near. He spoke of it to His gardener, Ismá'íl-Áqá. He told him about the last days of Bahá'u'lláh. 'Abdu'l-Bahá had been collecting Bahá'u'lláh's papers which were strewn about His room, when Bahá'u'lláh said to Him, 'It is of no use to gather them, I must leave them and flee away.' 'I also have finished my work,' said 'Abdu'l-Bahá to His gardener. 'I can do nothing more. Therefore must I leave it, and take My departure.'

On the last Friday of His life He went, even though He was so tired, to attend the noonday prayer at the mosque. Outside the mosque, the poor were waiting for Him as usual. They were expecting to receive alms from Him. He gave something to each of them. That day, He dictated some more Tablets. They were the last He revealed. He also blessed the marriage of one faithful servant in the family household. He insisted that the marriage should take place that day. In the evening,

He attended the usual meeting of the friends at His home.

On the Saturday He had a fever. And He was cold. He asked for a fur coat, to help Him to get warm. This was the coat which had formerly belonged to Bahá'u'lláh, a coat of which 'Abdu'l-Bahá was very fond. He went back to bed and asked to be well covered up. He was still feeling cold and had not been able to sleep that night because He was so cold. His fever lasted the whole day.

On Sunday He felt much better. The fever had gone. In the morning He took tea as usual with His family. In the afternoon there was a celebration at the Shrine of the Báb in honour of the Day of the Covenant. This feast was being offered by a pilgrim from India. 'Abdu'l-Bahá sent His family to attend it. He Himself could no longer do so. He received some visitors at His home that day, including the Mayor of Haifa. Later in the afternoon His sons-in-law returned from the commemoration at the Shrine. They told 'Abdu'l-Bahá that the pilgrim who had given the feast had been disappointed that He was not there.

He replied, 'But I was there, though my body was absent, my spirit was there in your midst. I was present with the friends at the Tomb. The friends must not attach any importance to the absence of my body. In spirit I am, and shall always be, with the friends, even though I be far away.' Would the members of 'Abdu'l-Bahá's family have understood the deeper meaning of His words?

In the evening, He enquired after the health of everyone in the household, the pilgrims and the friends in Haifa. 'Very good, very good,' He said when He heard that no one was ill. At eight o'clock He went to bed. First, He had taken a little nourishment. He then said, 'I am quite well.' He told them all to go to bed. Two of His daughters stayed with Him. 'Abdu'l-Bahá had gone to sleep very calmly. He had no fever now. At quarter past one He awoke, got up and went to a table to get a drink of water. He was feeling warm and took off His outer night garment. He went back to bed and when His daughter Ruḥá Khánum came to Him, He was lying peacefully. He asked for the bed curtains to be lifted a little. He had difficulty breathing, and needed more air. They brought a little rosewater. He sat up in bed to drink it. He lay down again and when they offered Him some food, He said in a clear voice, 'You wish me to take some food, and I am going?'

He gave Ruḥá Khánum a beautiful look. His face was so calm and serene.

It was Monday, 28 November 1921, early in the morning, an hour and a half after midnight. Ruḥá Khánum thought He was asleep. But He was not sleeping. His spirit had flown up to its eternal home. 'Abdu'l-Bahá was no longer on this earth!

In the room which 'Abdu'l-Bahá had left after one of His dreams, a pilgrim from America was staying. He was a doctor. He was quickly sent for. He found that 'Abdu'l-Bahá's heart was no longer beating. The doctor could do nothing more.

In their great sorrow, the family began to realize the meaning of what 'Abdu'l-Bahá had said in the past weeks. 'Now it is finished! It is finished.' Then they had not understood exactly what He had meant. Neither did they understand the real meaning of His dreams. But would they have been able to bear knowing that He was so soon to leave them?

# 64

## The Funeral of 'Abdu'l-Bahá

Some of the Western pilgrims were standing round 'Abdu'l-Bahá's bed. They were speechless and bewildered. Was it true that He would never again open His eyes? Would He not open them to look at them? Would He not open His mouth to tell them that He was not dead? Other doctors had now arrived to see whether He had, in fact, died. His heart had ceased to beat. Not even they could do any more. The mosquito net over the bed was lowered; now the pilgrims could see Him no longer. They left the room. The door closed behind them.

Munírih Khánum, the wife of 'Abdu'l-Bahá, and Bahíyyih Khánum, His sister, comforted the pilgrims. Even though their own sorrow was much greater. The whole family was overwhelmed with sorrow. In addition, the funeral must now be arranged. Where should the beloved Master be buried? No directions had been given for this. There was an empty chamber in the Shrine of the Báb. Bahíyyih Khánum decided that His body should be laid to rest there. News of His passing must also be conveyed to the Bahá'ís. Bahíyyih Khánum sent telegrams to the friends in other parts of the world.

That Monday morning, the news of 'Abdu'l-Bahá's passing soon spread around Haifa and the surrounding area. It was like an earth tremor, it caused so much consternation. The whole city mourned Him. The poor and the outcast were saying to one another, 'What will happen to us now? Who will look after us now? We have been orphaned. What can we do now but go away and die?'

That afternoon all were informed that the funeral cortège would leave His house at nine o'clock next morning. Everyone was invited to join the cortège.

On the Tuesday morning there was a huge crowd of about ten thousand people on the street. It would be a funeral such as no one in the Holy Land had ever seen. So many different people with such varied backgrounds. People from all sections of the population and of many religions were in attendance. The governors of Jerusalem and Phoenicia were there. The most senior representative of the British government had come by night on a special train from Jerusalem. There were people from the neighbouring countries and from Europe and America. All these different people were united in their sorrow at the loss of their Beloved. And they were all filled with gratitude for the fact that He had lived on this earth.

Slowly, the cortège with all these people wended its way up the mountainside. Precious Persian rugs covered the coffin. Many people kissed the coffin, which was carried by men who took it in turns to relieve one another. From a distance, it looked as if the coffin was being borne by invisible hands above the heads of the people. It was a sunny, cloudless day. On the official buildings in Haifa the flags were flown at half-mast. The city was silent. Only the Muslim call to prayer from the funeral cortège and the moving sobs and laments of the people could be heard. The poor, in particular, mourned the loss of their Friend. He had clothed and fed them and their children. During the war He had kept them from starvation. He had so often listened to their problems. With one voice they lamented, 'O God, my God! Our Father has left us! Our Father has left us!'

It took an hour and a half for the cortège to reach the Shrine of the Báb. The coffin was placed on a table covered in a white linen cloth. There were nine speakers: Christians, Jews, Muslims – they all spoke words of praise for ʿAbdu'l-Bahá. He had advanced the unity of religions. They praised Him for His knowledge and wisdom. He had guided the people. They spoke of His charity and generosity. Who was now to look after the poor and feed them? He had sacrificed Himself for others. They were full of praise for the nobility of His character.

A leading Jewish figure in Haifa said, 'As to his life, it was the living example of self-sacrifice, preferring the good and the welfare of others to his own . . . ʿAbdu'l-Bahá, and before him Baháʼu'lláh, have carried on their shoulders this glorious work – the establishment of universal peace . . .'

ʿAbdu'l-Bahá was praised so much that the Baháʼís needed to add nothing more.

After the eulogies, the coffin containing the body of ʿAbdu'l-Bahá was lowered into the empty chamber in the Shrine. Next to the chamber containing the remains of the Báb.

There were reporters from many countries present at the funeral. Articles about ʿAbdu'l-Bahá appeared in newspapers in many countries including in Europe, America, Egypt and India. Everywhere great appreciation for Him was expressed. From all parts of the world telegrams arrived conveying sympathy to the Holy Family.

For seven days after the passing, between fifty and a hundred poor people were given food at the house of ʿAbdu'l-Bahá. At the same spot where He had given them their weekly alms. On the seventh day, corn was distributed to about one thousand poor people, the people whose protector ʿAbdu'l-Bahá had been for so long. On the fortieth day after His passing, a banquet was given to over six hundred people from Haifa, ʿAkká and the surrounding places. The tables were decorated with purple and white flowers and bowls of golden oranges from 'Abdu'l-Bahá's own garden. There were no places of honour, just as in 'Abdu'l-Bahá's house. The guests were all equally welcome.

'Abdu'l-Bahá was no longer on this earth. But what had He said to His family on His last day? 'But I was there, though my body was absent, my spirit was there in your midst. I was present with the friends at the Tomb. The friends must not attach any importance to the absence of my body. In spirit I am, and shall always be, with the friends, even though I be far away.'

He had so often said or written to the Bahá'ís that He would always be with them. Whether He was in this world or in the next. When He said goodbye to the friends in Germany, He had also said that His heart and soul would always be with them. And to the pilgrims He had once said on their departure, 'I am with you always, whether living or dead, I am with you to the end.'

Do you remember Martha Root, 'Abdu'l-Bahá's ambassadress? She was the one who travelled four times around the world to spread the Faith. Some years after the passing of 'Abdu'l-Bahá she was on pilgrimage in the Holy Land. She had entered, with other pilgrims, the antechamber to the tomb of 'Abdu'l-Bahá. The other pilgrims laid their foreheads on the threshold of His tomb. At that moment Martha Root saw 'Abdu'l-Bahá standing beside the pilgrims. She heard Him say, 'Be happy! Be happy! Be happy!' And He said they could always be in contact with Him by reciting 'Yá Bahá'u'l-Abhá'.

And again He spoke the words, 'Remember I am with you always, whether living or dead, I am with you to the end.'

Will the other pilgrims who laid their foreheads on the threshold of 'Abdu'l-Bahá's tomb have noticed that He was so close to them?

# 65

## 'I am waiting, I am patiently waiting'

The Bahá'ís were very, very sad because 'Abdu'l-Bahá was not there any more. They had known that day would come. They had not dared to think then that it would ever happen. Now it was all past. To whom could they now bring their problems or who could answer their questions? How was the Faith to be guided now? Some were worried about this. That was understandable, because Mírzá Muḥammad-'Alí was sending letters far and wide saying that he was 'Abdu'l-Bahá's successor. He pointed out that in the Will and Testament of Bahá'u'lláh it said, 'Verily God hath ordained the station of the Greater Branch to be beneath that of the Most Mighty Branch.' Mírzá Muḥammad-'Alí was the Greater Branch and 'Abdu'l-Bahá the Most Mighty Branch. In another Tablet, Bahá'u'lláh wrote that the members of the Holy Family could only be regarded as branches if they remained faithful in every respect to the Faith. Could this be said of Mírzá Muḥammad-'Alí? Had he not for thirty years been breaking the Covenant?

'Abdu'l-Bahá had given His Will and Testament to Bahíyyih Khánum to keep. It was in safe hands there. And that was a good thing! For if the Covenant-breakers could get their hands on it, they would destroy it. Or perhaps falsify it.

The Will and Testament could not be opened or read until Shoghi Effendi, 'Abdu'l-Bahá's eldest grandson, was present. When he heard in London of the passing of 'Abdu'l-Bahá, it was an incredibly heavy blow to him. He was completely

overcome, so much so that he had to stay in bed for the first few days. He could not possibly travel at once. It was a month before he reached Haifa. Then the seal was broken on the Will and Testament and it was read first to him alone. It was a great shock to him. 'Abdu'l-Bahá had appointed him to be Guardian of the Faith. Shoghi Effendi knew what a tremendously heavy burden had been laid upon his shoulders. He was still a young man of twenty-four – and then to have to carry such a great responsibility. Especially since he was still so upset by the passing of 'Abdu'l-Bahá.

A few days later the Will and Testament was read to nine persons, mainly the older members of the Holy Family. On the fortieth day after the passing of 'Abdu'l-Bahá it was read to a group of Bahá'ís from various countries. After this, Bahíyyih Khánum sent telegrams, announcing to the Bahá'ís in other parts of the world that Shoghi Effendi had been appointed as Guardian of the Faith. The news was welcomed joyfully by the friends everywhere.

'Abdu'l-Bahá had written His Will and Testament before His journey to America. It is in three parts, each part having been written at a time when He was in great danger. Every time, Mírzá Muḥammad-'Alí and his accomplices had been the cause. After writing the first part, things were so bad that it had to be buried in order to keep it safe. In the second part 'Abdu'l-Bahá even wrote, 'O dearly beloved friends! I am now in very great danger and the hope of even an hour's life is lost to me. I am thus constrained to write these lines for the protection of the Cause of God, the preservation of His Law, the safeguarding of His Word, and the safety of His Teachings.'

'Abdu'l-Bahá describes in His Will and Testament how Mírzá Muḥammad-'Alí had always shown the greatest hostility towards Him, and calls him a highly unjust man, the Centre of Sedition and initiator of wrongdoing. He lists thirteen of his misdeeds. One of these was the falsifying of the holy text. Another was falsely denouncing 'Abdu'l-Bahá Himself. For instance when the Shrine of the Báb was being built, Mírzá Muḥammad-'Alí sent a report to the government that 'Abdu'l-Bahá was building a fortress and wanted to overthrow the government. He also accused the Bahá'ís and had some of them thrown into prison. Mírzá Muḥammad-'Alí did all these things because he wanted to be the Head of the Faith. But he not only harmed himself by all his wicked deeds but also caused others to be confused and poisoned. Could such a man ever head the Faith? Could the holy texts, in their pure form and without being tampered with, then be passed on to future generations?

What had 'Abdu'l-Bahá written in His Will and Testament about Shoghi Effendi? He called him 'the primal branch of the Divine and Sacred Lote-Tree, grown out . . . from the Twin Holy Trees'. By this He meant that Shoghi Effendi was a descendant of the two Holy Families: through His Father He was a descendant of the family of the Báb and through His mother a descendant of Bahá'u'lláh. 'Abdu'l-Bahá says that he is 'the sign of God, the chosen branch, the guardian of the Cause of God'. 'Abdu'l-Bahá wrote that after His passing all must turn to Shoghi Effendi. This applied to all the members of Bahá'u'lláh's family, all the members of the Báb's family, the Hands of the Cause of God and His loved ones. Shoghi Effendi is the interpreter of the Word of God. Whoever opposes him has opposed God. Whoever disbelieves in him, has not believed in God.

'Abdu'l-Bahá wrote in His Will and Testament about the Universal House of Justice. Its members must be chosen by the National Houses of Justice. Today, we still call them the National Spiritual Assemblies. Shoghi Effendi and the Universal House of Justice are both under the protection of the Báb and Bahá'u'lláh.

Through the Will and Testament of Bahá'u'lláh the unity of the Faith is safeguarded because 'Abdu'l-Bahá was appointed as the Centre of the Covenant.

Through the Will and Testament of 'Abdu'l-Bahá the unity of the Faith is maintained by Shoghi Effendi and the Universal House of Justice. The Will and Testament of 'Abdu'l-Bahá is extremely important to the unity of the Faith. So important that it may be a long time before we really become aware of how important it is.

Now 'Abdu'l-Bahá is no longer on this earth. In His Will and Testament He outlined how the Faith should be guided from then on. He also wrote there: 'It is incumbent upon everyone to show the utmost love, rectitude of conduct, straightforwardness and sincere kindliness unto all the peoples and kindreds of the world, be they friends or strangers. So intense must be the spirit of love and loving kindness, that the stranger may find himself a friend, the enemy a true brother . . .'

A call to love and unity. Had 'Abdu'l-Bahá not been doing that all His life? For example when He returned from America. He was then so weakened that many thought He had only a short time left to live. Then He wrote the following words to the Bahá'ís of the East and West:

Friends! The time is coming when I shall be no longer with you. I have done all that could be done. I have served the Cause of Bahá'u'lláh to the utmost of my ability. I have laboured night and day, all the years of My life. O how I long to see the loved ones

311

taking upon themselves the responsibilities of the Cause! . . . I am straining my ears toward the East and toward the West, toward the North and toward the South that haply I may hear the songs of love and fellowship chanted in the meetings of the faithful. My days are numbered and, but for this, there is no joy left unto me . . .

Ah me, I am waiting, waiting, to hear the joyful tidings that the believers are the very embodiment of sincerity and truthfulness, the incarnation of love and amity, the living symbols of unity and concord. Will they not gladden my heart? Will they not satisfy my yearning? Will they not manifest my wish? Will they not fulfil my heart's desire? Will they not give ear to my call?

I am waiting, I am patiently waiting.

# DATES AND EVENTS

The chapters in which these events are described are shown by the numbers in brackets.

| | |
|---|---|
| 1844 | 22/23 May: The Báb reveals Himself to His first disciple; 'Abdu'l-Bahá is born on the same night |
| 1846 | Birth year of Bahíyyih Khánum |
| 1848 | Birth year of Mírzá Mihdí |
| 1850 | 9 July: Martyrdom of the Báb (2) |
| 1852 | 15 August: Attempt on the life of Náṣiri'd-Dín Sháh. Bahá'u'lláh is imprisoned shortly afterwards in the Síyáh-Chál (3) |
| 1853 | January–March: Journey of the Holy Family from Teheran to Baghdad (4) |
| 1854 | 10 April: Bahá'u'lláh retires to the desert of Kurdistan until 19 March 1856(5) |
| ca. 1860 | Mírzá Mihdí is brought from Teheran to Baghdad |
| 1863 | April: Declaration of Bahá'u'lláh in the Garden of Riḍván (7) |
| 1863 | May–August: Journey from Baghdad to Istanbul (Constantinople) (7) |
| 1863 | December: Journey from Istanbul to Edirne (Adrianople) (8) |
| 1867 | September: Mírzá Yaḥyá is separated from the Holy Family and the Bahá'ís (8) |

313

| 1867–68 | Bahá'u'lláh reveals the Tablet of the Branch in Adrianople (8) |
| 1868 | August: Arrival of the Holy Family in the prison city of 'Akká. Mírzá Yaḥyá is banished to Cyprus (9,61) |
| 1870 | 23 June: Mírzá Mihdí dies after an accident (9) |
| 1870 | October: Bahá'u'lláh moves from the prison to a house in 'Akká (9) |
| 1872 | January: Murder of three Covenant-breakers in 'Akká (9) |
| 1873 | March: Marriage of 'Abdu'l-Bahá and Munírih Khánum (10, 11) |
| 1876 | Sulṭán 'Abdu'l-Azíz is dethroned and assassinated. Mírzá Abu'l-Faḍl becomes a Bahá'í (53) |
| 1877 | June: Bahá'u'lláh moves to Mazra'ih (12) |
| 1879 | September: Bahá'u'lláh moves to the Mansion of Bahjí (13) |
| 1889 | Ḥájí Muḥammad Riḍá is killed in 'Ishqábád; through the intervention of the Bahá'ís the murderer is not executed (25) |
| 1891 | Bahá'u'lláh shows 'Abdu'l-Bahá the place where the Shrine of the Báb is to be built (30) |
| 1892 | 29 May: Ascension of Bahá'u'lláh (14) |
| 1892 | December: Ibráhím Khayru'lláh leaves for America. (16) |
| 1894 | The first Americans become Bahá'ís (16) |
| 1896 | May: Assassination of Náṣiri'd-Dín Sháh; Varqá and Rúḥu'lláh are killed (17,18,19) |
| 1898 | 10 December: The first Western pilgrims visit 'Abdu'l-Bahá (20) |
| 1899 | The remains of the Báb arrive in the Holy Land (30) |
| 1899 ca. | Feb/March: 'Abdu'l-Bahá lays the first stone of the Shrine of the Báb (21,30) |
| ca. 1899 | Ali Kuli Khan, 'Abdu'l-Bahá's best translator, arrives in the Holy Land (22) |

| | |
|---|---|
| 1900 | Spring: Ibráhím <u>Kh</u>ayru'lláh severs his connection with the Faith (21) |
| 1901 | Summer: Thomas Breakwell declares his faith in Paris (23) |
| 1901 | August: Mírzá 'Abu'l-Faḍl arrives in America (54) |
| 1901 | 20 August: The order that 'Abdu'l-Bahá and His family must not leave 'Akká is again enforced (24) |
| 1901–08 | 'Abdu'l-Bahá writes His Will and Testament in three parts (65) |
| 1902 | 13 June: Thomas Breakwell dies of tuberculosis (23) |
| 1902 | November: The first stone is laid for the temple in 'Ishqábád (25) |
| 1903 | 7 March: The Assembly of the Bahá'ís of Chicago asks 'Abdu'l-Bahá for permission to build a temple (37) |
| 1904–05 | 'Abdu'l-Bahá is again troubled by Mírzá Muḥammad-'Alí's false accusations (24) |
| 1904–06 | Laura Clifford Barney puts her questions to 'Abdu'l-Bahá. His replies are collected in the book *Some Answered Questions*(26) |
| 1908 | July: 'Abdu'l-Bahá is freed after the Young Turk Revolution (28) |
| 1909–21 | March: The remains of the Báb are laid to rest in the Shrine on Mount Carmel. (30) In America the Bahá'ís decide to build the temple (37) |
| 1909 | Sulṭán 'Abdu'l-Ḥamíd is dethroned (28) |
| ca. 1909–10 | The family of 'Abdu'l-Bahá moves from 'Akká to Haifa (29) |
| 1910 | August: 'Abdu'l-Bahá leaves for Egypt (31) |
| 1911 | August–December: 'Abdu'l-Bahá's first journey to London and Paris. 'Abdu'l-Bahá's talks in Paris are collected in *Paris Talks*. (31–33) |

| | |
|---|---|
| 1912 | 25 March: 'Abdu'l-Bahá leaves Egypt on the *Cedric* for America (34) |
| | 11 April: Arrival of 'Abdu'l-Bahá in New York (35,49) |
| | 14 April: Sinking of the *Titanic* (34) |
| | 1 May: 'Abdu'l-Bahá lays the first stone for the Chicago temple (37) |
| | 5 May: 'Abdu'l-Bahá meets the children of Chicago (38) |
| | 19 June: The Tablet of the Branch is read in America; New York is named the City of the Covenant (39) |
| | 29 June: 'Abdu'l-Bahá gives a Unity Feast (41) |
| | August: Fred Mortensen comes to see 'Abdu'l-Bahá (42) |
| | 15 September: 'Abdu'l-Bahá and His companions miss the train which later crashes (44) |
| | 30 September: Thornton Chase, the first American Bahá'í, dies (46) |
| | 1–25 October: 'Abdu'l-Bahá visits California (44,46) |
| | 12 October: 'Abdu'l-Bahá speaks at the Synagogue in San Francisco (45) |
| | 19 October: 'Abdu'l-Bahá visits the grave of the first American Bahá'í (46) |
| | 24 November: White Bahá'ís serve black Bahá'ís at dinner (47) |
| | 5 December: 'Abdu'l-Bahá leaves New York on the *Celtic* (50) |
| | 13 December: 'Abdu'l-Bahá arrives in England (50) |
| 1913 | 21 January: 'Abdu'l-Bahá arrives in Paris (51) |
| | 30 March–1 May: 'Abdu'l-Bahá visits Germany, Austria and Hungary, and then returns to Paris (51) |
| | 13 June: 'Abdu'l-Bahá leaves France for Egypt (51) |
| | 5 December: 'Abdu'l-Bahá returns to the Holy Land (51) |
| 1913–14 | Lua and Edward Getsinger travel through India (40) |
| 1914–18 | First World War (55,57) |

| | |
|---|---|
| 1914 | 21 January: Mírzá Abu'l-Faḍl dies in Cairo (54) |
| | 29 June: 'Abdu'l-Bahá orders the pilgrims to leave the Holy Land (55) |
| | November: Bahá'ís flee from 'Akká and Haifa to Abu-Sinán (55) |
| 1915 | May: Bahá'ís return to 'Akká and Haifa (55) |
| ca. 1915–16 | Famine in Haifa, 'Akká and surrounding areas due to plagues of locusts (55) |
| 1916 | March/April: 'Abdu'l-Bahá reveals eight of the Tablets of the Divine Plan (57) |
| | 1 May: Lua Getsinger dies in Cairo (40) |
| 1917 | February/March: 'Abdu'l-Bahá reveals the remaining six Tablets of the Divine Plan (57) |
| 1918 | 23 September: The British Army takes Haifa. 'Abdu'l-Bahá is no longer in danger (56) |
| 1919 | April: All fourteen letters of the Tablets of the Divine Plan are read and discussed during the National Convention in America (58) |
| | 17 December: 'Abdu'l-Bahá reveals the Tablet to The Hague. (59) |
| 1920 | 27 April: 'Abdu'l-Bahá is knighted by the British government (60) |
| 1921 | 28 November: Passing of 'Abdu'l-Bahá (63) |
| 1922 | January: The Will and Testament of 'Abdu'l-Bahá is read to the Bahá'ís; Shoghi Effendi is appointed as Guardian of the Faith (65) |
| 1926 | 30 January: Martha Root's first visit to Queen Marie of Romania (58) |
| 1932 | 15 July: Bahíyyih Khánum, the Greatest Holy Leaf, dies (62) |
| 1939 | 28 September: Martha Root dies in the Hawaiian Islands (58) |

| | |
|---|---|
| 1945 | 51 countries sign the Charter of the United Nations in San Francisco (46) |
| 1948 | The temple in 'Ishqábád is badly damaged by an earthquake (25) |
| 1953 | 2 May: Dedication of the temple in America (37) |
| 1963 | April: The Universal House of Justice is elected for the first time (65). World Congress in London. |
| | The temple in 'Ishqábád is demolished (25) |
| 1992 | November: 27,000 Bahá'ís take part in the 2nd World Congress in New York, the City of the Covenant (39) |

# Bibliography

'Abdu'l-Bahá. *'Abdu'l-Bahá in London: Addresses and Notes of Conversations* (1912). London: Bahá'í Publishing Trust, 1982.

— *Memorials of the Faithful* (1915). Translated by Marzieh Gail. Wilmette, IL: Bahá'í Publishing Trust, 1971.

— *Paris Talks: Addresses given by 'Abdu'l-Bahá in Paris* 1911–1912. London: Bahá'í Publishing Trust, 12th edn. 1995.

— *The Promulgation of Universal Peace: Talks Delivered by 'Abdu'l-Bahá during His Visit to the United States and Canada in* 1912. Comp. Howard MacNutt. Wilmette, IL: Bahá'í Publishing Trust, 2nd edn. 1982.

— *Selections from the Writings of 'Abdu'l-Bahá.* Comp. Research Department of The Universal House of Justice. Translated by a Committee at the Bahá'í World Centre and by Marzieh Gail. Haifa: Bahá'í World Centre, 1978.

— *Tablets of the Divine Plan.* Wilmette, IL: Bahá'í Publishing Trust, 1977.

— *Will and Testament.* Wilmette, IL: Bahá'í Publishing Trust, 1944.

Abu'l-Faḍl, Mírzá. *The Bahá'í Proofs (Ḥujaja'l-Bahíyyih) and A Short Sketch of the History and Lives of the Leaders of This Religion* (1902). Translated by Ali-Kuli Khan. Wilmette, IL: Bahá'í Publishing Trust, 1983, facsimile of the 3rd edition (1929).

— *Miracles and Metaphors* (1900). Trans. Juan Ricardo Cole. Los Angeles: Kalimát Press, 1981.

*Bahá'í World, The.* Vol. 7, 1936–1938; Vol. 8, 1938–1940; Vol. 12, 1950–1954; Wilmette, IL: Bahá'í Publishing Trust, various years. Vol. 13, 1954–1963. Haifa: The Universal House of Justice, 1970.

Bahá'u'lláh. *The Hidden Words.* Translated by Shoghi Effendi. Wilmette, IL: Bahá'í Publishing Trust, 1985.

— *The Kitáb-i-Aqdas: The Most Holy Book.* Haifa: Bahá'í World Centre, 1992.

— *Tablets of Bahá'u'lláh Revealed after the Kitáb-i-Aqdas*. Comp. Research Department. Translated by Habib Taherzadeh et al. Wilmette, IL: Bahá'í Publishing Trust, 2nd edn. 1978.

Balyuzi, H. M. *'Abdu'l-Bahá*. Oxford: George Ronald, 1971.

— *Bahá'u'lláh, the King of Glory*. Oxford: George Ronald, 2nd edn. 1991.

— *Eminent Bahá'ís in the Time of Bahá'u'lláh*. Oxford: George Ronald, 1985.

The Bible. Authorized Version.

Blomfield, Lady. *The Chosen Highway*. London: Bahá'í Publishing Trust, [1940]. RP Oxford: George Ronald, 2007.

Braun, Eunice; Chance, Hugh. E. *A Crown of Beauty: The Bahá'í Faith and the Holy Land*. Oxford: George Ronald, 1982.

Brown, Ramona Allen. *Memories of 'Abdu'l-Bahá: Recollections of the Early Days of the Bahá'í Faith in California*. Wilmette, IL: Bahá'í Publishing Trust, 1980.

Esslemont, J. E. *Bahá'u'lláh and the New Era* (1921). Wilmette, IL: Bahá'í Publishing Trust, 5th rev. edn. 1980.

Gail, Marzieh. *The Sheltering Branch*. Oxford: George Ronald, 1968.

— *Summon Up Remembrance*. Oxford: George Ronald, 1987.

Garis, M. R. *Martha Root: Lioness at the Threshold*. Wilmette, IL: Bahá'í Publishing Trust, 1983.

Gollmer, U. *Mein Herz ist bei euch: Abdu'l-Bahá in Deutschland*. Hofheim-Langenhain: Bahá'í-Verlag, 1988.

Harper, Barron Deems. *Lights of Fortitude*. Oxford: George Ronald, rev. edn. 2007.

Hofman, David. *A Commentary on the Will and Testament of 'Abdu'l-Bahá*. Oxford: George Ronald, rev. edn. 1982.

Honnold, Annamarie (ed.). *Vignettes from the Life of 'Abdu'l-Bahá*. Oxford: George Ronald, rev. edn. 1991.

*In His Presence: Visits to 'Abdu'l-Bahá*. Memoirs of Roy Wilhelm, Stanwood Cobb, Genevieve L. Coy. Los Angeles: Kalimát Press, 1989.

Ives, Howard Colby. *Portals to Freedom* (1937). Oxford: George Ronald, 1983.

Maude, Roderic; Maude, Derwent. *The Servant, The General and Armageddon: The True Story of an Epic Adventure in the Footsteps of Prophecy*. Oxford: George Ronald, 1998.

Maxwell, May. *An Early Pilgrimage* (1917). Oxford: George Ronald, 1969.

Metelmann, Velda Piff. *Lua Getsinger: Herald of the Covenant.* Oxford: George Ronald: 1997.

Morrison, Gayle. *To Move the World: Louis G. Gregory and the Advancement of Racial Unity in America*. Wilmette, IL: Bahá'í Publishing Trust, 1982.

*The Mystery of God*. Comp. Írán Furútan Muhajír. London: Bahá'í Publishing Trust, rev. edn. 1979.

Nabíl-i-A'zam. *The Dawn-Breakers: Nabíl's Narrative of the Early Days of the Bahá'í Revelation*. Translated by Shoghi Effendi. New York: Bahá'í Publishing Committee, 1932.

Phelps, Myron. H. *The Master in 'Akká*. Revised and annotated. Los Angeles: Kalimát Press, 1992.

Rabbani, Rúḥíyyih. *The Priceless Pearl*. London: Bahá'í Publishing Trust, 1969.

Ruhe, David S. *Door of Hope: The Bahá'í Faith in the Holy Land*. Oxford: George Ronald, 2nd rev. edn. 2001.

Rutstein, Nathan. *Corinne True: Faithful Handmaid of 'Abdu'l-Bahá*. With the assistance of Edna True. George Ronald: Oxford, 1987.

Shoghi Effendi. *The Advent of Divine Justice*. Wilmette, IL: Bahá'í Publishing Trust, 1974.

— *God Passes By*. Wilmette, IL: Bahá'í Publishing Trust, 1944.

— *Messages to the Bahá'í World* 1950-1957. Wilmette, IL: Bahá'í Publishing Trust, 1971.

— *The World Order of Bahá'u'lláh*. Wilmette, IL: Bahá'í Publishing Trust, 1991.

— and Lady Blomfield. *The Passing of 'Abdu'l-Bahá*. Stuttgart: Wilhelm Heppeler, 1922.

*Star of the West* (8 vols.). Chicago: Bahá'í News Service, 1910–1935. Oxford: George Ronald. Reprinted 1978 and 1984.

Stockman, Robert H. *The Bahá'í Faith in America*. Vol. 1: *Origins, 1892–1900*. Wilmette, IL: Bahá'í Publishing Trust, 1985. Vol. 2: *Early Expansion, 1900–1912*. Oxford: George Ronald, 1995.

Taherzadeh, Adib. *The Covenant of Bahá'u'lláh*. Oxford: George Ronald, 1992.

— *The Revelation of Bahá'u'lláh*. Four volumes. Vol. 1: *Baghdád* 1853-63; Vol. 2: *Adrianople* 1863-38; Vol. 3: *'Akká, The Early Years* 1868-77; Vol. 4: *Mazra'ih and Bahjí*, 1877-92. Oxford: George Ronald, 1974-1988.

Thompson, Juliet. *The Diary of Juliet Thompson*. Los Angeles: Kalimát Press, 1983.

Ward, Allan L. *239 Days: 'Abdu'l-Bahá's Journey in America*. Wilmette, IL: Bahá'í Publishing Trust, 1979.

Whitehead, O. Z. *Some Early Bahá'ís of the West*. Oxford: George Ronald, 1983.

Whitmore, Bruce. *The Dawning Place*. Wilmette, IL: Bahá'í Publishing Trust, 1984.

*World Order*. A Magazine. National Spiritual Assembly of the United States. Various years.

Yazdi, Ali M. *Blessings Beyond Measure: Recollections of 'Abdu'l-Bahá and Shoghi Effendi*. Wilmette, IL: Bahá'í Publishing Trust, 1988.

Zarqání, Mahmúd. *Mahmúd's Diary: The Diary of Mírzá Mahmúd-i-Zarqání Chronicling 'Abdu'l-Bahá's Journey to America*. Translated by Mohi Sobhani with the assistance of Shirley Macias. George Ronald: Oxford, 1998.

# References

Page

2    'turn your faces . . .' : Bahá'u'lláh, Kitáb-i-Aqdas, v. 121.

2    'The object of this sacred verse . . .': Bahá'u'lláh, Kitáb-i-'Ahd, in *Tablets*, p. 221; see also Kitáb-i-Aqdas, note 145.

4    'We shall walk together . . .': quoted in Nabíl, *Dawn-Breakers*, p. 441.

7    ' . . . else, some day, he may give himself away': *Star of the West*, Vol. XIII, no. 10 (January, 1923), p. 272. See also Honnold, *Vignettes*, no. 40, p. 69.

8    'O Siyyid, this is not the time . . .': quoted in Blomfield, *Chosen Highway*, p. 22. See also Balyuzi, *King of Glory*, p. 64.

10    'The master, the master . . . : quoted in Blomfield, *Chosen Highway*, pp. 40–41.

12    'The little Bábi is fast pursuing us . . .': quoted in Nabíl, *Dawn-Breakers*, p. 616.

13    'Do not bring Him in here': quoted in Balyuzi, *'Abdu'l-Bahá*, pp. 11–12.

24    'It is good to be a spreader of the Teachings . . .': story told by 'Abdu'l-Bahá in Stuttgart, Germany, 4 April 1913; quoted in *Star of the West*, Vol. IX, no. 18 (February 1919), p. 201; see also Honnold, *Vignettes*, p. 118.

24–5    'There was a man . . .': *Star of the West* and Honnold, ibid.

34    Tablet of the Branch: quoted in Shoghi Effendi, 'The Dispensation of Bahá'u'lláh', in *World Order of Bahá'u'lláh*, p. 135.

42    'My brother . . .': quoted in Nabíl, *Dawn-Breakers*, p. 208.

44    'Far be it, for I am not worthy . . .': paraphrased from 'Episodes in the life of Munírih Khánum', in *Bahá'í World*, Vol. 8, p. 262.

46    'We have brought you into the prison . . .': quoted in *Bahá'í*

|     | *World*, ibid., see also Taherzadeh, *Revelation of Bahá'u'lláh*, Vol. 2, pp. 208–9. |
| 47 | 'I have brought a most wonderful gift . . .': ibid. |
| 48 | 'Oh Munírih! Oh my leaf! . . .': quoted in Blomfield, *Chosen Highway*, p. 88. |
| 51 | 'Are you one of the prisoners . . .': quoted in Balyuzi, *'Abdu'l-Bahá*, p. 33. |
| 53 | 'The palace at Mazra'ih is ready . . .': quoted in Esslemont, *Bahá'u'lláh and the New Era*, chapter 3; see also Balyuzi, *Bahá'u'lláh, The King of Glory*, pp. 358–9. |
| 59 | 'Then why do you say . . .': based on the account by Balyuzi, *'Abdu'l-Bahá*, p. 44. |
| 60 | 'The Sun of Bahá has set': ibid. p. 47. |
| 61 | 'Earthly treasures We have not bequeathed': Bahá'u'lláh, Kitáb-i-'Ahd, in *Tablets*, p. 217. |
| 66 | 'The Will of the divine Testator is this . . .': ibid. p. 221. |
| 70 | 'God sent you here . . .': quoted in Stockman, *Bahá'í Faith in America*, Vol. 1, p. 119. |
| 73 | 'My son-in-law . . .': quoted in Balyuzi, *Eminent Bahá'ís*, p. 83. |
| 74 | 'What have you been doing today? . . .': paraphrased from Taherzadeh, *Revelation of Bahá'u'lláh*, Vol. 4, p. 58. |
| 76 | 'We tell them that God has manifested Himself . . .': paraphrased from Taherzadeh, ibid. pp. 59–60. |
| 78 | 'This child is insulting holy divines . . .': quoted in Balyuzi, *Eminent Bahá'ís*, p. 90. |
| 82 | 'Now you have finally done . . .': paraphrased from Balyuzi, ibid. p. 96. |
| 88 | 'Abul-Qásim does not want you . . .': quoted in Maxwell, *Early Pilgrimage*, pp. 33–4. |
| 87 | 'We could not go . . .': ibid. p. 15. |
| 89 | 'I say unto you . . .': ibid. p. 40. |
| 89 | 'I am with you always . . .': ibid. |
| 97 | 'You have suffered much on your wanderings. . .': quoted in Gail, *Summon Up Remembrance*, pp. 108–10 |
| 99 | 'Eat these grapes . . .': ibid. p. 126. |
| 100 | 'You have been thinking . . .': ibid. p. 135. |
| 101 | 'Christ has come again! . . .': quoted in Balyuzi, *'Abdu'l-Bahá*, p. 75. |

104   'Cable your resignation': ibid. p. 76.

104   'Have you heard? . . .': ibid. p. 78.

105   'Grieve thou not . . .': 'Abdu'l-Bahá, *Selections*, no. 158, p. 187.

116   'My home is the home of peace . . .': 'Abdu'l-Bahá, quoted in *Star of the West*, Vol. XII, no. 13, p. 214; see also Honnold, *Vignettes*, no. 61, p. 172.

119   'She returned quickly. . .': Ives, *Portals to Freedom*, p. 85.

119   'Do you remember . . .': paraphrased from Gail, *Sheltering Branch*, pp. 26–9.

121   'O Jews, you are in truth . . .': in 'Abdu'l-Bahá, 'Religious Prejudices', *Paris Talks*, pp. 37–8.

128   'The meaning of the dream . . .': quoted in Shoghi Effendi, *God Passes By*, p. 271.

131   'This is impossible . . .': 'Abdu'l-Bahá, 'The Imprisonment of 'Abdu'l-Bahá', *Paris Talks*, pp. 30–31.

138   'Every stone of that building . . .': quoted in Shoghi Effendi, *God Passes By*, p. 275.

145   'I haven't given anything . . .': paraphrased from Thompson, *Diary*, pp. 175–6.

147   'Have you an appointment? . . .': paraphrased from Blomfield, *Chosen Highway*, pp. 159–161 (words of 'Abdu'l-Bahá are quoted exactly).

151   'Be kind to the strangers . . .': 'Abdu'l-Bahá, 'The Duty of Kindness and Sympathy towards Strangers and Foreigners', *Paris Talks*, pp. 1–2.

151   'This is my home . . .': quoted in *Star of the West*, Vol. II, no. 14 (23 November 1911), p. 3.

153   'Oh, how glad I am . . .': story from Blomfield, *Chosen Highway*, p. 185.

157   'No, you must do that yourselves': quoted in Thompson, *Diary*, p. 177.

158   'No, we will go direct . . .': quoted in Zarqání, *Maḥmúd's Diary*, p. 10.

163   'When 'Abdu'l-Bahá arrives . . .': story in Ives, *Portals to Freedom*, pp. 27–33.

167   'I consider you my relatives . . .': quoted in Thompson, *Diary*, p. 257.

168   'Assuredly, give to the poor . . .': ibid. p. 266.

171     'Mashriqu'l-Adhkár . . .': quoted in Rutstein, *Corinne True*, p. 60; see also *Bahá'í World*, Vol. 13, p. 847.

171     'Make a beginning . . .': ibid. p. 61; ibid.

174     'The temple is already built': quoted in Whitmore, *Dawning Place*, p. 65; see also *Bahá'í World*, Vol. 7, p. 219.

175     'O people of the world! . . .': Bahá'u'lláh, Kitáb-i-Aqdas, verse 31.

177     'You are the children . . .': 'Abdu'l-Bahá, *Promulgation*, pp. 91–2 (5 May 1912).

180     'Whoso turneth towards Him . . .': Bahá'u'lláh, quoted in Shoghi Effendi, 'The Dispensation of Bahá'u'lláh', in *World Order of Bahá'u'lláh*, p. 135.

185     'I appoint you, Lua . . .': quoted in Thompson, *Diary*, p. 313.

187     'See, I have cured Lua . . .': ibid. p. 325.

190     'When I return . . .': 'Abdu'l-Bahá, *Promulgation*, p. 206 (20 June 1912).

191     'This is a new Day . . .': ibid. pp. 213–4 (29 June 1912).

193     'What are the new teachings . . .': quoted in Zarqání, *Mahmúd's Diary*, p. 151.

194     'Peace be with you . . .': quoted in Thompson, *Diary*, p. 324.

195–200 Story of Fred Mortensen paraphrased from his own account in *Star of the West*, Vol. XIV, no. 12 (March 1924), pp. 365–7; see also Balyuzi, *'Abdu'l-Bahá*, pp. 248–51; Zarqání, *Mahmúd's Diary*, p. 214 (words of 'Abdu'l-Bahá are quoted exactly).

203–5  'There was once a traveller . . .': paraphrased from Ives, *Portals to Freedom*, pp. 123–4.

206     'Oh, it matters not . . .': quoted in Zarqání, *Mahmúd's Diary*, p. 265.

210     'How nice to dine in this way . . .': ibid. p. 293 (paraphrase).

211–2  Story of Juanita Storch from *World Order* magazine, Fall 1993, p. 34.

212–5  For 'Abdu'l-Bahá's talk at Temple Emmanu-El, see *Promulgation*, pp. 361–70 (12 October 1912).

218     'Welcome, Mrs Allen . . .': quoted in Brown, *Memories*, p. 36.

221     'Know ye not . . .': Bahá'u'lláh, Hidden Words, Arabic no. 68.

224     'Where is Mr Gregory? . . .': quoted in *Bahá'í World*, Vol. 12, p. 668.

224–5  Story of black rose paraphrased from Ives, *Portals to Freedom*, pp. 64–5.

| 227 | 'It is now more than two years...': quoted in Zarqání, *Maḥmúd's Diary*, p. 359. |
|---|---|
| 230 | 'nor do we keep rubies...': quoted ibid. p. 415. |
| 235 | 'Look at that imperial wave...': quoted in *Star of the West*, Vol. III, no. 16 (31 December 1912), p. 2. |
| 238 | Story of the black bread and shrivelled apple from Blomfield, *Chosen Highway*, p. 161–2. |
| 239 | 'Five years...': story of 'Abdu'l-Bahá in Stuttgart from Gollmer, *Mein Herz ist bei euch*, pp. 19–22; see also *Star of the West*, Vol. IV, no. 9 (20 August 1913). |
| 241 | 'I have promised the doctor...': ibid. pp. 100–101. |
| 245 | 'You are all very old!...': quoted in Blomfield, *Chosen Highway*, p. 169. |
| 246 | 'Look at me...': quoted in *Star of the West*, Vol. IX, no. 14 (23 November 1918), p. 161; slightly different version in Blomfield, ibid. p. 177. |
| 248–53 | Story of Mírzá Abu'l-Faḍl from Taherzadeh, *Revelation*, Vol. 3, pp. 93–104; Vol. 2, pp. 219–20. |
| 255–7 | Story of the Arabic dictionary from Abu'l-Faḍl, *Bahá'í Proofs*, p. 8, note. |
| 259 | 'Abu'l-Faḍl is not here': ibid. p. xii. |
| 260 | 'Where did you go...': quoted by Martha Root, interview with the Greatest Holy Leaf, in Garis, *Martha Root*, p. 211. |
| 269 | 'extend every protection...': quoted in Shoghi Effendi, *God Passes By*, p. 306. |
| 273 | 'No matter how much...': 'Abdu'l-Bahá, *Tablets of the Divine Plan*, pp. 42–3. |
| 275 | 'O that I could travel...': ibid. p. 39. |
| 276 | 'a gnat into an eagle...': ibid. p. 68. |
| 277 | 'Ambassadress': from Shoghi Effendi, *God Passes By*, p. 386: 'Leading Ambassadress of His Faith and Pride of Bahá'í teachers, whether men or women, in both the East and the West'. |
| 279 | 'Give something always...': quoted in Harper, *Lights of Fortitude*, p. 107, from Schoen, *A Love Which Does Not Wait*, p. 4. |
| 279 | 'These teachings are the solution...': quoted in Shoghi Effendi, *God Passes By*, p. 390. |
| 287 | Story of Isfandíyár from Blomfield, *Chosen Highway*, pp. 214–5. |
| 290 | 'My home is the home of laughter and mirth': quoted in |

Esslemont, *Bahá'u'lláh and the New Era*, ch. 4, section 'Last years', p. 62.

298    'This time is very sad . . .': quoted in Blomfield, *Chosen Highway*, p. 46.

299    'I seemed to be standing . . .': quoted in Shoghi Effendi, *God Passes By*, p. 310.

300    'Yes, Master, we think . . .': quoted in Shoghi Effendi and Lady Blomfield, *The Passing of 'Abdu'l-Bahá*, p. 4; reprinted in *The Passing of 'Abdu'l-Bahá: A Compilation* (Los Angeles: Kalimát Press, 1991), p. 5.

300    'It is of no use to gather them . . .': ibid. p. 5; quoted in Shoghi Effendi, *God Passes By*, p. 311.

301    'But I was there . . .:' ibid. pp. 8–9.

303    'What will happen to us now? . . .': quoted in Balyuzi, *'Abdu'l-Bahá*, p. 467.

304    'O God, my God! . . .': ibid. p. 465, from Shoghi Effendi and Lady Blomfield, *The Passing of 'Abdu'l-Bahá*, p. 11.

305    'As to his life . . .': quoted in *Star of the West*, Vol. 12, no. 17 (19 January 1922), p. 265; see also Braun and Chance, *Crown of Beauty*, p. 88.

306    'But I was there . . .'; quoted in Shoghi Effendi and Lady Blomfield, *The Passing of 'Abdu'l-Bahá*, p. 8.

306    'I am with you always . . .': quoted in Maxwell, *Early Pilgrimage*, p. 40.

306    'Be happy! . . .': quoted in Garis, *Martha Root*, p. 209.

307    'Verily God hath ordained . . .': Bahá'u'lláh, Kitáb-i-'Ahd, in *Tablets*, p. 221.

309    'O dearly beloved friends . . .': 'Abdu'l-Bahá, *Will and Testament*, para. 36.

310    'the primal branch . . .': ibid. para. 2.

310    'the sign of God, the chosen branch . . .': ibid. para. 16.

311    'It is incumbent upon everyone . . .': ibid. para. 23.

311    'Friends! The time is coming . . .': quoted in Shoghi Effendi and Lady Blomfield, *The Passing of 'Abdu'l-Bahá*, pp. 30–31.